THE NATIONAL TEAM

THE NATIONAL TEAM

THE INSIDE STORY OF THE WOMEN
WHO CHANGED SOCCER

CAITLIN MURRAY

ABRAMS PRESS, NEW YORK

Library of Congress Control Number: 2018936296

ISBN: 978-1-4197-3449-6
eISBN: 978-1-68335-527-4

Printed and bound in the United States
10 9 8 7 6 5 4 3 2 1

Abrams books are available at special discounts when purchased in quantity for premiums and promotions as well as fundraising or educational use. Special editions can also be created to specification. For details, contact specialsales@abramsbooks.com or the address below.

Abrams Press® is a registered trademark of Harry N. Abrams, Inc.

ABRAMS The Art of Books
195 Broadway, New York, NY 10007
abramsbooks.com

Contents

PROLOGUE

"Where Are All These People Going?"

When the national team boarded the bus and got ready to travel to the stadium for a game together, everyone had a different routine.

Some players listened to music on their Walkmans. Kristine Lilly would get so hyped she'd need slow, soft music that calmed her down. Kate Markgraf listened to hard-core rap to get pumped up.

Other players, like Mia Hamm and Julie Foudy, sat next to each other and just talked. There was no assigned seating, but Hamm and Foudy always ended up together.

Some players read the newspaper or did a crossword puzzle. Others just zoned out and looked out the window. It was always a quick, uneventful trip.

There was something different about this bus ride, though. Even though the bus had a police escort and was driving on the shoulder of the New Jersey Turnpike, the traffic was so overwhelming that day that the bus could barely navigate the roads.

The players worried they might be late for their game, the opening match of the 1999 Women's World Cup at the New York Giants' home stadium.

"It was the middle of the day and we left around 11 o'clock in the morning," remembers defender Brandi Chastain. "All the sudden, we're stopped, even though we had an escort. I'm wondering, *What the heck? What's going on in New York City that's causing all this traffic?*"

As the team bus turned a corner, it became clear what was going on. The players could now see that the cars clogging the turnpike had slogans like "Go USA!" painted in red, white, and blue on the windows. All the cars that dotted the New Jersey Turnpike were filtering into one destination: Giants Stadium.

For the players on that bus looking out the window, it was a sight they never thought they'd see. All those people—nearly 80,000 of them—were on their way to see the U.S. women's national team play a soccer match.

"When we got even closer, we saw tailgate after tailgate, from little girls to adults dressed in red, white, and blue playing pickup games and barbecuing in the parking lot," Chastain says. "I remember thinking to myself, *This is such a weird moment.* It was very surreal."

The team's starting goalkeeper, Briana Scurry, let out a gasp to herself as it dawned on her what was happening.

"They were waving at us and taking pictures. We were waving at them and taking pictures of them taking pictures of us," Scurry says, laughing. "It was amazing, because we went from, *Oh my gosh, where are all these people going?* to *We're going to be late!* to *Oh my gosh, these people are here for us!*"

For a team that not long before had been playing at high school stadiums and not even selling out, the excitement surrounding their first game of the 1999 Women's World Cup was something they could've never imagined. These were athletes who played on the national team for two primary reasons: They loved soccer, and they wanted to represent their country. Fame, money, and the sort of crowd that was spilling into Giants Stadium were not even remote possibilities in the players' minds. Most of the players barely made any money from playing soccer, and no one knew their names. But here they were, watching the crowd gather in droves right before their very eyes.

"We were in shock," defender Kate Markgraf says. "And I started to get terrified, because that's when I started to understand what it was all about."

This moment, as it turned out, was a big deal. A team that had been used to flying under the radar was about to be the talk of a nation. They were going to set records, inspire a new generation, and change the landscape of sports in America.

It was a moment that caught the national team by surprise, but whether the players realized it or not, they had been preparing for this for years.

PART I

CHAPTER 1

"We're Not Very USA-ish"

It was almost as if the national came together by accident.

In 1985, there was seemingly little reason for a U.S. women's soccer team to exist. There was no Women's World Cup and no women's soccer in the Olympics, and there were no major trophies on the line.

But there was a group of women who had been pushing to change that. With connections to the U.S. Olympic Committee and the U.S. Soccer Federation, Marty Mankamyer, Betty D'Anjolell, and Mavis Derflinger, among others, pushed decision-makers to take women's soccer seriously. Their goal was for it to one day become an Olympic sport.

"We warned them on more than one occasion: *You can't brush off recognizing women,*" Mankamyer remembers.

In the summer of 1985, the perfect opportunity arose for women's soccer to take a leap forward in America. That's when the National Sports Festival, a sort of mini-Olympics for amateur athletes, would be held in Baton Rouge, Louisiana. Even though women's soccer was still a long way off from becoming an Olympic sport, the Sports Festival organizers decided to give it a chance and include women's soccer for the first time.

A metallurgist from Seattle named Mike Ryan, who coached one of the regional teams there, was approached by officials from U.S. Soccer during the Sports Festival. They wanted him to pick 17 players from those competing at the Festival and coach the U.S. women's national team in its first tournament, which was due to start in Italy in one week.

The U.S. women's national team had existed on paper before that— some players remember making a list after regional tournaments in 1982, 1983, and 1984—but now there was a reason for the team to exist on the field. The national team had its first invitation to play in a real tournament, and U.S. Soccer decided before the Sports Festival that they'd pick a team from the players there.

"After the last game, they sat everybody down and said, *We're going to pick a national team and the team is going to train in New York and then you'll go to Italy.* That was the first anybody had ever heard of it," says Ann Orrison, who made the list and eventually played five times for the U.S. team.

The name of Brandi Chastain, a 17-year-old striker from San Jose, California, wasn't on the list. She was there in Baton Rouge too but had far less experience than the college players who made the cut. She also didn't even realize she had missed out on playing for the first national team.

"There weren't any hard feelings," Chastain says now, 192 appearances for the U.S. later. "Honestly, I didn't know anything about it. I had a great time at that tournament—my parents came, and I had lots of friends there."

The women who did make the list, plucked from the Sports Festival, didn't form a team so much as a mishmash of players. But it was a start.

They went to New York City and played scrimmages against local club teams from Long Island. The training camp lasted just three days, and then they were set to fly to Italy for the Mundialito, which is Spanish for "little World Cup."

The players didn't have any official uniforms, of course, so the federation rounded up some kits, ironed "USA" on the front, and gave them to the players. The uniforms were huge and appeared to be men's kits. Mike Ryan later recalled: "Everything came around their ankles—they looked like little gorillas walking around."

So, the night before their flight to Italy, the team was up late, cutting and sewing their uniforms and training gear, trying to make everything fit properly.

"We were trying to figure out who fit into which uniforms best," remembers Ann Orrison. "Our trainer was hemming warm-up pants so they would semi-fit."

They managed to make the clothes wearable, but they didn't look like what a U.S. national team should wear. The sweat suits were blue and pink while the white game shirts had only a little red trim around the collar and shoulders. None of the players had numbers.

"They weren't U.S. colors," recalled Michelle Akers, one of the only two players to make that team and keep playing long term. "I remember feeling like, *Well, I don't know what this national team is anyway, but we're not very USA-ish.*"

From New York, the group flew to Milan and then took a bus five hours to Jesolo, a small resort town outside of Venice. That was the site of the Mundialito, a four-team women's soccer tournament that was one of a kind at the time.

They may have been a ragtag bunch, but the national team was born.

* * *

When the national team's first games started, it was a rude awakening.

They finished their first official tournament by losing three of four games while drawing one. Having never played the likes of Italy, Denmark, or England before, the Americans didn't know what to expect— they weren't prepared for how hard the other teams tackled and tried to disrupt the game.

The U.S. team hadn't played good soccer, but it was the start of something, and they all knew it.

"We were just so happy to be there," forward Tucka Healy said later. "While watching the Denmark–Italy game, we grabbed an Italian flag and rushed to the sidelines, where we led a cheer. They were totally shocked that we'd cheer another team."

There was reason to be excited for all the teams there, though. Women's soccer had barely existed on a global scale by this point in 1985—these players were at the beginning of not just U.S. women's national team history but women's soccer history.

In 1971, only three international women's soccer teams existed, and just two international matches had been played. Progress was relatively slow from there, and it took until 1990 for just 32 national teams to exist. For reference, today, FIFA's world ranking includes around 180 women's teams.

"Women's soccer worldwide at that point wasn't very prevalent or supported," says Marty Mankamyer, who pushed to add women's soccer to the Olympics. "There were less than a dozen bona fide teams that participated in international games."

The lack of global women's soccer was not because women didn't want to play, though. It was partially because, for decades, they weren't allowed.

In England, the country that invented the modern game of soccer, women were effectively banned by the English federation until 1971. In Brazil—another famous soccer country known for producing Pelé, one of the greatest players in the history of the sport—it was illegal for women to play soccer until 1979. In Germany, women were finally allowed to play soccer in 1970, and even then, they were required to play shorter games, just 60 minutes instead of 90, and with a lighter ball.

While other countries were in the midst of repealing bans on women's soccer, the United States was going through a very different policy change. In 1972, Title IX became law and, whether everyone knew it or not, women's sports in the U.S. were about to undergo a rapid revolution.

Title IX was one sentence—a mere 37 words—tucked in a lengthy law dealing with reforming higher education: "No person in the United States shall, on the basis of sex, be excluded from participation in, be denied the benefits of, or be subjected to discrimination under any education program or activity receiving Federal financial assistance."

The words *sports* or *athletics* are never mentioned. On the face of it, the clause meant that any universities and schools that receive federal funding, which is most of them, must offer equal academic programming to men and women. But the language also extended to other programming, like athletics.

One of the bill's primary architects, Rep. Edith Green of Oregon, wanted the language to be subtle and broad. She believed the only way it would be approved was if her colleagues in Congress didn't actually grasp what it meant. She reportedly told her allies who planned to lobby for the bill: "I don't want you to lobby, because if you lobby, people will ask questions about this bill, and they will find out what it would really do."

It would take years before Title IX would start to be enforced, but the new law eventually meant that young women everywhere had access to competitive sports programs. It also offered a compelling financial incentive for girls to take sports seriously: If colleges offered male athletes scholarships, they had to offer them to women too.

With Title IX in effect, women's soccer exploded. In 1974, only about 100,000 girls across the country were registered with the U.S. Youth Soccer Association. Today, that number is in the millions.

By 1985, when the U.S. women's national team played its first official matches in Jesolo, Italy, the women of the national team were some of the earliest beneficiaries of Title IX.

Many of the players had been plucked from college teams, like Cindy Gordon, who played at Western Washington University and was on the national team from 1985 to 1986. She took up soccer in 1972, the year Title IX passed. Her brothers had played soccer, and she wanted to play too.

"I asked my mom if I could play, and she said that girls don't play sports," Gordon said. "When they passed Title IX, it was a big step forward."

* * *

After the Mundialito, U.S. Soccer never asked Mike Ryan to coach the team again. Instead, Anson Dorrance won the coaching job through a unique tryout that involved competing head-to-head with other coaches on a series of tests in front of a judging panel.

Dorrance came into the national team job as the head coach of the University of North Carolina women's soccer team and used his scouting work there to bolster the national team.

That included spotting a special player named Mia Hamm. While she was still in high school, on the recommendation of a colleague, Dorrance flew to Texas to see a 14-year-old Hamm play for the North Texas regional team. He didn't want to be told which girl she was beforehand—he went to watch the game without prejudice.

With Hamm's team kicking off, the whistle blew, and she instantly made her presence clear to Dorrance.

"She took off like she was shot out of a cannon, and that was all I really needed to see," Dorrance says.

He walked along the sideline and pointed to the girl he saw, asking his colleague if she was Mia Hamm. She was.

He continued his scouting and brought other players into the fold to build a team he thought could compete, including Brandi Chastain. Only two players from the original squad who played the national team's first game in Italy ended up staying on board with Dorrance: Michelle Akers and Lori Henry.

Dorrance wasn't sure when the first Women's World Cup would happen, but he wanted to be ready for it.

"We went into everything with guns blazing, with the ambition to be as good as we could be," Dorrance says. "Back then, we had no idea how far we were behind other teams or what we'd need to overcome to compete. But it wasn't a big adjustment to envision the possibility of a Women's World Cup. We weren't naive about what the potential was."

In 1988, the world governing body of soccer, FIFA, planned a new tournament as a case study for whether a Women's World Cup was a viable idea. The event was called the FIFA Women's Invitational Tournament and featured 12 teams from around the world.

When Dorrance asked a 17-year-old Julie Foudy if she could join the team for the tournament in Panyu, China, she initially lied and said she was busy. She claimed she had summer school classes at Mission Viejo High School, because she wanted to spend her summer at home in California.

"Julie, do you understand what I'm asking you?" Dorrance replied. "I want you to play for the United States of America."

"What do you mean?" Foudy asked him, confused.

That's how new and strange the concept of the U.S. women's national team was. The players who were on it didn't even know what it was. All Foudy knew was that she kept getting call-ups—first to the state team, then to the regional team, and finally to the national team.

But before Foudy knew it, she was on a plane to China for the first-ever FIFA-hosted women's tournament. There, the U.S. beat Japan in their opening match and then settled for draws against Sweden and Czechoslovakia, which allowed them to advance to the knockout round. But in the quarterfinal, Norway beat them, 1–0, and eventually went on to win the whole tournament.

Three weeks after the Women's Invitational ended, FIFA announced it had been successful enough that the first women's world championship tournament would be held in 1991.

They called the event the "1st FIFA World Championship for Women's Football for the M&M's Cup." FIFA worried the women's event might not be worthy of the "World Cup" label. (They've since retroactively bestowed it with the "Women's World Cup" name.) The matches were also planned to be 10 minutes shorter than normal soccer matches, running just 80 minutes each, an indication of FIFA's scaled-back expectations.

The name was confusing and the rule changes were insulting, but the national team was excited to have a world championship to compete in.

"We were acutely aware of the men's World Cup, so we were just waiting for our chance," Dorrance says.

The national team was getting better on the field—they won all six of the games they played in 1990—but that's not to say everything had been figured out quite yet by the time the first Women's World Cup got close.

At the 1991 Women's World Cup qualification tournament in Haiti, the players of the national team were given white roses by U.S. Soccer officials to throw out to the spectators.

"We walked out to throw these roses to the crowd and we tossed them into the stands," remembers midfielder Tracey Bates, who played on the team from 1987 to 1991. "As we turned around, they threw them back at us. I just remember covering my head and running."

The effort to win over the Haitian crowd didn't go as planned—Dorrance urged his players to shake it off and focus on the first game—but by the end of qualification, the crowd was cheering for the U.S. national team anyway. The Americans outscored their opponents 49–0 over five games in Haiti. (Yes, they scored 49 goals, with 12–0 wins over both Mexico and Martinique and 10–0 wins versus both Haiti and Trinidad & Tobago.)

"I remember in the local newspaper the next day, it said something like: *The Americans tried to seduce us with white roses, but instead they seduced us with their style of play*," Bates recalls.

The women's game was still new, and the U.S. Soccer Federation was still figuring out how to navigate it. Alan Rothenberg, who was elected president of the federation in August 1990, admits he didn't know what to do with the women's side of the game when he first came into office.

"The blunt truth is, I didn't even know the women's side of the game existed in the United States at that time," he says.

Luckily, Anson Dorrance and his assistant coaches, Tony DiCicco and Lauren Gregg, had been putting together a competitive team, even on a shoestring budget. As the U.S. women's national team was forming its own identity, it looked to the styles it had encountered elsewhere in the world: Germany's combination play, Norway's direct attack, and so on.

When the first Women's World Cup finally arrived in 1991, the Americans were not the all-around best team. While women's soccer was still in its infancy around the world, the teams from Europe had technical skills and tactical acumen the Americans did not. But what the Americans discovered in that tournament is something they've held on to ever since: a winning mentality.

"If you would've compared us player for player, we might've been a bit more athletic, but it was really our mentality," says Shannon Higgins, a UNC midfielder who earned 51 caps for the U.S. from 1987 to 1991. "All of us, we had to fight for what we got. We had a mentality that we weren't going to lose and we were going to fight."

The national team steamrolled through the tournament. They won every game and outscored their opponents 25–5 across all six games. The closest match came in the final, when the U.S. beat Norway, 2–1.

It was a standout tournament for April Heinrichs, a forward from Colorado. She scored four goals and drew on her own experience as the head coach of the women's soccer team at the University of Maryland to be an effective captain of the national team.

"My role is to be the liaison between what the players want and need and feel, and getting that message to the coach," she once explained. "Occasionally, I help out with coaching decisions: When should we practice? How long should we go?"

Heinrichs helped mold the captain's role—she was the national team's first captain, having been appointed to the job by coach Anson Dorrance in 1986. Dorrance coached Heinrichs when she was a student at UNC before the national team existed, and it impressed him how she didn't ease her way into the team or try to make friends. As he once put it: "She came in and crushed everyone."

"The thing I admired about April is, she wanted to be liked, wanted to be on a team that got along, but she wouldn't sacrifice her level of excellence to be like everyone else, wonderfully mediocre," Dorrance said. "We took her mentality and framed the culture of the national team around her."

Back stateside, virtually no one knew about the first Women's World Cup or the fact that the USA won it. The games weren't shown on television, email was not in widespread use yet, and landline phone calls were expensive, so players sent loved ones faxes to let them know how the tournament was going. Back home, recipients distributed them like newsletters, the early 1990s equivalent of status updates on Facebook.

Midfielder Julie Foudy quips now: "When we won in '91, we came back and no one even knew about it. There were two people at the airport to greet us—it was our bus driver and our operations guy."

The players did get some recognition from U.S. Soccer, though. After they became the first-ever world champions in women's soccer, the federation sent them all cards in the mail.

The note inside went something along the lines of: *Congratulations on your success. We're so incredibly proud of what you and your teammates have achieved. You're changing women's soccer forever. Enclosed is a $500 bonus for winning the World Cup.*

When Brandi Chastain saw that $500 check, all she could think was: "Cha-ching!"

"I thought, *Whoa, this is incredible!* And now when I look back and tell this story today, people are like, *That is horrible*," Chastain says. "And it *was* horrible, to be honest, in hindsight. But in that moment, I remember thinking how lucky we were, because I didn't know anyone who was doing what we did on the national team to make money."

That's right: The national team's bonus for winning a world championship in 1991 was $500 each, and at the time, the players were thrilled about it—even though FIFA offered prize money of around $50 million for teams at the men's World Cup. The players were thrilled because there wasn't any money in women's soccer, and they knew it.

CHAPTER 2

"I Just Want to Play Soccer"

It was December 1992. Mia Hamm, a 20-year-old student, was sitting at the Rathskeller, a bar just a stone's throw from the University of North Carolina campus.

Nicknamed "The Rat," it looked every bit the college bar it was. Previous patrons had scrawled their names or other graffiti all over the booths, and tables had old-time jukeboxes that looked as though they didn't work—and no one wasted their loose change trying.

Hamm was with her coach from UNC and the U.S. national team, Anson Dorrance. Like many of the national team players, Hamm started representing her country while she was still in college—it was Dorrance who scouted her to join UNC and, when he became the national team coach, named her to the 1991 World Cup team. She asked him to join her that day because she was meeting with a representative from Nike at The Rat.

The meeting was unexpected, to be sure. At the time, the company had barely positioned itself in American soccer and had no presence in women's soccer. But something told Joe Elsmore, an enterprising young employee at Nike, that he should talk to Hamm about a possible endorsement deal.

Elsmore moonlighted as a referee, and it was while he was officiating UNC games that he got to know Hamm. He was the referee at the 1992 NCAA championship game—North Carolina walloped Duke, 9–1, and Hamm led the scoring with a hat trick. After the game, Elsmore told her she should talk to Nike before she made any decisions about her future, and a week later she called him to set up the meeting.

He didn't have a specific plan for the sit-down. He worked on the retail side of Nike at the time, not in marketing. But there was something special about Hamm. She was the best player on the field, yet she always put her teammates first and deflected the spotlight. She was down-to-earth, spoke with a soft shyness, and blended in—just another brown-haired, ponytailed all-American girl—but she also had an elusive star quality.

"Mia, what's important to you?" he asked her at the Rathskeller. "What do you want to do in life?"

Her answer was simple: "I just want to play soccer."

But there was no clear way for her to do that. National team players weren't paid more than a small stipend at the time. There was no professional league for her to join in order to make a living wage.

Elsmore slid a small square napkin in front of him, pulled out a pen, and asked Hamm to list off her expenses to live. Her car insurance, laundry, groceries—anything she had to be able to pay for went on the napkin. At the end, the total came out to about $12,000 a year.

The meeting ended with no promises, but Elsmore took the napkin with him to his office at Nike and set out to sell his bosses on the idea that Mia Hamm was worth signing as a Nike athlete.

"I kind of did it on a whim," admits Elsmore, now the director of North American soccer marketing at Nike. "I wasn't really sure what was going to happen. I was in sales and just transitioning into marketing at that point. I talked to many Nike executives, and I said, *I know we're not really in soccer that deeply, and we're definitely not in women's soccer, but there's something about this woman that Nike needs to be connected with.*"

It took some convincing to get his bosses on board, but Elsmore eventually came back with an offer: He could offer enough to cover everything listed on the napkin plus a bit more, and Nike would sign her after she graduated college in 1994 so it wouldn't affect her NCAA eligibility.

It was a huge moment, not just for Mia Hamm but for women's soccer. Though Hamm sought Anson Dorrance's input, he says he left the decision entirely up to her.

"She didn't need my opinion to guide her one way or the other," Dorrance says. "I really trusted her, and I knew she was going to be fine."

For the first time ever, a female soccer player wasn't going to need to think about getting a "real" job after college or getting financial help from family so she could keep playing the sport she loved.

Michelle Akers, however, was the first women's soccer player to sign an endorsement deal that was worth more than free gear or a couple hundred dollars. Unlike Hamm, who had her deal waiting for her at college graduation, Akers's deal was a long-coming payoff she could've never expected. Akers was 25 years old when Umbro signed her, and by that point she had already patchworked her finances for years to be able to play, even though she was the best player in the world.

Akers was hard not to notice on the field: at 5-foot-10 and 150 pounds, she was like a wrecking ball on the field when she wanted to be. She had curly golden-brown locks that she let flow freely when she played, unlike all her U.S. teammates, who always put their hair back with a hair tie.

Her endorsement deal wasn't too far behind Hamm's in terms of its compensation. But it came about in a very different way than Hamm's did.

It started with Mick Hoban, a former pro soccer player who bounced around small-time American clubs before finishing at the Portland Timbers in 1978, a time when soccer offered meager pay. He was working at Umbro in 1991 when he saw Akers speaking at an annual conference for the Sporting Goods Manufacturers Association in Arizona.

In her speech to an audience of executives from the largest sporting apparel companies in the world, Akers used her platform to make an impassioned plea: Please invest in women's soccer. As she talked about how difficult it was as a female soccer player to make ends meet, it struck a chord with Hoban, who remembered scraping by in the 1970s.

"When this person steps up, who is known as the dominant player in the world, and she's telling us a story about how she's having to piece together a career, it resonated," Hoban says. "She's pleading: *I just want to be able to play*. It paralleled what I had experienced."

Before the trade show ended that evening, Hoban approached Akers and gave her his business card. He told her: "We're interested in getting involved in the women's soccer movement, and we think you'd be a great spokesperson for it." Weeks later, Akers had an offer to be Umbro's first paid female endorsee and the first one in women's soccer.

It wasn't a huge sum of money, but it meant Akers could keep doing what she loved. Akers, a fiercely passionate competitor, had lasted longer than some players who couldn't keep scraping by—players who hung on because they loved it but eventually had to get "real jobs."

After all, there was never any expectation for the earliest members of the U.S. women's national team that they'd make any money—not when Hamm started, not when Akers started, not when any of them started. The possibility of making a living from soccer—professional league contracts, endorsement deals, bonuses for World Cups or Olympic Games—never even entered the players' minds.

They played, quite simply, because they loved it.

* * *

There were few perks for being on the national team in those days. Even traveling the world was less exciting than it sounded.

When the U.S. players took their flight to the 1991 World Cup in China, they were confused as to why they were flying the opposite way around the world. In an apparent money-saving move, the plane from the U.S. stopped to pick up the Swedish and Norwegian teams along the way.

"Then when we went home, instead of just crossing the Pacific Ocean, we went all the way back around to drop everybody off and then landed in New York," remembers Brandi Chastain, who first became a national team regular in 1986.

Shannon Higgins, a member of the 1991 World Cup–winning team, says the players didn't have their own uniforms for years—they wore hand-me-downs from the men's national team that didn't fit. Higgins, all 5-foot-something, 120 pounds of her, wore No. 3, which meant she had to wear the uniform of whichever player was No. 3 on the men's team. That was John Doyle, a 6-foot-3, 200-plus-pound giant. The 1991

World Cup was the first time that the women didn't have to wear old men's uniforms.

While the men's team got USA-branded tracksuits in the country's signature red, white, and blue colors, the women each got a purple-and-green jacket from U.S. Soccer. The players weren't exactly sure why that's what the federation gave them, but they were *something* and they cherished them.

"We all came to the conclusion that it was the last thing they had at the warehouse," says Chastain, who played for a boys' soccer team in junior high because her school in San Jose, California, didn't have a girls' team.

Before the Women's World Cup or the Olympics came into the picture, the national team actively looked for exhibition games known as "friendly matches" they could play. The goal wasn't just to get better—the games also helped the national team figure out where it stood against the rest of the world, because there were no major competitions. But there wasn't much money to do it.

"The early days were sort of thin for us in terms of commitment from U.S. Soccer to develop the team," says Anson Dorrance, who was the national team coach from 1986 to 1994. "Finances were a huge issue for all of us, but our enthusiasm was certainly not lacking."

Higgins, a native of Kent, Washington, remembers playing friendlies in France at the same time the men's under-23 team was there. The women's senior national team stayed in a sort of bed-and-breakfast lodge where the German woman who owned it would cook meals for them and the players all slept in one giant room together. The men's U-23 team stayed at a nearby hotel.

When the women's team went out for a run one day, they passed the U-23 men's bus—it was a luxury liner that dwarfed the tiny shuttle bus the women were carted around in.

"We'd look at them and say, *Gee, can we put our luggage in your bus?*" Higgins remembers, laughing.

The players weren't upset about the treatment they received, though. They didn't know any different and couldn't have expected more. After all, the women's team was still new and the U.S. men's team had existed decades longer, playing its first official match in 1916.

"You never knew if the electricity was going to be on at the hotel or if you were going to get a shower, but no one was high-strung," Chastain says, laughing. "We played cards by candlelight. We took showers in the pool. We had flooding in the bathroom."

"It was fantastic," Chastain adds with a wistful hint of nostalgia. "It was exactly how it was supposed to be. How do you learn to be resilient as a team without going through things like that?"

The players also didn't make any money, though. The sorts of deals Mia Hamm and Michelle Akers signed were rarities, and some players had difficulty making ends meet.

While each player on the men's team got a $10,000 bonus for qualifying for the 1990 World Cup, the women received only a couple of T-shirts for qualifying for the 1991 Women's World Cup. The shirts featured the logo of Budweiser, a U.S. Soccer sponsor, and the players sarcastically called them their "$5,000 T-shirts."

The women remember being paid a $10 per diem when they were with the national team domestically and $15 when they traveled abroad. At the same time, the men's national team received a $25 daily stipend. The women ate only during team meals and then squirreled away their per diem so they'd have something to show for their trips with the national team.

"We were getting $10 per day. There was absolutely no ulterior motive other than dying to represent your country," says Tracey Bates, who earned 29 caps between 1987 and 1991. "There was real purity in that."

Before the 1991 World Cup tournament started, the federation bumped up the stipend for the women to $1,000 a month—at least while they were in camp. But that small stipend didn't change the fact of the matter: To compete in the tournament, players were spending money to be part of the team, not making it. Time with the team meant leaving jobs that paid livable wages and sacrificing the opportunity to advance in whatever career they had started outside of soccer.

"This team has probably given up more money for this run at the World Cup than any team ever," Michelle Akers told reporters in 1991. "The players have all quit their jobs two or three times. Nobody has any money."

Carin Jennings, the Golden Ball winner of the 1991 World Cup, was one of them. Unlike the younger players at the tournament, such as Julie Foudy and Mia Hamm, Jennings was out of college and needed to make a living. She had a marketing job in Irvine, California, but when she asked for a three-month leave of absence for national team duty, her employer said no. She quit so she could keep playing and compete in the 1991 World Cup.

"Carin quit multiple jobs to continue on with the team. Thank god—she was so amazing for us," Bates says with a laugh. "She just chose to make the national team her priority. It was kind of the running joke: *Well, Carin quit another job!*"

Many players made ends meet by continuing to live with their parents after they finished college or, if they were married, relying on their spouse's income. But after a while, some players just couldn't do it anymore. They were making little money, and they didn't know if they would ever make more, even as they tried to juggle national team duties and their careers.

For Shannon Higgins, it was becoming more and more difficult to leave her job as a coach at George Washington University for short stints to play for the national team. She could've moved back in with her parents, but she didn't want to keep putting her future on hold. At just 23 years old, right after winning the 1991 World Cup, she retired from playing soccer—not because she wasn't good enough anymore but because she couldn't keep scraping by.

"If I moved back home with my parents and got a waitressing job, I could've probably been okay, but that wasn't where I wanted to be," Higgins says. "I was trying really hard to make the ends meet at that time. I either had to commit myself to the next four years or walk away."

And so she walked away.

Every player has to call it quits at some point—April Heinrichs was forced to retire after the 1991 World Cup due to injuries—but being broke shouldn't be the reason for it. The injustice of seeing talented teammates quit playing the game they loved—a game they were so good at—planted an idea in the minds of the players who were able to stick around. They needed to take control of their own futures.

"If you didn't have a means to supplement it, then a lot of players decided they were going to retire," Julie Foudy says. "That's what got us thinking this way in the first place. I remember thinking: *This does not seem right. Players have years and years of time left in them to play physically and mentally but are having to make an economic decision.*"

That eventually led to the first big, public fight the players had with U.S. Soccer.

* * *

By the time the 1996 Olympics were set to be played in Atlanta, Georgia—the first time women's soccer would be an Olympic sport— the U.S. national team was the favorite to win gold. Even though they fell short at the 1995 World Cup, coming in third, expectations remained high.

As such, the U.S. Soccer Federation, which paid them $1,000 per month when they were in camp, would offer a bonus only if the women won a gold medal. The women were outraged—the men had been offered a bonus for *any* medal, and the women wanted the same.

The players didn't know how to respond until they gained some inspiration from a fellow athlete in another sport: tennis legend Billie Jean King. At a small closed event hosted by the Women's Sports Foundation, Julie Foudy was one of eight female athletes who sat down to exchange stories and ideas. Foudy listened intently as King talked about the fight within tennis for women to be paid equally to the men, and a lightbulb went off for Foudy.

"I was like, *Oh my god, that's us,*" Foudy remembers. "*We're going through the same problems.*"

If anyone was going to take the story from Billie Jean King and run with it, it was Foudy. Her teammates nicknamed her "Loudy Foudy," and she jokes that as the youngest of four kids growing up in San Diego, California, she learned to speak up for herself from a young age. When Reebok later approached her about endorsing their soccer balls, Foudy wanted to know how they were made first and visited Pakistan to tour the manufacturing facilities herself. She wasn't one to quietly brush things aside.

In other words, Julie Foudy was a team captain for a reason. On the plane ride back from the event with Billie Jean King, all she could think about was how the team was about to sign a new contract with U.S. Soccer that didn't improve working conditions and didn't offer them anywhere remotely near what the men were paid.

So, after that meeting with the Women's Sports Foundation, she called King to ask her how the national team could get the federation to listen to them.

"You just don't play. That's the only leverage you have," King told Foudy. "They depend on you, you're representing them, you make them money, and you have to say no."

And that's exactly what the veteran players did.

Julie Foudy, Mia Hamm, Briana Scurry, Michelle Akers, Joy Fawcett, Kristine Lilly, Carla Overbeck, Carin Jennings, and Tisha Venturini rejected U.S. Soccer's offer for a contract for 1996, and the nine players did not attend a training camp in December 1995, just months away from the Olympics.

Hank Steinbrecher, U.S. Soccer's secretary general, told reporters that the players were being greedy, quipping that they were more worried about lining their pockets—or, rather, shoes.

"Our team is favored to win it all and we cannot award mediocrity," he told the media. "It seems some players are more concerned about how green their shoes are, instead of bringing home the gold."

When a reporter asked him what he meant by that, he added: "Bonuses are paid for superior performance. Our expectation is to be playing for the gold and winning it. That's where the bonus should go."

Steinbrecher's comments incensed the players. Their resolve to boycott the Olympics if necessary was only strengthened. Michelle Akers responded in the press by calling an Olympic boycott a "definite reality."

"If we medal or win, the opportunities for our sport will be wide open," she told reporters before a media blackout between the two sides. "We understand how big the Olympics are. We hope the federation keeps that in mind."

The U.S. Soccer Federation seemed baffled by how difficult the players were being. From Steinbrecher's view, the federation had increased its spending on the women's program and spent more than other countries did around the world on women's programs.

"They didn't understand the level of angst happening among the group," Foudy says, "especially because you had a team that had been together for so long. You have some teams that play together for a couple years and then they cycle off. But this group, we'd been through everything together for a while."

Foudy adds: "We'd joke in the beginning, *Oh, it builds character.* But by the end, it was like, *Okay, I am up to my fucking eyeballs in character.*"

The nine players holding out for bonuses equal to the men's were willing to go on strike, but U.S. Soccer made the decision for them when the federation locked them out of a pre-Olympics training camp. As Steinbrecher put it: "This camp is for people who have come to agreement with the federation."

For players like Brandi Chastain and Shannon MacMillan, who had fallen out of favor and didn't make the 1995 World Cup team, it was a chance to earn their way back into the fold.

Chastain had struggled with back-to-back ACL tears, but was determined to get back on the national team. She had been carefully monitoring every detail—her diet, her sleep, her training—and waited for an opportunity to return. Even though accepting a call-up made her a "scrub" or a "scab," her former teammates were supportive. Julie Foudy encouraged her to go.

MacMillan had been on a similar path. After she lost her spot on the national team, she went back to Portland, Oregon, and sobbed in the office of Clive Charles, her former college coach. Once she was finished crying, he told her: "All right, I'll see you this time tomorrow, and I'm going to kick your butt in training." She was confused. She had been told she didn't have a spot on the national team, and she also didn't have a club or school to play for. What would she be training for?

"You're going to have an opportunity, and you're going to be ready for that opportunity," he told her sternly. "So, you have 24 hours to mope and feel sorry for yourself, and then I'll see you on the field."

At their first national team camp since being cut, Chastain and MacMillan played well while the veterans were locked out. Coach Tony DiCicco saw a spot for both of them on the team—but not at their usual positions. Both had been forwards all their lives, but if they wanted to play for the national team, that was about to change. DiCicco told Chastain she'd need to become a defender while he told MacMillan she had to move to the midfield. Both players agreed and never looked back.

Months after the dispute started, the federation and the locked-out players reached a compromise. The women would receive a bonus if they won gold or silver. The men still got bonuses for winning gold, silver, or bronze, but at least the women were no longer limited to just gold.

Of course, they won gold anyway, which was worth a $20,000 bonus each for the players—and both Chastain and MacMillan were among them—but being heard by U.S. Soccer was a small victory that would prepare them for the clashes to come.

DiCicco, the team's beloved coach, generally stayed out of money matters. After all, it wasn't his place. But he did tell U.S. Soccer: "If you want this team to achieve special things, you've got to treat them special."

CHAPTER 3

"Screw You, We'll Show You Differently"

When the national team's bus got snarled in traffic midday on the way to Giants Stadium, that's when the players knew something special was happening. At first they didn't realize it, but the gridlock was caused by an unprecedented groundswell of fans flooding into the stadium to see the opening of the 1999 Women's World Cup—and it was only a sampling of what was yet to come.

The tournament would go on to be a pivotal moment in history, one that changed the sports landscape of the United States forever. It was unprecedented in its scale and its reach, with records for TV ratings and attendance shattered. Millions of people—young and old, male and female, in the United States and abroad—saw women athletes in a new light.

But before that happened, few people believed it was possible—and the naysayers had been loud.

Julie Foudy was sitting in front of a room full of reporters in San Jose, California, for the World Cup draw months before the tournament was set to begin. Carla Overbeck, her national team cocaptain, was seated at a table with her in front of a wall of cameras, ready to take questions. The first one came from Jamie Trecker, an ESPN columnist.

He stood up and suggested the players and the World Cup organizing committee were lying about ticket sales. They were trying to position the Women's World Cup as a major world event but, as he later put it, "I don't see any evidence that the world cares." The organizers, he theorized, were making a mistake by trying to make the event about more than just soccer.

"Good way to start off the press conference," Foudy quipped.

Overbeck smiled politely and jumped in. "Well, we still have six months to go, and we think people will show up," she said. "And we do think it's bigger than soccer. It's empowering in a lot of different ways, and that's why we play."

For the 1999 Women's World Cup to be a success, a defiant approach needed to be taken against the naysayers, whether they were journalists or executives at the highest rungs of the sport. FIFA, the all-powerful governing body that oversees soccer throughout the world, didn't see much potential in a Women's World Cup. Initially, they vehemently opposed putting games in large, marquee venues like Giants Stadium.

FIFA had already made the men's World Cup one of the most profitable sporting events on the planet, but by 1999, expectations were still low for the Women's World Cup. The women's tournament had been hosted only twice before, and both times it was relatively small.

By 1995, FIFA finally called the tournament the FIFA Women's World Cup—no longer the "FIFA World Championship for Women's Football for the M&M's Cup"—but it was still treated as minor. With Sweden as host country, three of the 1995 tournament's five venues seated just 10,000 people or less. The U.S. played their opening match versus China in front of only 4,635 people, which would be the largest crowd they saw the entire tournament.

"You hardly knew the World Cup was there," says JP Dellacamera, a broadcaster for ESPN who covered the tournament. "There was really no media presence. There were no signs anywhere. I didn't get a sense that this was a big event, and the crowds they got showed that. The venues were small, and I would describe them as more of high school stadiums."

For the players, it felt like participating in friendly matches—not competing for the top prize in the sport.

"It was a Podunk tournament, and just like any other overseas trip, at best," recalls Tiffeny Milbrett, a forward who scored 100 goals for the national team over her career.

So, when the 1999 Women's World Cup came around and the United States prepared to host, FIFA continued to have low expectations for the tournament.

At the time, FIFA was run by Sepp Blatter, who these days is known more for his sexist comments and for being banned from FIFA over accusations of corruption and bribery. But back then, as the most powerful man in soccer, Blatter worked closely with Alan Rothenberg, the former president of the U.S. Soccer Federation who oversaw the 1999 Women's World Cup organizing committee. Rothenberg quickly got a sense of how Blatter felt about the women's version of the sport.

"Sometimes he was trying to be funny, but he talked about the girls in cute uniforms—silliness, but offensive nonetheless," Rothenberg says.

Rothenberg remembers that when the U.S. asked to host the event, FIFA didn't need much convincing—they were happy to have someone volunteer and worried more about preventing financial losses.

"When we went to FIFA, they insisted that we do it with small stadiums all in the northeast in order to minimize travel costs," Rothenberg says. "We argued the time was right and the interest in the United States was high enough that we could do more than that. They just said no."

The U.S. organizing committee didn't relent, but the most FIFA was willing to concede was that the final—the biggest game of the tournament—could be hosted at RFK Stadium, a venue that seated around 50,000 people.

That is, until they saw the 1996 Olympics in Atlanta. The crowds to see the U.S. women gradually built over the tournament, and by the time the gold-medal match arrived, a massive crowd of 76,489 showed up to see the U.S. win. The gold-winning match wasn't aired live on TV, so most Americans didn't even know about it, but it proved Americans were willing to pack a stadium for a big event.

"They finally said, *Okay, you guys can go ahead and do it in big stadiums.* Of course, they gave us permission, but they didn't give us any money, so we had all the risk," Rothenberg says. "They took no additional financial risk, so from their standpoint, they had nothing to lose. Honest to god, I think it was like, *Here are these crazy Americans. They think they can do this, so godspeed, go do it.*"

Ticket sales would be the main source of revenue, particularly due to a lack of major sponsors. Both Coca-Cola and McDonald's, who had spent hundreds of millions of dollars sponsoring men's World Cups and the Olympics—including the 1994 men's World Cup held in the U.S.—weren't interested in the Women's World Cup.

But there was no blueprint for selling hundreds of thousands of tickets for a stand-alone women's soccer event. That had simply never been done before.

In the months leading up to the Women's World Cup, the crowds showing up to see the national team's warm-up matches weren't remotely close in size to the lofty goals the World Cup organizing committee had set. In the last friendly matches before the tournament, the team played in front of 6,767 people in Milwaukee, Wisconsin, against the Netherlands on May 13, 1999, and 10,452 people in Orlando, Florida, against Brazil a week later. Other than one gold-medal match at the Olympics three years earlier, Americans had never turned up to see the team in numbers that could fill Giants Stadium.

With no track record of attracting the massive crowds they wanted, the organizing committee devised a "plan B" early on in case ticket sales didn't pan out.

"We were concerned as to whether it would actually be successful or not, so when we went around to stadiums to sign them up, we blacked out time for concerts," Rothenberg remembers. "We figured if ticket sales were lousy, we could have a concert beforehand and fill the house."

Marla Messing, the CEO of the organizing committee, built out a conservative ticketing model to see if the tournament could be put in big stadiums without losing money. If tickets didn't sell, she planned for decorations to block out empty sections in the upper bowls of the stadiums so the games' atmospheres wouldn't suffer.

FIFA, an organization that was seeing profits in the hundreds of millions of dollars at the time, didn't help the organizing committee market the event. Marketing was left to the organizing committee, which had a budget that was only about 1/10th of the budget for the men's World Cup in the United States five years earlier. Promoting the event would require some creativity. The organizers quickly realized that their best asset to spread the word about the event was the national team itself.

Says Donna de Varona, the chair of the tournament's organizing committee: "We knew with the personalities on the team, they would be the draw."

Most Americans didn't know much about the national team yet, but the players were about to change that.

* * *

In 1999, if there was a soccer camp for young girls in a city scheduled to host a Women's World Cup game, there's a good chance that Mia Hamm was there. She would've been handing out flyers and letting the girls know: *Hey, there's a big soccer tournament coming up—you should ask your parents to take you.*

For the players of the national team, making the Women's World Cup a success became a personal mission. They canvassed their way across the country, visiting every youth soccer team, school, clinic, and event they could find. It was the sort of relentless boots-on-the-ground technique you might expect from an upstart campaign for political office. But with no marketing budget, it was the only way to do it.

"It was the equivalent of being a door-to-door salesperson," recalls goalkeeper Briana Scurry, a native of Minneapolis. "That's how we sold it: On the ground, in the grass roots, here and there. We spoke to as many people as possible, especially in the cities that would be hosting World Cup games. We were the ones doing the soccer camps for kids, personally going from club to club to hand out flyers and to make these kids and their parents feel like they knew us so they would come to our games when they were in their area."

It's difficult to imagine players going out and selling their own games now. For perspective, the 2015 Women's World Cup in Canada set a tournament attendance record of 1,353,506 total. Organizers spent more than $200 million to host the event—about 10 times the budget in 1999. The Women's World Cup is now a big-time event. For the players to campaign for ticket sales now would be like Tom Brady showing up to youth football clinics to convince kids and their parents to come see the Super Bowl.

But these players wanted to do it. They were eager to make the 1999 Women's World Cup a hit and prove to everyone—from skeptical reporters at press conferences to the dismissive executives at FIFA—that they could and would succeed.

"If you have ownership of what it is you're doing, then it's not being put on you, it belongs to you," says Briana Scurry, who became the first black woman inducted into the National Soccer Hall of Fame in 2017. "And we had ownership of that World Cup. It was ours to put on and it was ours to win."

The reason the grassroots campaign worked, however, was the players themselves.

The women of the national team were the sort of athletes America hadn't seen before. Young girls had role models just like them for the first time. Julie Foudy, a Stanford graduate, says when she was growing up, she had no choice but to look up to male basketball players—as she puts it: "My sports role models were 7 feet tall and 300 pounds."

But even more than that, the national team players were humble and relatable to average Americans. After games and practices, they would stay and sign autographs until every single fan waiting got one, sometimes for hours.

As soon as tickets for the World Cup went on sale, it became apparent the players' efforts were working. In the end, more than 660,000 people bought tickets and packed into stadiums for the 1999 Women's World Cup, far exceeding even the most optimistic sales projections CEO Marla Messing built into her models.

Some doubters, like the reporter in San Jose, thought the sales figures announced ahead of the tournament were false.

"I do remember there was a sense that we were lying about our numbers, which, by the way, we never did," says Messing.

FIFA's communications director, Keith Cooper, was honest about the organization's surprise: "We have to admit we never thought it would be this successful," he told reporters once the tournament ended.

The players who believed fans would show up had the last laugh, of course. Foudy couldn't help but think of that reporter in San Jose who put the players on the spot and accused them of lying about the ticket sales.

"When we walked out onto the field at Giants Stadium and it was an 80,000-people packed house and they gave us a standing ovation, I literally, in my brain, was like, *Where the hell is that goddamn Jamie Trecker?*" Foudy recalls, laughing. "*I want to grab him by the neck right now.*"

Foudy was used to doubters by that point, and like the other women on the memorable "'99ers" team, she never let the naysayers stop her.

"There's always going to be the Jamie Treckers," she says now. "There are a lot of people who listen to those doubters and never take that next step, they never get out of their comfort zone and pursue their dreams because they've got those types in their lives telling them they can't do it. That's what was amazing about that team—whenever anyone did that to us, we were like, *Screw you, we'll show you differently.*"

* * *

As the players of the national team took on roles as spokeswomen to help sell the Women's World Cup, they couldn't forget their primary job: winning.

After all, they worried, if they lost at the World Cup they'd worked so hard to promote, all the momentum they had been building might crumble. For star players like Mia Hamm, Julie Foudy, Brandi Chastain, and others, that meant pulling double duty to train for the World Cup while promoting it.

It was a huge ask of the players—they not only had to make the tournament a business success but an on-field success. Lauren Gregg, who was the assistant coach of the national team at the time, remembers it being a delicate balance for the coaching staff. But Gregg and head coach Tony DiCicco understood how important it was to the players that they could promote the tournament.

"They wanted to sell the game, and they did it happily," Gregg says. "But when you're also trying to compete and be the best in the world, hours every day selling the game—doing media events and interviews or school appearances or commercials—that's time you have to calculate in."

"Every minute and every second is planned toward becoming a world champion. It's not something that just happens. But the pressure to sell out the stadiums was enormous."

As much as the players wanted to prove doubters wrong and put on a successful women's tournament, they also had to consider their own futures. If the 1999 Women's World Cup wasn't a success, their hopes for launching a women's professional league—the first opportunity for players like Mia Hamm and Brandi Chastain to be true professional athletes—would disappear.

Despite the pressure that came with being a national team player, it wasn't a full-time job. They weren't paid much and only competed with the team a few months out of the year. Many players made extra income by coaching clinics or holding part-time jobs because there was no professional soccer league for women yet in the United States.

A successful World Cup figured to change that. If the national team could sell out stadiums, hoist the trophy, and show America how exciting the sport was, a professional league could come next.

"We had to make players available every day just for media," Gregg says. "We had to sell the game and sell our story and sell the sport. The beautiful thing about it is the players wanted to carry the sport on their backs. They wanted to inspire the next generation of boys and girls."

Sure, the players managed to sell tickets, but that was only half of the task. They still needed to win.

CHAPTER 4

"From Darkness into the Light"

There is something fascinating in sports about the tunnel—the dark and often dingy area where players are tucked away inside the belly of a stadium before they walk onto the field before a game.

It's the place where a player's wildest dreams can linger for a final moment and, shielded from the crowd and the light, she can collect her composure. It's also the place where nerves can kick into their highest gear. All that's left is anticipation and what feels like an endless wait in purgatory before players can step on the pitch and get to work.

At Giants Stadium on June 19, 1999, the tunnel had a bit of everything to offer. It was a more heightened version of any wait in the tunnel the players had experienced before.

"The tunnels in the stadiums are very dark—you kind of go from this cave-like environment to walking out into this brilliant bright light," defender Brandi Chastain says. "It's an almost blinding light with the incredible green grass and the explosion of colors in the stadium and the crowd."

"I remember looking at Kristine Lilly, and we both had tears in our eyes. *Oh my gosh—this is actually happening.* I will never forget that moment of the darkness into the light," Chastain adds wistfully.

As the players emerged from the shadows of the tunnel and onto the grass field in New Jersey, they were immediately surrounded by a view that gave them chills. It was the largest crowd that had ever come to see the U.S. women's national team—and everyone was there to see *them*.

On that day, 78,972 people packed into Giants Stadium. The Giants themselves had never packed the stadium like that. No one else had either, except on one occasion five years earlier, when the Pope drew a crowd of 82,948.

The players had seen the crowds tailgating, they heard the ticket sales figures, and they knew it would be a massive crowd. But experiencing it was something else—something unfathomable. It was the tangible proof that all their campaigning had worked. Americans became invested in their story and had come to watch them play.

"When you come out of that canopy, it's a very interesting thing to hear a crowd that big go from talking amongst themselves to when they see players come out," says goalkeeper Briana Scurry, who played at the University of Massachusetts from 1989 to 1993. "It's a very powerful change of sound. It really gets your heart. When we started to come out, people started to clap and pictures were snapping and there were all these flashes. The enormity of that stadium, and all those people were there for us—it was such an overwhelming feeling."

On that afternoon, Giants Stadium sounded different than it usually did, too. As Donna de Varona, the chair of the organizing committee, puts it: "It was the sound of young voices." Children and young women made up a bigger part of the chorus than at any game held in that stadium before.

"It's one of those moments that gives you chills and you think, *Oh my gosh, this is real*," says midfielder Shannon MacMillan, who won the prestigious MAC Hermann Trophy in college at the University of Portland. "The first time you come out of the tunnel and step on the field, that roar just truly sucks the breath out of you."

If you could pinpoint the moment women's soccer started to change the sports landscape in the United States, it would perhaps be when the players emerged from the tunnel at Giants Stadium.

And yet, the players hadn't even touched a ball. That was the whole reason they were there. The players were experiencing one of the most intense, powerful moments of their careers, but their journey at the World Cup hadn't even started yet. Their emotions couldn't get in the way.

"We were all either laughing uncontrollably or crying," Scurry remembers. "And then we had to play a soccer game. So, the funny thing about selling it so well was now we had to go out there and win the damn thing."

The players had long prepared for this moment, and the crowd at Giants Stadium quickly got to see the dominance that the national team was known for.

* * *

Only 17 minutes into the opening match of the 1999 Women's World Cup, Mia Hamm scored in a splendid bit of skill. The ball bounced toward her on the right flank, and she tapped it with her right foot, around a Danish defender, onto her left foot, and, off the bounce, fired a half-volleyed shot. It was a powerful blast that hit the roof of the net, and the national team's path to winning the World Cup was firmly underway.

Hamm ran toward the team bench, screaming and pointing her finger in the air until her teammates caught up with her and jumped on her, creating a massive group hug. The players' emotions were bubbling at the surface and, in that moment, it was a release—equal parts excitement and relief.

From there, the U.S. bulldozed their way through the group stage. After a 3–0 win over Denmark in the opener, they went to Chicago and walloped Nigeria, 7–1, in front of a sellout crowd of 65,080 on June 24, 1999.

By the time the Americans prepared to play North Korea in the final match of the group stage three days later, Shannon MacMillan and Tisha Venturini had jokingly discussed what they might do if they scored. MacMillan scored first in that game. Venturini, who scored next, wanted to do a backflip, but she didn't get the chance.

"I didn't know she was going to do the backflip," MacMillan says. "I assisted her goal, and I jumped on her back before she could do it—it was just pure adrenaline."

When Venturini scored again a few minutes later, she made sure no one got in the way.

"After her second goal, she waved everybody off and pulled out this crazy flip," MacMillan says. "We were like, *Where did that come from?* We'd never seen her do that before."

The Americans were having fun, outscoring their group-stage opponents by a whopping 13–1. They easily topped Group A and advanced to the quarterfinals, where they would face one of the best teams in the world: Germany.

That was when the fun stopped.

The German team was one of the world's best, and four years earlier at the 1995 World Cup in Sweden, they had finished as runners-up to Norway.

"We are no more afraid of the Americans than they are of us," said German goalkeeper Silke Rottenberg before the quarterfinal. "We don't want to hide from the Americans."

But it wasn't the Germans who hurt the Americans first—it was the Americans themselves. Just five minutes into the quarterfinal in Maryland outside of Washington, D.C., defender Brandi Chastain tapped the ball back to Briana Scurry in goal with the German attacking line pressing. But Scurry was already coming out of goal, and the ball rolled right past her, back into the USA's own net.

Chastain remembers: "I thought, *I'm just gonna make a simple play and pass it back to Briana Scurry*, and Briana was thinking, *I'll just come out and get the ball and make a simple play*, and we didn't communicate."

It was an own goal, and Germany was ahead, 1–0. All of a sudden, on July 1, 1999, the Americans were in danger of being knocked out of the tournament.

Chastain instantly blamed herself. But Carla Overbeck, the team's cocaptain and the mother of a 2-year-old, wouldn't let that feeling linger.

"That could've been the most awful moment—and it wasn't great, that's for sure," says Chastain, "but after we raced back to the goal and we got there just too late, it was almost instantaneous that Carla grabs me and says, *Don't worry about it; there's a lot of game left. We're going to win, and you're going to help us.*

"Not for one second longer—and I mean it—did I think about the fact I just scored an own goal. I never let myself think, *Oh my gosh, I just lost the game.* When you trust people and they're there for you in moments like that, you can only feel empowered. Carla empowered me to move forward."

The Americans equalized 10 minutes later when a Michelle Akers shot was deflected and Tiffeny Milbrett fired the loose ball into the net. Chastain's own goal had essentially been canceled out and the two sides were square again.

The first half dragged on, and the Americans felt that if they could get back to the locker room for halftime with the score level, they could win it in the second half. But in stoppage time before the halftime whistle blew, German striker Bettina Wiegmann fired an absolute rocket from some 25 yards out, and a diving Briana Scurry couldn't get a hand on it. The U.S. was down again, 2–1, and it looked like it could be the dagger that ended their World Cup on home soil.

"When the halftime whistle blew, that was the first time I saw panic," remembers midfielder Tiffeny Milbrett, a native of Portland, Oregon. "We didn't panic in terms of, *Oh, we're going to collapse*—but I saw stress like I hadn't seen. It was probably a remembrance of losing in 1995. It was a moment of realization that we could lose."

The Americans came out of the locker room with fight and energy in the second half. They pressed the Germans hard to win the ball back and they were quick in transition, pushing numbers forward to create chances in the attack.

It was only four minutes into the second half when the Americans found another crucial equalizer. And it came from Brandi Chastain, who scored by firing a volley in the box. She credits Carla Overbeck with allowing her to be ready to score when the moment arrived.

"I always talk about it in a funny way, like, *Woo, thank goodness Carla plays for our team.* But she allowed me to be ready for my moment, and that was the moment my team needed," Chastain says. "I just feel like that is one of the most important moments I've had in my life.

"I always say, you're going to make mistakes, so embrace that fact. What are you going to do when that happens? Are you going to quit? That has been my life ever since that moment."

Chastain fell down on the grass after her goal and lay there for a moment with her eyes closed and arms out while her teammates rushed over and piled on top of her. Redemption.

With the score tied at 2–2, a chance for the Americans to move on was there for the taking. Shannon MacMillan was watching from the bench, and she noticed that Joy Fawcett wasn't being marked well on set pieces.

"When you're on the bench, that's just one of the hardest places to be, because you can't really affect the game," MacMillan says. "So for me, I was watching the game and realizing Joy's open on the near post. I kept seeing her on the near post—there was this massive gap."

In the 65th minute, with the game stopped as the Americans lined up for a corner kick, MacMillan came on as a substitute for Julie Foudy. At first, MacMillan thought Tiffeny Milbrett would take the corner kick, but Milbrett waved her over. MacMillan's first touch of the game would be serving a corner kick into the box.

She looked for Joy Fawcett.

"I just knew Joy was going to be there," MacMillan says. "I drilled the ball into that near post and, as soon as it left my foot, I knew."

Fawcett redirected the ball into the goal with her head and the Americans were back on top. MacMillan ran straight to Fawcett for a hug.

Live television cameras caught Bill and Hillary Clinton celebrating the goal in a suite overlooking the field at Jack Kent Cooke Stadium. They laughed as they clapped, almost in disbelief of the USA's tenacity.

"To come off the bench, and have that be my first touch, and get the ball to Joy, who was my rock on the team, I couldn't get to her fast enough to celebrate," MacMillan says. Joy Fawcett, a defender, was, along with Overbeck, the only other mother on the team. Fawcett had two daughters, and she raised them around her teammates, reinforcing the family atmosphere of the national team.

After finishing the job against Germany, the U.S. blew past Brazil in the semifinals, winning 2–0. At the Brazil game, the U.S. women played in front of 73,123 fans, and by the time D.C. United, the men's pro club team, took the field as part of a doubleheader—an extra measure to ensure the games could attract crowds—60,000 people got up and left. It was clear who the crowds had come to see.

With that, the Americans had landed their spot in the final versus China.

* * *

Once the World Cup final arrived, the U.S. women's national team players were more popular than they had ever been by orders of magnitude. Suddenly, more people were showing up to watch team practices than had come to games one year before. Police barricades had to keep the fans at bay.

Tiffeny Milbrett remembers getting off the team bus in Los Angeles with Michelle Akers and joking to her teammate: "Whoa, now we know how it feels to be animals in the zoo."

Everything the players of the national team did elicited a reaction from the massive crowds that came to watch them train. The smallest moments would prompt whispers or laughter or cheers from the crowd.

"There were so many people that were so interested in us," Milbrett says. "That to me was the weirdest feeling and pivotal moment to say: *Wow, I've never experienced attention like this before.* That was the moment you realize these people were here for you and they were interested in you."

As the U.S. national team continued through the tournament, the attention grew bigger and bigger, which meant new experiences along the way. One of them happened during the group stage in Chicago. One fan, a girl maybe around 10 years old, chased the team bus for blocks until the players finally urged the bus driver to stop. They figured they should reward the young fan for her effort somehow.

"That girl probably chased us for four or five blocks before we finally yelled to the driver, *Stop, stop, stop!*" Shannon MacMillan remembers. "We were like, *What should we give her?* Brandi pulls out her shoes and tosses them to the poor girl. She probably had a heart attack right there when the bus pulled away."

A women's soccer event that started with doubts about ticket sales, followed by worries about how long the excitement could last, was showing no signs of slowing down.

"Halfway through the tournament, you started to see it snowball," says Julie Foudy. "I thought maybe Giants Stadium was a one-off, and we were worried about how we could sustain those levels. But you just saw the frenzy escalate as the tournament went on. We'd have 2,000 people lining the practice field in this frenzy, just screaming at us. That's when we started figuring out we had hit a nerve."

By the end, the players knew the stakes. The 1999 Women's World Cup final against China had legitimately become a major event both in the U.S. and globally.

At the time, diplomatic relations were tense because the U.S. had bombed a Chinese embassy in Yugoslavia, killing three Chinese citizens, which the U.S. government said was an accident. JP Dellacamera, the play-by-play announcer for ESPN and ABC during the tournament, remembers there being an unusual heightened sense of concern.

"The night before the final we had a big production meeting and we were told, god forbid if something happens, make sure you guys are safe—safety is the first priority—but if you're in a position where you can help describe what's going on, then that's what we expect you do," he recalls. "I remember thinking that was unusual."

For the players, the final got off to a rocky start because television scheduling left almost no time between the third-place match and the final. When Norway and Brazil were stuck at a 0–0 deadlock after 90 minutes, instead of the third-place game continuing into extra time, as it was supposed to, it went straight to penalty kicks. But that still took longer than the TV schedule allowed, and while that game dragged on, the Americans started to warm up for the final inside the stadium in sneakers, instead of on the grass in cleats, as they were supposed to.

"The bulk of our pregame warm-up was in our running shoes on cement underneath the Rose Bowl bleachers," Tiffeny Milbrett recalls.

"But the third-place game didn't even get to extra time—they had to go to PKs immediately because of TV time. How unfair is that?"

The American players needed to ignore that disruption to their usual routine and forge ahead. They quickly were shuffled out on the field, where the pop-rock band Hanson sung the national anthem, jets raced overhead, and the whistle blew for kickoff.

In front of a record crowd of 90,185 people at the Rose Bowl in Pasadena, California—the largest ever to see a women's sporting event—the players of the U.S. women's national team were about to play the biggest game of their lives.

* * *

The match started like many high-stakes finals: It was tight, it was scoreless, and both sides just wanted to minimize mistakes. The occasion was huge, and neither side was willing to push too hard and risk giving up a goal on a counterattack.

Michelle Akers was a marauding presence in the midfield as she sniffed out potential attacks and shut them down. Her teammates nicknamed her Mufasa after the *Lion King* character, ostensibly because of her wild mane of curly hair, but it was also fitting for the way she prowled the midfield and pounced after the ball. China managed just two shots on goal after 90 minutes.

As Akers put it in 1999: "I play hard and people just bounce off me or I go through them. I don't notice it until after I get hit in the face."

But seconds before the fulltime whistle blew, forcing the 0–0 match into extra time, Akers collided with Briana Scurry in the box on a corner kick. Akers crumbled to the turf and stayed down in a heap.

She was woozy from an apparent concussion and dehydration. Doctors checked on her to see if she needed to be taken to the hospital, but either way, she needed to come out of the game. She, of course, tried to convince the coaching staff otherwise and to let her keep playing.

"That's Michelle," assistant coach Lauren Gregg says. "She would die for this team. We had our physician assess her, and the decision was that her health was in jeopardy. There was nothing that would allow us to put her on the field."

As extra time started, Akers was on a stretcher in the U.S. locker room, with an IV in each arm and an oxygen mask over her face.

For as tough as Akers was, she suffered from chronic fatigue syndrome, a condition that sapped her of energy when she did the most mundane tasks. She fought her way through it, but her concussion left her especially woozy. Out of sorts, she kept asking for the score, even though the game was on a TV that she was watching in the locker room.

Back on the field, losing their midfield enforcer changed the way the Americans played. Sara Whalen replaced Akers and took Joy Fawcett's spot on the back line while Fawcett shifted to defensive midfield. The Chinese looked revived by the change. They attacked more freely through the midfield and found another three shots on goal during extra time.

One of those shots should have sealed a victory for China. Ten minutes into extra time, China executed a perfect corner kick: a lofted ball toward the top of a six-yard box followed by a driving header toward the far post. Briana Scurry, stationed at the near post, had been beat, and there was no way she was going to get a hand on the ball.

"I was like: *Uh-oh, the ball's behind me*," Scurry said after the game.

If the ball went into the net, China would win because, at the time, the golden-goal rule was in effect: the first goal scored in an overtime period would be the game-winner.

Kristine Lilly, meanwhile, was stationed at the far post, her feet on the goal line. It was a job assigned to her on corner kicks. As the ball went across the face of goal for the corner, she drifted away from her post, but as the ball headed past Scurry and toward the open net, Lilly was in the exact perfect spot to lunge upward and head the ball away from the goal.

It was pure instinct. Lilly single-handedly denied China a game-winning goal.

"It happened like that," Lilly later said, snapping her fingers. "I did not even know what was going on."

The Americans held on after that and, with the score stuck at 0–0 at the end of extra time, the match would be decided on penalty kicks—a fitting final act of drama for a World Cup full of thrilling performances.

* * *

Penalty kicks. PKs. Spot kicks. A penalty shootout. Whatever nomenclature you choose, deciding a game via penalty kicks is an excruciating and oftentimes cruel twist in soccer. Some call it a crapshoot based on pure luck. Others think it's a legitimate test of skill. But a penalty shootout is very different than the 120 minutes of soccer that precede it.

The penalty shootout is all about psychological tricks.

There's not enough time for a goalkeeper to read a shot and react after the ball is kicked, so they often choose a side before the player even shoots and then lunge in the chosen direction as the player connects their foot to the ball. Goalkeepers often memorize which side certain players prefer and run through the odds before they choose which side to lunge for.

Most of the time, goalkeepers stretch their arms out in goal as the player walks up to the spot—the goalkeeper wants to look bigger and thus make the goal look smaller. Maybe, then, the shooter will become rattled or overthink the placement of the ball.

For the kickers, the key when shooting is to not give away whether they are opening up their stance to shoot outside, or whether they're shooting across their body inside. Some players might stutter-step in their run-up to the ball to throw the goalkeeper of her rhythm. Some will make eye contact with the goalkeeper to show they are fearless, while many will block the goalkeeper out and focus only on the ball.

Lauren Gregg helped Tony DiCicco prepare the team to take penalty kicks, and she had a journal full of penalty kick observations just in case of a moment like this.

Michelle Akers would've taken a penalty kick, but her concussion left Gregg with a choice: Should Brandi Chastain take her spot or Julie Foudy? Gregg was worried because earlier that year, in a friendly against China and goalkeeper Gao Hong, Chastain had a penalty kick and missed—it went off the crossbar. Chastain also tended to kick to the right side with her right foot. If Chastain was going to take another kick against the same Chinese goalkeeper in a World Cup final, it would need to be an attempt that Hong would not expect.

Gregg leaned toward choosing Foudy, but DiCicco had an idea—one that might be enough to throw China's goalkeeper off. Could Chastain take it with her weaker foot? DiCicco told Gregg to find out.

"I went up to her and said, *We want you to take a kick, but are you comfortable taking it with your left foot?* She said, *Hell yeah!* She wanted it," Gregg remembers.

Chastain had never taken a penalty kick with her left foot before, but she didn't hesitate. She didn't really know why she was asked to kick it with her left foot—all she knew was that she was ready.

Mia Hamm was less enthusiastic about the shootout. She was the star of the team and arguably the team's best, most reliable player. But she tried to get out of being one of the first five penalty kick-takers.

Hamm looked Gregg in the eyes and said: "I don't think I should take the kick."

"I remember it like it was yesterday," Gregg says. "I remember thinking that I cannot flinch a muscle and I cannot show anything but a mirror of confidence to this kid."

Gregg was surprised by Hamm's self-doubt in taking a kick but played it cool. She told the player: "We need you. You're one of the best goal-scorers in the world." Hamm nodded and said, "Okay."

The Americans and the Chinese went back and forth exchanging successful attempts for four straight kicks. Someone needed to miss eventually to break the deadlock.

For Briana Scurry, just one save would've been good enough. For a goalkeeper in a penalty-kick shootout, getting even just one save is considered a huge success. Saving one shot means giving your own team of kickers the chance to pull ahead and win. Whether the goalkeeper's team wins or loses, if she saves one penalty kick, everyone will say the goalkeeper did her job.

As one of her psychological tricks, Scurry never watched her own team during penalty kicks. During the 1999 World Cup final, she waited to hear the crowd's reaction to tell her it was time to go back into the goal.

As she puts it now: "Whether we scored or not is not relevant to me at the time because it's not in my control, and I don't let it filter into my thinking."

Scurry also never looked at the kicker until she stepped into the goal and was ready for the shot. But when Liu Ying, China's third kicker, stepped up to the spot, something felt different.

"I was walking from my place where I wait into the goal and something in my mind said, *Look*," Scurry remembers now. "I looked at her and I knew she was the one. How do I know that? I felt like—and I still feel this way 20 years later—I just knew. There's certain times in sports where you have a surreal, otherworldly feeling about stuff. I had an audible sound in my mind that said, *This is it*. I just knew."

"Players talk about being in the zone and the net looking big or whatever, and it was like that," she adds. "It didn't matter where she kicked it—I was going to save it."

Liu Ying took her shot, and Scurry lunged out to her left and palmed the ball away. As the crowd let out a deafening roar, Scurry erupted with an explosion of fist pumping and screaming as she walked back to her place to wait while kicks proceeded. Suddenly, the Americans had a chance to pull ahead.

Lilly went next, putting the U.S. ahead, but China answered. Hamm followed, looking nervy but burying her shot, and again China scored. It came down to Brandi Chastain, the last kicker in the USA's rotation. If she made it, the U.S. would win and become the biggest success story of perhaps a generation. If not, China could still come back and win it.

"It was such a heavy moment," Chastain says. "The feeling was that the future of women's soccer depends on the outcome of this game."

Chastain settled the ball at the spot, took a few steps back, and waited for the whistle to blow. When it did, she waited for a moment and then ran up to kick the ball. With her left foot, she fired it across her body to the right side of the goal. The Chinese goalkeeper, Gao Hong, was diving the correct way, but Chastain's placement was too good. The ball tucked just inside the post and out of Hong's reach.

The ball hit the back of the goal loudly enough to make a loud thump. And then the Rose Bowl filled with the roar from the crowd in unison.

The U.S. had just won the 1999 Women's World Cup. Chastain ripped her shirt off without a moment's hesitation, waved it around her head, and then dropped to her knees. The image of her on her knees behind the penalty spot, both fists in the air—jersey clenched in her right fist—was captured by photographers. It instantly became one of the most iconic images in American sports.

The players rushed Chastain, who lunged to her feet and pointed in the air with a huge smile spread across her face. Michelle Akers, still woozy, yanked the IVs from her arm and charged out onto the field to celebrate.

The players of the national team were world champions again—and this time, everyone knew about it.

CHAPTER 5

"Babe City, Ladies and Gentlemen"

There was one specific moment when Briana Scurry knew something had changed for her after the 1999 World Cup.

She was still in Pasadena, California, where the team had won the trophy in front of a record crowd at the Rose Bowl and for a record TV viewing audience. ABC said 40 million people watched some or all of the final, and the overnight TV ratings were more than double the network's expectations. The national team had just finished its media obligations for the moment—they were the stars of a parade down Disneyland's Main Street the morning after the final and were quickly being booked by everyone from David Letterman to the White House.

With some downtime, Scurry was on her way to lunch with friends who were in town for the tournament. She wasn't wearing any U.S. Soccer–branded gear, and she certainly wasn't wearing goalkeeper gloves and cleats—there was no obvious hint as to who she was. But as she walked down a sidewalk, she heard a man yelling her name.

"Scurry! Scurry! SCURRY!" The man slammed on his brakes in the middle of the street, put the car in park, opened his door, and ran over to her.

"I just had to come over and shake your hand and tell you that you were awesome," he told her. His car was still sitting in the street with the door hanging open and cars were waiting behind. The man looked close to Scurry's own age at the time, 27.

He shook her hand enthusiastically and then, as quickly as he appeared, he left. He ran back to his car and drove off.

It was a whirlwind encounter that would become increasingly common to her. In the days after the tournament, she'd be stopped by as many as a dozen people every day, a change of pace from the very sporadic fan encounters she'd had before. For the first time, many of the fans approaching her were grown men.

"People would buy me lunches and dinners and come up to me and say, *Oh my gosh, you're Scurry!*" she says. "We knew we were doing something amazing, but all we were trying to do was win that final. I don't think we really understood how many people had seen it and how it impacted people."

Among the team's fans was the First Family of the United States. After their victory, the players went to the White House to be honored, and Hillary Clinton made an offhand comment about a shuttle launch in Florida she was headed to and asked if the players wanted to join her on the trip. The players turned to Aaron Heifetz, their press officer, for permission. He said their schedule was free, and they turned back to the First Lady and said, "Okay!"

So, off the U.S. women's national team went for a flight on Air Force Two with Hillary Clinton and a group of female senators.

"I think we looted the plane. Everything that wasn't bolted down—little boxes of M&M's to the napkins with the presidential seal—we took," says Shannon MacMillan with a laugh, noting she recently came upon the boxes of M&M's she had saved from that trip some 19 years later.

The tournament and the frenzied attention surrounding it introduced the players to a new lifestyle at a time when neither soccer nor female sports had been in the public consciousness much. Suddenly, they were all celebrities.

The team took up entire floors of hotels and had to use code names for their hotel rooms. Julie Foudy chose the name Julia Gulia, after a character from the movie *The Wedding Singer*. Shannon MacMillan was Gina Von Amberg, after a character on the soap opera *Day of Our Lives*. Kate Markgraf was Stifler, named after the *American Pie* character who tended to say inappropriate things. Some code names weren't so much names as inside jokes. Mia Hamm chose "How *You* Doin'," which was Joey Tribbiani's catch phrase on the sitcom *Friends*. Michelle Akers was Pig Farmer.

Without such code names, fans could've easily called players by asking for them at hotels—and they probably would have. Tiffeny Milbrett remembers that shortly after the World Cup, her home phone in Portland, Oregon, rang and, when she answered, it was the voice of what sounded like a teenage girl.

"Is Tiffeny Milbrett there?"

"Yeah, this is Tiffeny."

"OH MY GOD! It's *you!*"

The girl started crying. Although Milbrett was flattered, she changed her number and made sure it wasn't published after that. She also learned to brace herself before going out.

"You realized every time you stepped out that someone might recognize you," Milbrett says. "Every time I stepped out in public, I remembered, there is going to be one or multiple people who will know you and they'll be watching, and it was that way for years."

Eric Wynalda, the striker for the U.S. men's national team that came in last place at the World Cup one year prior, now credits the women's team with saving soccer in America. The men embarrassed themselves at the 1998 World Cup in France and made American soccer look like a joke, but the women in 1999 made it something everyone wanted to be a part of.

"Nobody ever says this out loud, but I'm going to: Not until Brandi Chastain saved it in 1999 did we have a good feeling about this sport," Wynalda says. "The boys had blown it."

* * *

Brandi Chastain remembers vividly the first time she saw the *Sports Illustrated* cover. It featured what is now a famous image: She was on the grass field of the Rose Bowl, shirt in hand, muscles flexed, celebrating her winning kick at the 1999 Women's World Cup.

Days after the World Cup had ended, she was in New York City for an event Nike held near Times Square with the streets blocked off, and as she stood on stage, someone handed her a huge blown-up image of the magazine in a frame. Chastain, who had been nicknamed "Hollywood" by her teammates because of how dramatic she could be when appealing to refs, was speechless.

"Never in my wildest imagination was this happening in my future," Chastain says. "In a way, I feel really proud about that because I never once put on a pair of cleats or put on my uniform with this underlying goal of being famous. That was never a part of it. I fell in love with soccer and sports as a young girl and I just loved playing."

But that visual of her celebrating in her sports bra took what was already a big moment and turned it into a cultural phenomenon.

Suddenly, Chastain became the world's most famous bra-wearing athlete and, with that, she found herself in the middle of a conversation about female sexuality in sports. Everyone wanted her to weigh in, and it was bewildering to her.

"I became a person who got asked a lot about sexuality in sports, or can you be feminine and be athletic?" she says. "These were discussions that, gosh, prior to those questions, I never spent very much time thinking about. What we all collectively consumed ourselves with was, how can I personally improve so I can help my team? The sexualization of sports or the defeminization of women in sports never crossed my mind."

Men ripped off their shirts to celebrate goals all the time in soccer. It was so common that a couple of years later FIFA passed a new rule that removing a shirt during a goal celebration would be an automatic yellow card. But a woman doing it sparked a debate. It got its own "hot topics" segment on *The View* and became fodder for late-night TV.

In an article titled "U.S. Women Win World Cup and Promptly Tarnish It," one columnist in Indiana wrote that Chastain "was the worst the U.S. had to offer." Another column in Iowa, "Stripping Down to Sports Bra No Big Deal," fired back to the outcry: "Well, you would think she mooned the queen the way this has been reported."

That moment, for a time, could've defined her. It followed her around, and there was no escaping it. But she refused to feel burdened by it.

"There's no doubt that every interview I did for a very long period of time included that moment," she says. "And understandably so, because never before had a women's sporting event garnered that many fans in one location or around the world watching. So, it makes sense that would be a lead question or a follow-up question."

"I always reminded myself: That question allows me the opportunity to walk through the door, answer the question, and then give more information about women's soccer than I had ever been offered before."

In 1999, the American public and the sports landscape itself still seemed unprepared for the rise of a team of female athletes. Individual female athletes—tennis players, gymnasts, and figure skaters—had captured America's attention before, but for the first time, a team of women was commanding the spotlight. Yet, the soccer was almost secondary at times.

During the tournament, Christine Brennan of *USA Today* asked Brandi Chastain: "If you were all ugly, if you were not wholesome, attractive—words that have been attached to you—would this team be as popular?"

Chastain didn't scoff or tell the columnist to take a hike. Instead, she had little choice but to answer this like any other question: "There are those people who come purely for the soccer. There are those people who come purely for the event. And there are those people who come because they like us, to look at us. Those are three great reasons to come."

Just by the virtue of being female athletes who competed with the same passion and competitiveness of the men, the players of the national team were redefining what it meant to both be a woman and an athlete. For many of the fans, including young girls, who followed the team's journey, it was a new way to look at what women could do, an expansion of what it could mean to be athlete.

"Up until then, there were limited gender-appropriate ways to express yourself as a female," says defender Kate Markgraf, who broke into the team in 1998 after graduating from Notre Dame. "For the most part, our team fit into that traditional female look, but in terms of our personalities on the field and how we expressed ourselves and how we joked around and how we weren't quiet, that was at odds with some of the lessons of how females were supposed to be."

"That's where I think those questions were coming from," she adds. "No one had the culturally appropriate language for women who were bucking the norm."

The players' looks became a topic all its own. A small sampling of newspaper headlines in 1999:

- U.S. Women's Team Looking Good: Sex Appeal Part of the Story (*Boston Herald*)
- Uncover Story: Soccer Has Sex Appeal (*Chicago Sun-Times*)
- Get Real: Sex Appeal Does Count (*Washington Times*)
- Talented, Athletic, Sexy—That's U.S. Soccer Team (*Memphis Commercial Appeal*)
- Talented and Sexy: U.S. Team Has It All (*Orlando Sentinel*)
- Success of the '99 Women's World Cup Is . . . Looking Good (*Los Angeles Times*)
- The Babe Factor In Soccer Team's Success (Scripps News Service)

The debate teetered between whether sex appeal was driving the team's popularity and whether the players' traditional femininity—wearing makeup and posing in magazine spreads, all while being strong competitors on the field—was feminist or not. One columnist for the *San Francisco Examiner*, like others, was unable to reconcile the team's girls-next-door image with its athleticism—writing that the 1999 Women's World Cup was played "like the talent competition in the Miss America pageant, rather than as a sporting event."

Chastain landed herself in that conversation not just because she celebrated in her bra, although that became the biggest flash point. Just before the 1999 World Cup, she posed for *Gear* magazine covered with nothing except some strategically placed soccer balls. That photoshoot—not anything she did on the field—prompted David Letterman to invite her on his late-night talk show before the 1999 World Cup started. He displayed her photo to his audience and remarked: "Soccer moms? Soccer mamas!"

While much of the national team's attention came after the Women's World Cup had started, Letterman was ahead of the curve, and he was credited by organizers as helping drum up excitement for the tournament. But he seemed less enthralled by the soccer than by the women themselves.

After Chastain's segment, Letterman told his audience: "The U.S. team—and this may come out wrong, but I'll just say it and forget about it—is Babe City, ladies and gentlemen. Babe City!"

Whether it was sex appeal or not, the national team was connecting with men in a way it never had before. That didn't come as a surprise to the 1999 Women's World Cup organizers, though. Marla Messing, the CEO of the organizing committee, says everyone assumed their target audience would be "soccer moms," but they instead targeted men who had daughters who played soccer.

"Back in '98 and '99, the image was a soccer mom in her minivan—it was a whole cultural thing," Messing says. "But we decided that, back then, it was men who bought tickets to sporting events, and this was an opportunity for them to do something with their daughters."

Men showed unprecedented interest in the team, whether they had soccer-playing daughters or not. According to ESPN, two-thirds of the TV viewers who watched the Women's World Cup were men.

The players certainly noticed, and Shannon MacMillan recalls seeing more and more men at their practices asking for autographs.

"The older guys would be like, *It's for my granddaughter*, and I'd say, *Oh, what's her name?*" MacMillan remembers. "They'd say, *Oh, don't put her name on it—I'll put it on later.*"

MacMillan laughs because she knew there was no granddaughter. She would joke back to the men: "We can sign it for you—that's fine. You don't have to come up with a story."

But just as quickly as the excitement was building around the team, critics were quick to write off their success as a one-off—a big event but hardly a blueprint for sustained interest in women's soccer.

Shaun Powell, a columnist for *Newsday*, summed up the sentiment in the bluntest of terms: "For those living in the good ol' male-dominated sports world, fear not. By tomorrow, you will reclaim the sports pages. You can turn on ESPN and not mistake it for the Lifetime Channel. No more athletes with first names that end with 'i.' And from now on, you only get Hamm between rye and Brandi after dinner, thank you. Hey, the Women's World Cup was nice. But, please. It's time to be realistic, at the risk of sounding chauvinistic. The whole event was overhype at its best, or worst, whichever you prefer."

While that sort of rhetoric could be dismissed as run-of-the-mill sexism, the players undoubtedly faced a major uphill battle. Suddenly, millions of Americans were aware they existed for the first time, and the lingering question was: What comes next? There was no blueprint for what the players needed to do to sustain their careers.

What was clear, however, was that it would be up to the players to try to figure it out. Otherwise, it would become increasingly difficult for them to keep playing. For all the fanfare surrounding the players and the prestige they brought to the U.S. Soccer Federation and FIFA, their rewards were relatively small.

The players earned bonuses of around $50,000 each for winning the World Cup. Most of that payout came as an unplanned gesture from the organizing committee, which made off with an unexpected profit, and U.S. Soccer offered $12,500 per player.

FIFA didn't offer any prize money for the Women's World Cup. Meanwhile, one year earlier, FIFA had given awards to the U.S. men of around $25,000 each for simply qualifying for the World Cup. If the men had won, they would've gotten $388,000 each, but instead, the U.S. men lost all three group-stage games, came in last place, and FIFA still rewarded them.

For the women, who earned small salaries at the time, a onetime bonus wouldn't be enough to sustain their careers. They had proven in front of record audiences that they were serious athletes—but money, air time, and respect in a crowded sports landscape weren't a given.

The players had to fight for it. They had already proved they could do it on the field, and they were about to show they could fight off the field, too.

CHAPTER 6

*"Oh S***, These Women Are for Real"*

On the morning after the national team won the 1999 World Cup, the celebrations continued. While the players were off to do a victory parade at Disneyland, officials from the U.S. Soccer Federation opened the sports pages of local newspapers, eager to see the coverage of the victory.

The *Los Angeles Times* used the headline "America the Bootiful" alongside a large photo of Briana Scurry's penalty-kick save. Some of the U.S. Soccer brass probably cracked a smile at the pun. But when they turned to page 5, they saw a different headline—one that would touch off a bitter dispute and mark a permanent change in the relationship between the players and their boss, the federation. It was on a full-page advertisement for an indoor victory tour the national team players had scheduled for that fall.

Hank Steinbrecher, the secretary general of U.S. Soccer, was shocked. The players were calling themselves the All-American Soccer Stars but essentially planned to travel to 12 cities as the World Cup–winning U.S. national team to play exhibition games against an all-star team of world internationals. Robert Contiguglia, the president of U.S. Soccer, was furious.

But if the heads of U.S. Soccer were shocked, as they claimed, it was only because they hadn't been paying attention—not just to notices the players gave them about the tour but to the players' demands for more respect in general.

It was only one year earlier the players had to get their new lawyer, John Langel of Ballard Spahr, to chase down bonus payments they had been owed for more than a year. He first agreed to represent the players on a pro bono basis and met with them in September 1998, about 17 months after the national team won all six games and sold out three in a Nike-sponsored tournament. Langel was stunned to learn the players were still waiting for the $3,000 each they were owed by U.S. Soccer for that tournament.

"To women who weren't making a lot of money, $70,000 collectively, or about $3,000 per player, was a lot of money," Langel says.

He and the players decided they should come up with a list of grievances and bring all their complaints to the federation. Much of the list came simply from looking at what the men's team had and comparing it to the women's. Did they have physical therapists? How many? What about massage therapists? Did the men have equipment managers? Across the board, the men's team had more.

While the women carried their own equipment, the players on the men's team didn't have to worry about such things. While the men's team traveled to games in luxury buses, the women traveled in vans. The men stayed in better hotels and had better accommodations for flights, too.

"We were staying in hotels that had cockroaches in them, and we had to drive to games in hotel shuttle buses. We actually went to a game on a Holiday Inn shuttle bus once," Julie Foudy says. "I'd take pictures of us in every single middle seat going up the plane. Back then they had the smoking section, and our seats were always the ones before smoking—we were sitting 10 hours in smoke-infested quarters on long flights. Little things became big things."

At one team training session in Florida in 1998, Langel visited the team and noticed Kristine Lilly wasn't there.

"Where's Lil?" he asked.

"Oh, she went to get us some bagels and fruit because we have two-a-days," the answer came. "Our nutritionist says we should eat an hour after our first training and an hour before our next one."

Langel was again stunned. The players had double training days, and in between sessions, a player had to run out and get food because U.S. Soccer didn't provide catering like they did at the men's training sessions. That went on the list, too.

Other small things added up. Players weren't allowed to keep their jerseys after they played—they had to give them back to the federation, which was unusual in the world of soccer. There were no provisions that covered childcare for mothers on the team. Joy Fawcett and Carla Overbeck had children that they often took to national team camps.

Armed with the list and the complaint of late bonus payments, Langel told U.S. Soccer they had breached their contract and the players wanted a new one. The federation disagreed and refused to budge, even as it eventually paid the overdue bonuses.

By January, when the draw came around for the 1999 Women's World Cup—the event the women would campaign so hard to promote—the players were still angry at U.S. Soccer. Langel threatened the federation: Mia Hamm, the star of the team, would not to appear at the draw unless the federation made some concessions. The draw, which would determine the matchups for the tournament, was a major promotional event, and it would've been a public embarrassment if Hamm didn't show up. The federation relented and made a deal.

"It wasn't a major deal, but it set the table for equivalency on some noneconomic items with the men's team, like training tables and doctors and physical therapists and massage therapists," Langel says. "Nothing got out to the media, and no one knew that Mia might not show up to the draw."

After that ordeal, the players learned not to expect U.S. Soccer to look out for them—the players felt they needed to take care of themselves. With the 1999 Women's World Cup on the horizon, the players, with Langel's help, set out to find ways to capitalize on the tournament.

The inspiration for the indoor victory tour—the one advertised in the *Los Angeles Times* after the 1999 Women's World Cup—came from an unlikely, tragic source.

After the 1996 Olympics, even though the gold-medal match wasn't aired live and most Americans didn't see the national team win, Mia Hamm's star power started to break through. Her sponsorship agreement with Nike blossomed into heavy-rotation ads, and she picked up other deals, including Pert Plus shampoo and Gatorade. She was named to *People* magazine's "50 Most Beautiful People" list. Everything seemed to be going right for the goal-scorer.

But amid all that, she lost something she would've given all of it up for. Her 28-year-old brother, Garrett, died from an infection after a bone-marrow transplant eight months after she won the gold medal. Garrett joined Hamm's family when she was 5 years old—her parents adopted Garrett, an 8-year-old Thai American orphan—and they grew incredibly close. As children, they played soccer together.

Garrett was diagnosed with a rare blood disorder called aplastic anemia at 16. Even when he was very sick in his final year and doctors told him there was nothing they could do to help his worsening condition, he was there in Atlanta for the 1996 Olympics to watch his sister win a gold medal, tears streaming down his face.

"He kept telling me how proud he was of me. That meant so much to me," Hamm later said. "It wasn't so much that he had high standards for me, but I always looked at him as setting a standard that I could never reach. Having him say that meant the world. It meant so much to me that my family was there. It wouldn't have been complete without Garrett. And it never will be."

After he died, Hamm made it her mission to honor him. She founded the Mia Hamm Foundation and launched an annual fundraising event called the Garrett Game, where she and her teammates competed against all-stars from NCAA college teams.

Hamm just so happened to mention the all-star game fundraiser to John Langel, and something clicked. An all-star game was the post–World Cup opportunity the national team was looking for.

After all, the players had already asked U.S. Soccer how the federation planned to capitalize on hosting the Women's World Cup on home soil. The answer they got back, essentially, was that the federation wasn't really thinking about that.

"We pressed them on it and said, *Hey, what are you doing? What are the plans?*" remembers Julie Foudy. "They said we were going to Africa. We were like, *Africa? We need to grow the game here. Why are we going to Africa?* We had never even been to Africa."

Yes, for some reason, U.S. Soccer president Robert Contiguglia and secretary general Hank Steinbrecher wanted to send the players on tour in South Africa and Egypt after the 1999 World Cup, when interest in the team at home would be at an all-time high. To this day, the players don't understand what U.S. Soccer's higher-ups were thinking.

To say the federation lacked foresight or ambition to help the national team keep up its momentum is to put it mildly. There was no strategy to grow interest in the sport from the federation responsible for it, to say nothing of cashing in and hosting games that would sell lots of tickets. It was a strange response from the federation that only deepened the team's mistrust of their boss.

"They had nothing for us," Kate Markgraf says. "They had no plan. They didn't think the World Cup would be what it was."

So the players started talking through the details of a tour they could put on themselves. They agreed to hire event-marketing firm SFX, which could handle logistics of the tour. But it wasn't done in secret behind U.S. Soccer's back, as the federation later made it seem.

Langel and the players sent letters to U.S. Soccer notifying the federation of their plans, but officials just ignored their messages. The team attempted again just before the Women's World Cup to see if U.S. Soccer wanted to have anything to do with the tour.

"They just kept ignoring us," Langel says. "I said, *Look, we're going ahead with this. Do you want to do it with us?* But they didn't believe we could get it off the ground. They essentially told us: *Try.* So we decided to go ahead with the tour on our own."

For the national team, the tour represented a unique opportunity to make some real money: a guaranteed $1.2 million for the 12-city tour. Most important, it was income shared equally among all the players, $60,000 each, because the top players—those like Mia Hamm and Julie Foudy—insisted it be that way.

It was another step toward securing financial independence as more individual players started to earn their own endorsement deals and didn't need to rely on U.S. Soccer as much. By then, Nike had expanded its footprint in soccer beyond Mia Hamm. They'd added Brandi Chastain, Briana Scurry, Tiffeny Milbrett, and Tisha Venturini to their roster of sponsored athletes and featured all five of them in advertisements that promoted the Women's World Cup. Nike's expansion into women's soccer was a game-changer for the players who benefited from it.

"Soccer was my side hustle. There was no money in it originally. But I came right when Nike came in, and I started to get a little bit of money," says Briana Scurry. "It was impeccable timing because if it wasn't something that would allow me to pay my bills, I would've had to stop—we all would've had to, and that would've really been a shame."

Not everyone had that same opportunity for sponsorship, but now, with this collective group effort to launch a tour—by the team and for the team—financial freedom was available across the board. It was a payday for all players.

And in another sense, the players were doing the federation's job for them. The tour allowed the national team to play in front of fans who did not attend World Cup games, which would grow a fan base at home in America. Yes, it gave the players money, but it also spread the gospel of the Beautiful Game, as soccer is known around the world. It did everything that U.S. Soccer's haphazard plan for an African tour would not.

As Julie Foudy put it in a press statement after the tour was announced: "The one thing we've learned recently is that our fans want to see more of us and more of soccer. We're answering their call."

So there were Hank Steinbrecher and Robert Contiguglia opening their newspapers on the morning of July 11, 1991. They were "shocked" by the tour the players warned them about and furious the players weren't going along with the African tour, which would've certainly pushed the national team back into relative obscurity.

"U.S. Soccer went apoplectic," Langel says. "They immediately hired a Chicago law firm, and they sent a complaint to my law firm that they're going to go into federal court to get an injunction."

An injunction, if granted, could have stopped the tour in its tracks. John Langel and his legal team worked through the night to prepare their responses to try to stop the federation from seeking a court-ordered moratorium on the tour. Then came two days of marathon meetings between Langel and Alan Rothenberg, the head of the 1999

Women's World Cup organizing committee. Rothenberg, who had been the president of U.S. Soccer through 1998, played a sort of mediator role.

"They had achieved success and popularity, and they had to properly take advantage of that," Rothenberg says. "But to go around on tour as a unit, no matter what they call themselves—effectively as the national team—that right belonged to the federation."

In a panicked move to retake control, U.S. Soccer offered $2 million to essentially buy out the tour from the national team and send them to Africa as planned. Even though this would be more money than they had ever been paid for playing soccer, the players were having none of it.

"We were like, *You haven't spent any time on this. You expect us to jump ship and go with you guys?*" Foudy says. "*After this marketing group invested in us, not even knowing if the World Cup was going to be a success or not? They're the ones who believed in us, and you never did. No, screw you.*"

Negotiations with U.S. Soccer became incredibly tense and acrimonious. It was as if everything—contract disputes, lack of communication, and perceived slights—was finally coming to a head. When Mia Hamm, Julie Foudy, and John Langel met with U.S. Soccer president Robert Contiguglia and federation counsel John Collins in Washington, D.C., the players were ready to stand up.

At one point during a meeting, Contiguglia was dismissive of the planned victory tour and accused the players of "adulterating the sport" by playing at indoor venues. Mia Hamm threw the comment right back at him.

"You used the word *adulterate*," she said. "Well, I'll use the word *adultery* because we feel like you cheat on us all the time."

Contiguglia was taken aback. The players, who felt like U.S. Soccer was too worried about the men's team, had had enough, and they weren't going to back down, even under the threat of a lawsuit.

"If you sue us, I'm prepared to never play for U.S. Soccer again," Hamm told Contiguglia. Then she turned to her teammate.

"I don't know about you, Julie, but I feel pretty good about what we've done with our careers," Hamm said. "I won a World Cup in '91, I won a World Cup in '99, I won an Olympics in '96. I'll call it a day."

Foudy nodded.

"Yeah, me too," she replied. "I'm pretty happy walking away from the game."

"I'm sure Nike will like that you're walking away from the game, too," Foudy said to Hamm. Foudy was deftly calling out the federation's coveted sponsorship with Nike, which was then worth about $15 million per year.

Asked about these specific negotiations now, Contiguglia says he doesn't remember them, but he does recall that over the years, the relationship between the federation and the players was hostile. At one point, he admits, "I did lose my cool," but he adds: "The last thing I ever wanted was an adversarial relationship with our athletes."

"That's what happens in collective bargaining when you don't have a relationship of mutual trust," Contiguglia says. "It was a horrible, horrible environment. It was not healthy, but I blame lawyers."

While the federation was certainly unhappy the players defied them by moving forward with the indoor tour, there were other practical considerations behind their opposition to the tour. The federation had its own sponsors at the time, and if the national team was going on an unsanctioned tour where they used a competitor's equipment or wore another company's uniforms, it could damage U.S. Soccer's existing business relationships.

After two days of meetings in D.C.—and some sharp-tongued exchanges between the federation and the players—the two sides worked out an understanding: The tour would incorporate all of U.S. Soccer's existing sponsors. The tour the players had worked on was going to happen after all.

After that concession, the players and Langel were fired up. They knew they had some real leverage for the first time. Outside the second meeting, Foudy and Hamm joked with Langel: "Who's driving the bus? We're driving the bus! That's right, we're driving the bus!"

The tour belonged to the players, not U.S. Soccer, and it gave them a new collective revenue stream that wasn't controlled by the federation. It was set to earn them $2.4 million over two tours—one after the 1999

World Cup and one again after the 2000 Olympics—and, in addition to the ticket sales, the team also signed balls and photos, which generated another $250,000 to be shared. Eleven of the players appeared in a Chevrolet commercial together. The players were finding financial freedom they had never experienced before.

As part of the final understanding to make U.S. Soccer happy, the players gave the federation the opportunity to take over the tour afterward if they wanted to do it again. Now, it is built into the national team's contract, and to this day, after major tournaments, the team still goes on the same victory tour. It started with the 1999 team and a "shocking" full-page ad, and it has lasted two decades.

*   *   *

Although the indoor-tour dispute got settled, the conflicts were far from over.

The national team's contract with the federation was set to expire at the end of 1999, which was barreling closer and closer. John Langel had been trying to work out terms for a new deal since the World Cup ended, but U.S. Soccer was uninterested.

The federation had declined to meet for negotiations in the months before the deal was set to expire, from September through November, which angered Langel and the players. Alan Rothenberg flew to Philadelphia to let Langel know that U.S. Soccer would not be making a deal with the players.

"You should've saved your money and called me to tell me that," Langel told him.

Just before the deal was to expire, the federation suggested the players just extend their existing deal, which had been agreed to in 1996. That was a nonstarter for the players, who had still not gotten everything on their list and still earned far less than the men.

The players' demands included better conditions and noneconomic issues, but the sticking points largely came down to compensation. For the months when the players had games to play, the federation was paying the most veteran players a modest $3,150 per month while newer players earned even less. The players had earned about $5,000 per month during the World Cup—a combined wage between U.S. Soccer and the World Cup organizing committee—and that's what they wanted in their new contract.

Even more of an issue than the amount of compensation was the reliability of it. Payment was contingent on the team's schedule, which U.S. Soccer set, so if there were no camps or games in a month, the players got nothing. If a player got injured and couldn't play, she no longer got paid, either.

"We're not going to mortgage our future for one team," Hank Steinbrecher told reporters. "We have the men's team, the U-17s, U-18s, and all the other teams we have to put on the field. Some people think we just have the women's team."

The national team was supposed to go to Australia in January 2000 for a tournament, but they threatened to strike. In return, the federation threatened to send a "B team" in their place, comprised of players from the under-20 youth national team.

The federation spun the ordeal as a positive—as Jim Moorhouse, U.S. Soccer's spokesman, put it: "We will use this trip to Australia as an opportunity to get the next generation of players some valuable playing experience."

The average age of the roster for that Australia Cup, excluding 1995 World Cup defender Thori Bryan, was just 19.9 years old. For some players, it was indeed a huge opportunity to be seen at the senior national team level.

One of those players who crossed the proverbial picket line was Danielle Slaton, who would remain in the national team picture for years afterward. When she was called up for the Australia Cup, she was aware it was due to a dispute the national team was having with U.S. Soccer. Because she knew Brandi Chastain from Santa Clara University, she spoke with her before going.

"It's not a problem," Chastain told her. "Go play in the tournament."

The national team veterans in the thick of the dispute didn't begrudge younger players seizing an opportunity to represent their country. But the veterans could tell U.S. Soccer was hoping to pit the current team against the young up-and-comers. When the reserve team won the tournament in Australia, it looked like a real possibility the federation could simply refuse to give in to the senior national team's demands and keep turning to youth players.

After Slaton got back from Australia, she got a phone call from Chastain: "Look, they're going to ask you to go to the next tournament, and now we need you to say no."

With some guidance from Billie Jean King, the national team realized they needed the younger players to see the bigger picture and join them in the fight. If the federation had the option to replace the national team rather than offer better working conditions, no one—not the current generation nor the next ones—would ever have the power to convince U.S. Soccer of anything.

"I remember that phone call with Brandi—her taking the time to explain, this is what's going on, here's the history, this is what we're fighting for," Slaton says. "These were the women who were your idols growing up. You respected that and felt it was for something bigger."

It wasn't just Slaton who received a call—all the players who went to the Australia Cup and all the players on the U-20 team were contacted by players from the senior team who were on strike. In a sort of quasi-phone tree, every veteran was assigned a youth player to call. They didn't stop until the U-16 team was on board, too.

They spoke to younger players one-on-one and invited them to join a large conference call. Many of these youth players were teenagers, so their parents were invited to join, too.

"We're doing this for you," Foudy told them. "We're trying to build the future, and we need you to say no if they ask you to come in because we're going to say no. We ask that you support us because ultimately, you'll gain the benefit of this. It's not us being greedy like Hank Steinbrecher is saying—we're just trying to make conditions better."

None of the younger players resisted. Instead, all the players agreed to present a unified front to U.S. Soccer.

"There was total cooperation," John Langel says. "It was pretty amazing how it happened."

With practically the entire women's national team program on board, team leaders Julie Foudy and Mia Hamm continued to push for a new team contract. Merely extending their expired contract wasn't an option, so if they couldn't get a new one, they weren't going to play.

Hank Steinbrecher's standby answer to that threat had already been made clear at the Australia Cup, and the players were ready for it. He told them the federation would bring in the U-20 team again. Foudy and Hamm were unfazed.

"You can't. They're with us now," they responded. He countered that they could call in the U-18 team. Again, Foudy and Hamm said they had already spoken to those players. Before he could even mention it, they told him they had the U-16 players on their side, too.

"I think that's when they were like, *Oh shit, these women are for real*," Foudy says now.

With the 2000 Summer Olympics approaching and the federation out of leverage, a landmark deal finally got done.

For the first time, players were guaranteed compensation for at least eight months out of the year, so they didn't have to worry about when their next national team paycheck would come. That basic structure, which offered better financial stability for on-contract players and some protection against the whims of the federation, still exists within national team contracts today.

The tension between U.S. Soccer and the players would continue, however, and it had the knock-on effect of bringing others into it.

Tony DiCicco, a coach beloved and respected universally by his team, always stayed out of contract negotiations. A coach has no role in contract negotiations between a team and their federation—a coach is only there to coach. Besides, DiCicco viewed the players more like an extension of his family than workers he was there to manage.

It wasn't unusual for Tony DiCicco to host the players at his house for big pasta dinners with his wife, Diane, and the couple's three sons. He was passionate about coaching and seemed to care for his players deeply as human beings. At the start of training sessions, he'd walk out onto the grass and shout up to the sky with his arms out: "I LOVE MY JOB!" The players would echo the call and giggle, starting practice with smiles on their faces. And when the players prepared to go out onto the field for a game, his last words were always: "Play hard, play to win, have fun."

But one day, amid contentious talks between the players and U.S. Soccer, DiCicco tried to talk to Julie Foudy about the ongoing negotiations, which she believes was prompted by the federation.

"I understand where you're coming from, but don't get in the middle of this, because you will lose every player on the team," Foudy warned him. "We don't fuck with your negotiations, so don't fuck with ours. I know they're pressuring you, but I'm telling you, this will ruin your relationship with every player, because we care that deeply about this. The respect will be gone if you're seen as being on the side of the federation."

DiCicco told her he understood, and he backed off. He went back to staying out of contract negotiations. It was a decision that may have saved his relationship with the players of the national team, even as it hurt his own relationship with the federation.

CHAPTER 7

"Is That the Starting Team? Am I Not on It?"

After the national team won the 1999 Women's World Cup, it seemed like U.S. Soccer would be eager to keep a good thing going: The federation would obviously work to sign a new contract with its players and make sure Tony DiCicco would stay on as coach.

Except, neither happened.

The contract dispute seemed inevitable after the victory-tour debacle, but why the World Cup–winning coach didn't return to the team is the matter of some debate, even all these years later.

Four months after winning the World Cup, DiCicco announced he would resign to spend more time with his family, and indeed, the job took him away from his wife and three boys for weeks at a time for tournaments around the world. His family was relieved that he wouldn't disappear for such long spells anymore. DiCicco admitted he missed watching his own kids' soccer games and spending more time with Diane, his wife.

But factoring into DiCicco's decision seemed to be the lukewarm, at best, attitude the federation had toward the national team coach who brought success at the highest stage.

Sources recall DiCicco confiding the details of meetings he had with the heads of the federation shortly after the 1999 Women's World Cup. The federation's leaders expressed dissatisfaction with the style of soccer the team played. They wanted the players to engage in more one-touch passing. The team didn't look dominant enough in the final, they said. DiCicco told those close to him about the discussions, but sources spoke on the condition of anonymity because DiCicco, who died in 2017, never publicly spoke about it.

What was public, however, was how unenthusiastic the federation seemed about keeping the World Cup–winning coach around.

With DiCicco's contract set to expire at the end of 1999, when reporters asked him what was going on, he admitted he didn't know if U.S. Soccer would keep him: "They have been up-front and honest with me and very much noncommittal in either direction."

U.S. Soccer dragged its feet on offering a new contract—waiting three months until after the '99 World Cup—and when they finally did, it was a short, one-year deal that looked more like a stopgap measure than a vote of confidence. DiCicco was reportedly insulted by the offer.

That attitude from U.S. Soccer could also be explained by the federation's apparent impression that DiCicco wasn't iron-fisted enough with the players. Whether that perception was right or wrong, it may have stemmed from his unwillingness to take the federation's side during contract negotiations and insert himself into the process.

"I remember the word on the street was they thought he was too soft with us," says Julie Foudy, who later went on to be president of the Women's Sports Foundation from 2001 to 2002. "That's what we heard—that he gave us too much power. And I remember thinking, *How stupid is that? This is a coach who is a good player manager.*"

"He would have a leadership council of the captains, the veterans, and younger players, and he'd ask what you think and get the pulse of the team," she says. "He'd often disagree with us, but he'd let us have a voice, and I think any good leader does that."

Now, Contiguglia says there was a combination of reasons that kept the federation from pushing to keep DiCicco as coach.

"One of the decision-makers felt very strongly that you don't keep a national team coach for two cycles," he says. "Some players, who I spoke to, wanted a change. There were issues with the style of play. There were a number of factors."

Whatever the reasons, DiCicco would not be the coach again after leading the national team to an astonishingly successful 103–8–8 record. Suddenly, the federation was without a coach less than eight months from the start of the 2000 Olympics in Sydney, Australia.

On his way out, DiCicco recommended the job go to Lauren Gregg, his assistant, who helped lead the national team to winning the 1999

Women's World Cup. Gregg, along with assistant coach Jay Hoffman, managed the national team on its trip to the Australia Cup, where the young Americans won even as the veterans boycotted the tournament.

"Lauren would give the team the best chance of winning at the Olympics," DiCicco told reporters. "And the one-two punch of winning the World Cup and the Olympics could launch the sport to the next level: a pro league."

Gregg was seen as a frontrunner, along with University of Portland coach Clive Charles, but April Heinrichs, who had become the first woman inducted into the National Soccer Hall of Fame two years earlier, was asked to apply later in the candidate search.

After retiring from the national team in 1991, Heinrichs built up a coaching résumé both within U.S. Soccer and at the collegiate level, including four seasons at the University of Virginia, where her teams always made the postseason, though they never reached a semifinal. At the time she was invited to interview, she was coaching the under-16 women's national team for U.S. Soccer.

There was no question that Heinrichs, the captain of the 1991 World Cup team, had the leadership qualities for the job. Taking charge seemed natural for her.

Take, for instance, her reaction when she saw a hit-and-run in 1991. Heinrichs was driving back to a national team residency camp in North Carolina with teammate Tracey Bates when the highway traffic suddenly started to merge into one lane. An accident had just occurred, and, as the players neared the accident scene, a truck that was involved—and missing a back tire—sped away.

Heinrichs immediately followed the truck in pursuit, calling out to her teammate: "Get the license plate number! Get the license plate!" In the passenger's seat, Bates was having trouble seeing it because sparks and debris were flying from the spot where the truck was missing its tire.

They followed the truck to a gas-station exit, and a Ford Pinto pulled in front of the truck and stopped. Out of the car stepped three uniformed marines. With the national team players behind and the marines in front, the hit-and-run driver was cornered. As Heinrichs got out of her car and approached, the truck driver went into reverse.

"He's backing up!" Bates shouted. Heinrichs ran back to her car and tried to get it out of the way, but the truck smashed into it. The marines swarmed the truck and tackled the driver while Bates ran to call the police on a pay phone. She also called coach Anson Dorrance to explain why she and Heinrichs would be late returning to camp.

After the police arrived, the players asked the marines if they realized she and Bates were in pursuit of the truck. The marines said they did notice what Heinrichs and Bates were up to, but they were worried about what would happen when the mom and her little daughter stopped the truck.

"They thought April was the mom and I was like 12 years old," Bates says, laughing.

Bates adds: "The next day at practice, everyone on the team was calling us the North Carolina Highway Patrol."

What April Heinrichs's teammates knew about her was that she was a doer. But how she got that way—how she was molded into the person she became—wasn't something she talked about very much.

She was born April Minnis, but she never met her father. She grew up in a self-described "dysfunctional family," and her sister ran away from home when she was a teenager. The name Heinrichs came from her stepfather, Mel, a Denver firefighter. Her mother divorced him, and when April was a high school freshman, she chose to live with him. She went on to have little contact with her mother and later said they just never connected.

"You hear stories all the time about people tracking down missing fathers or mothers," Heinrichs once explained. "The thing about me is, I don't spend too much time on the past or the absence of it. I spend a lot of time on goal setting, which is all about the future. I know now as an adult that it's a real good coping mechanism."

She has said she doesn't think her background affected who she always was. But whatever the reason for the way she approached everything, Heinrichs was someone her former teammates could tell was destined to move into coaching after her playing days ended.

Still, Heinrichs's opportunity for the national team coaching job came sooner than anyone expected. U.S. Soccer was gambling on someone who had limited experience managing at the international level. Another wrinkle was that Heinrichs had been teammates with many of the veterans still on the team.

But federation president Robert Contiguglia, who had followed her career since the 1980s, was impressed by her. When he was the president of Colorado Youth Soccer, she was a teenage standout for an academy team in Denver—on multiple occasions, he had presented her medals. He asked Heinrichs to submit a written proposal for the job.

Tracey Bates remembers reading Heinrichs's paper before she submitted it to the federation. Even though Heinrichs was her longtime friend, Bates didn't need to feign enthusiasm. When she finished reading and put down the paper, she told her: "You are going to get this job, April."

Not only was Heinrichs hired in January 2000, but she got the multiyear contract that Tony DiCicco did not get. She signed a four-year contract that would take her into the next World Cup–Olympics cycle.

"We are talking about building a program and not an event," Contiguglia told reporters on her introductory conference call. "It involves success on the field, but it's more than that. We're building a program and a sport."

* * *

Players quickly learned that April Heinrichs was a very different kind of coach than they'd had over the past few years. Tony DiCicco held frequent team meetings and was eager to include veteran players in decisions, which created an atmosphere that many players say felt like a family. But Heinrichs was more businesslike in her approach.

She wanted players to feel like they were competing against one another for spots on the team. That approach would force players to always give their very best—no one could take their spot for granted. But some players took it as Heinrichs pitting them against one another, especially since the veterans and younger players stayed in separate housing at the residency camps.

"We want to make sure there's no complacency," Heinrichs told reporters early on. "We want to make sure we're not stagnant, make sure we're still growing."

The roster of Heinrichs's first camp made it clear that she was turning the page on a new chapter. Tiffany Roberts, Danielle Fotopoulos, and Tracy Ducar—members of the '99 World Cup–winning team—were left out of Heinrichs's first camp, where she invited a large crop of 35 players.

For the younger players who were brought in, it represented a huge opportunity to impress a new coach who was examining the player pool with fresh eyes.

"Quite frankly, what I remember from that camp was trying to survive," says Danielle Slaton. "It was like, *Holy cow, these were the girls I saw at the Rose Bowl when I was watching as a fan, and now, oh my god, I have to try to mark Kristine Lilly!*"

But for the most established players in the group, their standing quickly felt threatened. In Heinrichs's first games as the head coach, a pair of friendly losses to Norway, the stars who carried the team to the 1999 World Cup—Mia Hamm, Julie Foudy, Brandi Chastain, and others—found themselves starting on the bench.

"It was just uncertain," Mia Hamm told reporters. "You start to overanalyze everything. She puts a team out there, and you're like: *Is that the starting team? Am I not on the starting team?*"

"That camp was very competitive, and there was not a lot of feedback in camp," Hamm added. "Everyone was going: *Am I doing all right? Is this what she wants?*"

Heinrichs did have a plan all along: She wanted to evaluate the newer players and get a sense of where the program was overall. The problem, however, was that she didn't explain that to anyone.

In her first match as head coach, Heinrichs didn't put Carla Overbeck, the team's longtime and beloved cocaptain, in the starting lineup.

The move came with no warning, and it sent ripples of anxiety throughout the veteran contingent of the team.

Overbeck worried she was losing her spot on the team and knocked on the coach's office door to ask directly what was going on.

"I just had questions," Overbeck later said. "I was wondering a bit about my future, just because there weren't meetings and it wasn't communicated to me."

There wasn't a lot of time for the players and Heinrichs to adjust to each other, though. The 2000 Olympics were around the corner, and the expectations for the national team were enormously high after the 1999 World Cup victory.

On top of a quick turnaround for a new coach, the team was dealing with a bit of a hangover from the intense previous few months. Some of the players had more demands on their time than ever before with media requests and sponsorship opportunities. The protracted and bitter dispute with U.S. Soccer over a new contract was also emotionally draining for the team.

"We had been marketing ourselves on our own, because U.S. Soccer didn't, for a good six months, and we had just finished contract negotiations," says Kate Markgraf, who played her early years under her maiden name, Sobrero, and grew up north of Detroit, Michigan. "We were tired. Any new coach wants to hit the ground running, but psychologically we were fatigued."

On top of it all, Heinrichs was overseeing many players who had been her peers on the 1991 World Cup team, which she captained. It offered an unusual dynamic that was jarring for some of them.

"The big thing with April was that she played with a lot of us," says Shannon MacMillan, who wasn't among that 1991 World Cup group. "That's a tall order, to switch off of being teammates and friends to now saying, *I'm your coach*. I think that was a lot to ask of her."

By the time the 2000 Olympics arrived, everyone had to block out whatever else was going on with the team. The team had to keep its momentum going to maintain its place in the sports landscape. Only a win would suffice. NBC wasn't going to repeat its mistakes from the

1996 Olympics—each of the national team's games would be aired live on MSNBC and CNBC, despite the time difference.

They would have to somehow do it without Michelle Akers, their heartbeat in the midfield. A shoulder injury and her ongoing battle with chronic fatigue syndrome caught up with her. Three weeks before the Olympics, she announced her retirement at age 34.

Akers had been considering retirement for years, but she kept going and pushed for a spot on the 2000 Olympics team because, as she later put it, "I would beat myself up with second-guessing for the rest of my life." She made the team but determined she couldn't actually play on. She left as the national team's second all-time leading scorer, behind only Mia Hamm, with 105 goals and 37 assists.

"I found myself at the end—physically and mentally—with a body ready for a M*A*S*H unit," she said.

Otherwise, the squad was mostly the same one that won the World Cup less than a year earlier—but there were some notable changes.

Briana Scurry had lived it up a little too much after the 1999 World Cup victory. By the time she returned to the national team fold, she had gained 20 pounds and lost several inches on her jumping ability. She made the 2000 Olympic team but lost the starting job to Siri Mullinix.

In addition to the three 1999 World Cup players she cut as soon as she took over as coach, Heinrichs also cut veteran midfielder Tisha Venturini. Meanwhile, two young players were added: midfielder Michelle French and defender Danielle Slaton.

The core of the team was largely intact, but Heinrichs asked players to play slightly different roles. She shifted the team away from DiCicco's favored 4–3–3 tactical system and into a 4–4–2 that would allow the team to defend deeper and control the midfield.

Once the games got underway in Australia, the team comfortably got out of the group stage, buoyed by a 2–0 win over rival Norway in the opening match. It seemed like a positive omen. Norway was the team that knocked the U.S. out of the 1995 World Cup and the team the Americans hated most. In fact, the 1995 loss to Norway had been the USA team's only loss in a major tournament up to that point.

Many of the top players on the 2000 Norwegian team had competed in the 1995 World Cup, which gave Norway bragging rights for years. Norway captain Linda Medalen gleefully told reporters: "It's fun to beat the Americans because they get so upset, make so much noise, when they lose."

What irked the Americans most, however, was Norway's celebration: "The Train." The players would crawl on all fours in lockstep, each player holding the ankles of the player in front, chugging their way around the field as a train. That's what they had done after winning in the 1995 World Cup as a crushed U.S. team watched.

"You had just lost one of the biggest tournaments of your life, didn't even get to the final, and to see your opponent rubbing it in your face like that, it made your stomach turn," Carla Overbeck later said. The Americans had nicknamed the Norway team "the Viking Bitches" for a reason.

So after the Americans sailed through the first rounds of the 2000 Olympics having beaten Norway once already, it was a theatric twist that the Americans were forced to face them once again in the gold-medal match.

Again, the Americans looked dominant to start. It took them just five minutes to strike first on an exquisite Mia Hamm run. She passed the ball to Tiffeny Milbrett in the box for an easy one-touch tap-in. The U.S. looked poised to head into halftime with the lead until Norway, playing their villain role to a tee, equalized right before the break on a Gro Espeseth goal.

By the 78th minute, Norway had worked their way into the match again and took the lead on a looping Ragnhild Gulbrandsen header. If the Americans wanted to win another world championship at the Sydney Olympics, they were running out of time to do it.

The clock ticked past the 90th minute and into injury time. The whistle was going to blow at any moment. Tick . . . tick . . . tick . . . and then Tiffeny Milbrett scored again. Deep into injury time, it was again Mia Hamm serving a ball for Milbrett to score, this time with her head, in a dramatic equalizer to put the match at 2–2.

The American fighting spirit—the team's core identity—was carrying them to extra time.

"I think there was 30 seconds left in the game and everyone was going nuts," Kristine Lilly later recalled. "It goes to overtime once again, and we were like, *Okay, we're going to win this.*"

The Americans had every reason to believe it. They were playing well, and they were built to thrive in these high-stakes, extra-time situations.

And maybe they should have won. Maybe they would have if the game went the full 120 minutes of extra time. But 11 minutes into it, Dagny Mellgren took the ball out of the air with her arm. The play should have been whistled dead for a hand ball, but the ref let it play on and she scored. The golden-goal rule—first goal in extra time wins the game—was in effect, and the match was over. The U.S. had lost.

Julie Foudy went to the referee afterward and told her: "You're going to see that video and you're going to want this back. You crushed every damn dream I ever had, so sleep well tonight."

After everything they had been through in the lead-up to this tournament, the national team was left with a heartbreaking loss. It was only the second time the team had lost a game in an Olympics or World Cup, and, again, it came at the hands of rival Norway.

While the American players cried in the locker room, Norway was next door in their locker room, singing in celebration. The Americans could hear it through the wall. It stung just as badly as watching Norway do "The Train" in 1995.

"Because of who we were as a team, the expectation was gold or nothing. If you don't get gold, it's a failure," Shannon MacMillan says. "For us to come off the World Cup and take silver, it was extremely disheartening and frustrating for us. We felt like we underachieved."

As devastating as the loss was, the national team would eventually have something else to focus on and something to look forward to: a league of their own.

CHAPTER 8
"We Kind of Bled to Death"

It was April 14, 2001, and it felt as though everyone in Washington, D.C., knew what was about to happen that day. A new women's professional league—the Women's United Soccer Association, or WUSA—was about to launch, and the Washington Freedom would host the Bay Area CyberRays in the inaugural match.

Or, if Washingtonians didn't know all that—even if they couldn't name either of the teams—they at least knew that Mia Hamm and Brandi Chastain were in town playing against each other.

The nation's capital had been sprinkled with billboards and bus banners announcing "MIA vs. BRANDI," while full-page ads with the same tagline ran in magazines. Television commercials depicted the pair of national team stars sizing each other up, as if getting ready for a heavyweight fight. In one such TV ad, the two players stared at each other with fiery expressions for a few seconds until Hamm broke the silence:

"Did you get bangs?" Hamm asked.

"Yeah," replied a flattered Chastain.

"Cute," Hamm sneered back.

The promoters of the WUSA were counting on fans to care that two of the national team's biggest stars were facing off as opponents for the first time. Thankfully, it worked.

As kickoff got closer, an unexpected rush of 7,000 walk-up fans overwhelmed ticket booths as frazzled sales associates tried to keep up. Another 11,000 fans had placed orders over the phone in the days prior that had to be picked up at will call, adding to the gridlock.

Fans would still be streaming in as halftime approached. In the end, attendance tallied 34,148, easily setting a new record for the biggest crowd at a domestic women's soccer match anywhere.

The WUSA was not announcing itself quietly. The inaugural match was a spectacle to behold before the soccer actually started.

Billie Jean King, the tennis legend and unofficial adviser to the national team in their legal battles, presided over the inaugural coin toss. The national anthem featured an American bald eagle swooping across the sky at the final note of "The Star-Spangled Banner." And for good measure, there were also fireworks and three female parachutists.

While Chastain and Hamm were on the field ready to play, the rest of their national teammates, who were playing for other teams in the league, were on the sidelines, where they were announced one by one to the crowd. Julie Foudy had her video camera, of course, and she filmed her teammates hugging and giggling with excitement.

"How cool is this?!" Tiffeny Milbrett called out to her teammates.

A ball hadn't been kicked yet, but already a sense of accomplishment washed over the players: It was really happening. The women of the national team finally had a league to play in.

"What I remember about that day most vividly was standing there with the captain's armband thinking, *This is a forever moment,*" Chastain says.

Quickly, Chastain and Hamm had to snap out of it. There was a game to be played. What happened on the field, however, would end up being the least memorable part about the day.

It was a tight and chippy affair, but the soccer was disjointed as both of the brand-new teams were getting used to playing together. Scoring chances were few and far between.

The fans seemed to grow restless, and they clearly wanted see something from the stars they watched during the World Cup. The crowd roared when Hamm put a header on top of the net in the second half, but in truth, the effort wasn't really that close to resulting in a goal.

Jim Gabarra was tapped as the Washington Freedom's first head coach after he coached the World All-Stars during the 1999 indoor victory tour. He was focused on winning the match, but he admits there was more than that on his mind.

"I felt a huge responsibility to put on a product that lived up to all the euphoria and excitement that the World Cup and the victory tour had," he says. "We had everything in place to live up to it as far as the crowd, the presentation, the marketing, the operations, the players. Then we had this soccer game that was probably the only part that didn't live up to it. It wasn't a very good game. It was the kind of game you'd expect between two new teams that had never played together."

The game's only goal came in the 70th minute. With Hamm dribbling through the box with the ball at her feet, Chastain stepped to her to cut off her angle. Hamm went down, and the referee pointed to the spot for a penalty kick. Brazilian forward Pretinha took it and buried it.

It was perhaps a cheap way for the Washington Freedom to win the match. These days, no one on either side really disputes that it was a questionable penalty call from the referee. But the game got a much-needed goal and the home team won, which wasn't the worst thing as far as script writing goes.

When the match ended, Hamm walked over to Chastain and told her: "I'm sorry the game had to be decided like that."

Chastain cried. She was upset to have given up the penalty. Still to this day she believes it was an incorrect call. ("The referee blew it and gave them a penalty kick!" she jokes.)

But her tears were about more than just losing a game. They were about the stakes, the expectation, the moment. This was everything the players had dreamed of, and now they had to make the most of it.

After the game, Chastain told reporters: "People asked me this week, *What would make this league a success?* I said, *We've already been successful. We started a league.*"

* * *

The first women's pro league in the United States was actually supposed to start three years earlier. After the relative success of the 1996

Olympics, where the U.S. won gold, the national team and its most ardent supporters saw a domestic league as a real possibility.

The league, which was going to be called the National Soccer Alliance, or the NSA, had some key pieces in place by early 1997 for a launch the following year.

Much of the national team that won gold at the 1996 Olympics had committed to playing in the NSA, including Mia Hamm, Brandi Chastain, and Julie Foudy. The commissioner was set to be Booth Gardner, former governor of Washington state. Anson Dorrance would chair the advisory board. Preliminary talks had started with some potentially big sponsors, including Nike and Reebok. A search was underway to identify the eight markets that would have teams on both coasts.

"I'm not just excited about this league, I'm ecstatic," Julie Foudy told reporters as details of the proposed league emerged in February 1997. "To remain dominant in the world, this is a necessity."

In the months that followed, the league picked eight cities for teams, and the budget was set at $15 million for operations. That included player salaries ranging from $15,000 to $30,000 and ticket prices averaging around $10 each. The league also secured key investments, including support from John Hendricks, the founder of the company behind the Discovery Channel.

But while the organizers were moving ahead with the idea of the NSA league, U.S. Soccer officials were skeptical.

"I think they are moving a little faster than prudent," said Alan Rothenberg, the president of U.S. Soccer and chief architect of Major League Soccer, or MLS, the men's professional league that had launched in 1996, nearly three years after its planning began.

For everything the organizers had gotten in place, they couldn't get one thing they really needed: the support of U.S. Soccer.

U.S. Soccer was supposed to vote at the end of 1997 on whether the National Soccer Alliance should be sanctioned for Division I status—earning Division I status would mean the NSA was the top level of the sport, which comes with financial and competitive benefits—but instead the federation pushed back the vote. That was enough to cause some of the league's investors to question whether a 1998 launch was realistic anymore. With the World Cup planned for 1999, it wouldn't be able to launch that year, either.

Just like that, with one delayed vote from U.S. Soccer, the National Soccer Alliance was essentially dead.

"It wasn't a lack of planning, a lack of financial support, or a lack of support of the players, and we had the interest of TV," said Jennifer Rottenberg, a consultant who helped spearhead the effort. "I felt some tension from U.S. Soccer—actually, some hostility."

Some sensed the federation was reluctant to sanction a new women's professional league while Major League Soccer, the men's league, was still only three years old. MLS itself was struggling with attendance and attracting investors, and a women's league threatened to compete for the same market share.

But Rothenberg said all along he just thought it was too soon for a women's league to launch. Asked about it now, Rothenberg says launching a women's league before the 1999 Women's World Cup would've been a mistake—the women's league needed to be postponed until after a World Cup, just as MLS had been.

"I had the same view of the men," he says. "When FIFA granted the U.S. the rights to host the 1994 World Cup, they were granted on the condition that we would start a pro league. FIFA's intention was that it would happen before the '94 World Cup. But when I looked at everything we had to do, I convinced FIFA they needed the hype of a successful '94 World Cup to launch it."

So, the idea of a women's league would have to wait until after the national team's stunning 1999 World Cup win. But similar animosity from U.S. Soccer and MLS would creep into the planning again the second time around.

On one hand, some of the people who had been involved with the NSA returned to develop the WUSA, including John Hendricks, who led the effort. On the other hand, U.S. Soccer had asked MLS to submit a business plan for a women's league.

With the WUSA and MLS groups pitted against each other, it felt like a reprise of the recent battles between the national team and U.S. Soccer.

"I am aware of the women's desire to have a league of their own, and I can sympathize with that," said Robert Contiguglia, who became president of U.S. Soccer after Rothenberg while talks of a women's league continued. "But they have to respect our needs as well."

The national team players felt the federation had thought about its own needs enough already. They were wary of following the federation's lead fresh off the contentious disputes over the victory tour and their contracts.

"We didn't trust anything U.S. Soccer did. We didn't trust they had our best interests in mind," says Julie Foudy. "Everything we fought for, we had to scrape and claw for. They had given $10 million for MLS and we couldn't even get them to support a women's league."

"So, whether it was right or wrong, we felt that, with them having a huge hand in MLS and being part of it, they were trying to bottle what we were doing. We were concerned that them inviting us to join forces with MLS was them actually wanting to kill us off."

If MLS or U.S. Soccer were worried about the WUSA hurting MLS, they had their reasons. At the time, MLS was in the midst of discussions about folding two of its teams and the overall health of the league was questionable. It was rapidly hemorrhaging money, attendance was declining, and television ratings remained dismal. Just as there was little reason for the women to believe affiliating with MLS would ensure success, there was little reason for MLS to believe the WUSA wouldn't be a threat.

Meanwhile, the WUSA seemed to have the momentum that MLS at the time was lacking. Hendricks had quickly managed to get deep-pocketed investors from the cable industry to run each of the eight teams. The national team had been attracting plenty of media attention, and its individual players were attracting bigger sponsors than anyone on the men's team did.

The national team players were the key, and the WUSA had the support of all of them. There wasn't going to be a successful women's league without the likes of Mia Hamm, Brandi Chastain, and Julie Foudy. In the end, there was nowhere for MLS to go without the support of the players.

There would be a new women's league, the WUSA, and John Hendricks, who believed in them even before the 1999 Women's World Cup, would lead the way.

* * *

When John Hendricks and the investors involved in the WUSA put together the 200-page business plan for the league, the revenue projections were built on having 10 core corporate sponsors. They believed there were 10 categories where they could realistically find sponsors.

So, once the plan was finalized, Hendricks then set out to secure those sponsorships. Hyundai signed on immediately. The automotive category was already checked off, and it seemed like the other nine categories would be filled in no time.

"It came lightning fast. Hyundai loved it, and they were going to be the official car of the league," Hendricks says. "So we were like, *Okay, we're going to do this. We'll find the 10 sponsors that each put in $2 million per year.* And that $20 million was vital to the business plan."

By the first kickoff on that historic day, April 14, 2001, the league had attracted about $64 million from investors. On paper, that was an impressive number, but the fact is, they hadn't secured the other core sponsorships they wanted—the sponsorships the business plan depended on.

They ended up with only Hyundai at the commitment level they wanted, plus some smaller sponsors, which put the league about $15 million behind where they wanted to be annually. The longer the league went on with that deficit, the deeper the hole would become.

There was cautious optimism, though. Surely the other sponsorships would come soon enough. The product on the field was too good, and the players were too likable.

"We always had great meetings," Hendricks says. "The participants from the sponsors were all fans, so it stood out on their schedule when they had a meeting that featured Mia Hamm and Brandi Chastain and Julie Foudy. So, we tended to have really great meetings."

Hendricks, who founded the Washington Freedom, recruited an impressive batch of investors—friends of his in the cable television industry—to put in $5 million each to run teams in seven other cities. The investors, who came from Cox, Time Warner, Comcast, and Continental Cablevision, could tolerate losses and weren't expecting immediate profits, which is how investing in start-up sports leagues usually goes.

Many of them agreed in part to invest in the league because John Hendricks was well-liked and respected. But many also, as Hendricks did, saw it as an investment that could be beneficial in the long term.

"We said, *Let's give this thing a try and see how it goes,*" says Jim Kennedy of Cox Enterprises, who ran the Atlanta Beat franchise. "I didn't ever envision it to be a moneymaker for us. We were hoping it'll break even and maybe create some value down the road for all the owners."

The thread that ran through all the backers of the league was that, on some level, they all believed the women of the national team deserved a league to play in. They had all seen the 1996 Olympics or the 1999 World Cup, and it affected them in some way. Some of the investors had daughters. Some were fans of the players. But they saw it as a worthwhile investment, even if it fit more into the nice-to-do category than the moneymaking category.

By the time the WUSA held a huge launch event for the players, the investors, and their families in Washington, D.C., everyone felt good about the investment. At the dinner, held at a hotel event space, the players stood up one by one and shared what the launch of the WUSA meant to them.

"They knew little boys had sports heroes growing up—little boys could see a path pursuing a career in sports, but girls couldn't see that kind of path," Hendricks remembers. "There was hardly a dry eye in that room. All the owners were welling up with tears. We were all just so excited. We thought maybe 10,000 people would show up to the first game, but 34,000 people—it was at a level above MLS, so we were just on a high."

For all the national team had accomplished—selling out the Rose Bowl, forcing TV networks to air their games live, and securing better contracts from their federation, championship trophies, and sponsorship deals—the league was coveted in a way nothing else was. It was supposed to be the crucial step toward sustainable careers.

"The league was the most important piece," says Tiffeny Milbrett, who debuted for the national team in 1991. "You can't be a professional athlete for six months out of the year or work two weeks out of every month or every other month. That's not professional. You need a week-in and week-out daily environment. That's called work."

The opportunities created by the WUSA weren't just for the U.S. national team players, though—they were for all women playing soccer. Americans who excelled in the college game and top players from around the world now had a highly professional league to play in.

Some players owed their own national team breakthroughs to the WUSA. The league started as a place for the national team players to go and became a place where national team players were made.

Take Angela Hucles, for instance. When she graduated from the University of Virginia in 2000, for all she knew, her soccer career was over, despite scoring 59 goals, a Cavaliers record, 19 of them game-winners.

"I went out and did your normal get-a-job type of procedure: Going to the career center, looking at opportunities, and talking to counselors," she says.

As she heard rumors of a possible league forming, she started training for a management role at Ferguson Enterprises, where she was learning to operate a forklift, coordinating refrigerator deliveries, and performing other tasks to learn every aspect of the business. She was there just three months before she abruptly quit to enter the draft.

She was selected 93rd overall, but her solid play in the league earned her call-ups under April Heinrichs. She eventually went on to earn more than 100 caps for the national team.

The league also created new opportunities for the national team's opponents. Bringing in superstar internationals was seen as crucial, not just to bolster the league's quality but to ensure a deep pool of club talent outside of just the U.S. national team players. With most players at the time quitting soccer after college, the dilution of talent was a concern that international players could address.

"We had a lot of best players in the world—players like Birgit Prinz [Germany] and Sun Wen [China]," says Julie Foudy. "That was an interesting change because we had never interacted with them like that. All the sudden we were teammates with them."

Lauren Gregg, Tony DiCicco's assistant coach at the 1999 World Cup, was tapped to head player personnel for the league front office, where she signed nearly 70 international players during her time with WUSA.

To have top world talent alongside one another was a new experience for all the players. It made all of them better competitors, and it led to some memorable lost-in-translation moments. At one point with the San Diego Spirit, Foudy was getting to know Chinese defender Fan Yunjie when the conversation went something like this, at least as far as Foudy heard:

"What's your husband's name?"

"Who?"

"Your husband."

"Yeah."

"No, what's his name?"

"Who?"

"YOUR HUS-BAND. WHAT. IS. HIS. NAME?"

Yunjie finally looked at Foudy and said: "Julie, my husband's name is Hu."

Everyone burst out laughing.

"Foudy was crying because she was laughing so hard," teammate Shannon MacMillan remembers. "All of us were like, *Oh my gosh, Jules.* We caught on after, like, the first round, but she kept going and starts talking louder because she thinks she can't hear her."

But the cultural exchange that was happening in the WUSA was bigger than that. Some of the international players were coming from countries where they too felt their federations were failing to support them. By becoming teammates with the U.S. national team players, players around the globe were being exposed to the American mentality of banding together and standing up to demand more.

"They got to see how feisty we were with our federation and how involved we were in advocating for change," Foudy says.

Those planted seeds would take some time to grow—and indeed, the U.S. national team would inspire other national teams around the world for years to come—but the WUSA may have been where the U.S. team's influence started.

Through it all, however, those rooting for the WUSA's success felt MLS was actively trying to hurt it.

"MLS was a hostile force to what we were doing," says Amos Hostetter Jr., who founded the Boston Breakers. "There was no element of cooperation from them and, in fact, they were against us. A lot of scheduling was set up to conflict with our games. They were of the view that if anyone was going to have a successful soccer league, they should do it."

* * *

The signs were there by the time the first season ended. Financially, the league was on an untenable path it could continue on for only so long.

With Hyundai as the only major corporate sponsor, the advertising revenue the league projected and needed to break even never came over the course of that first season. And as attendance trended downward, it was even tougher to sell sponsors on the idea that an investment in the league was worth making.

While the Washington Freedom, the Atlanta Beat, and the Boston Breakers looked to be hitting their numbers with crowds of 8,000 or more per game, not everyone attending games had paid full price for tickets, which cut into the revenue teams counted on. It was only going to get harder in year two after the newness had worn off.

"I was concerned that we were doing too many promotions to get people there," says Jim Kennedy of Cox Enterprises and the Atlanta Beat. "I thought we ought to just find out if there would be true paying fans who will to pay to come to games."

The situation was dire in other markets, though. The New York Power, San Diego Spirit, and Carolina Courage averaged below 6,000 fans per game in the first season. That was well under the league's initial projections and, again, not everyone was paying to get in the door.

At one point, Joe Cummings, the general manager of the Boston Breakers, was asked to take over as GM for the New York Power. He was stunned when he arrived and took a closer look at their budget. The team was spending $800,000 annually on marketing in metro New York City even though it was averaging only about 2,500 paying fans per game at $15 per ticket. At that rate, with 10 home games per season, breaking even was impossible.

The Boston Breakers were arguably the closest franchise to being on a break-even path. After all, running a sports team wasn't new for Cummings. Before taking over as general manager of the Breakers, he had been the assistant general manager of the New England Revolution in MLS.

Every Tuesday, a spreadsheet would go out to all the teams showing the financial performance of each franchise. The Breakers were consistently in the top three in attendance and spent far less money than many of the other franchises to get people to the games.

"Nobody ever called and said, *Joe, what are you doing?*" he says. "No one at the executive level ever called and asked for best practices."

That worried Cummings because a lot of people running franchises in other markets didn't have experience in professional sports.

It also became evident to some of most active investors that not everyone had the same level of interest in running a sports team, either.

"It became clear to me fairly soon that having corporate ownership wasn't the best thing," says Kennedy. "You really need a passion when you own something like this—you need to really care about it. Here in Atlanta, we really did. We wanted it to be successful. But I don't know it was that way in other markets."

Because of the league's single-entity structure, when some franchises lost money, all franchises shared the cost. The franchises that were doing relatively well—franchises like the Washington Freedom, the Boston Breakers, and the Atlanta Beat—still ended up losing money as other teams floundered.

After the first season ended, the league took drastic steps to cut costs. The WUSA headquarters were moved from an expensive New York City office to a space at Cox Enterprises in Atlanta. The league's CEO, Barbara Allen, who took few steps to rein in spending or help teams stay on track, was replaced by a more business-savvy Lynn Morgan.

Those changes, plus a championship attendance of more than 21,000 people, led to some optimism that the league would be able to course-correct. But just two weeks after those reforms were implemented during the offseason, the unthinkable happened: The terrorist attacks of September 11, 2001, changed the world overnight.

For the WUSA, that meant corporate sponsor dollars dried up almost instantly.

"After 9/11, it was such a shock to the economic system," says John Hendricks. "Most companies continued advertising, but they cut back dramatically on nice-to-do corporate sponsorships. All our sponsorship leads came to an end. It was extremely hard to even get a meeting after 9/11, let alone close them."

At one point, Hendricks went to the McDonald's corporate headquarters in Chicago with Mia Hamm and Brandi Chastain. He pitched the company hard about how soccer was a popular and growing sport with American families. The players talked about how empowering it was for young girls to have soccer. But the McDonald's executives didn't budge.

"They were apologetic," Hendricks says. "They told us they were cutting back—they were not doing golf tournaments they used to do and they were not doing as much in sports."

The hope of the revenues and expenses ever coming in line was rapidly disappearing. Without new revenues, the league continued to cut expenses.

By the third season, the only major expense left to cut was personnel, and there was talk of pay cuts across the entire league. For non-national team stars like Shannon Boxx—players who already weren't earning very much money—the thought of retirement loomed.

Boxx, a Notre Dame alum, wanted to work in child psychology, and that was her plan for when she stopped playing soccer. Before she knew she'd play in the WUSA, she had started gathering recommendation letters and applying to graduate schools.

One day, at a team meeting with the New York Power, Boxx told her teammates: "I don't know I can do this anymore. I would love to, but I can't."

She was ready to quit before her third season in the WUSA. But the national team players told her they would cut their salaries so players like her wouldn't be affected as much. The founding players of the WUSA—the national team players—realized if they lost the league's best talent, the league would never thrive.

For the third season, they took pay cuts of as much as $25,000 each, and salary caps league-wide were cut by 25 percent, reducing the average salaries to about $37,235. Minimum salaries for first-year ($25,000), second-year ($26,250), and third-year ($31,500) players remained untouched. Rosters were trimmed from 18 players to 16.

Boxx ended up staying to play in that third WUSA season, and it's a good thing she did. That was the season she broke through to the national team under April Heinrichs. Boxx eventually went on to represent the national team in 195 games.

In the end, though, cutting expenses was never going to be enough for the WUSA. Running a professional soccer league cost what it cost.

"The fundamental issue, frankly, wasn't expenses," says Ben Gomez, who ran the investment firm of Breakers founder Amos Hostetter Jr. and helped run the WUSA team. "Obviously, building a team and doing it in a high-quality way was expensive, but the fundamental issue was the revenues just didn't show up. Ticket revenues were lower than expected, advertisers didn't show up, and there were no TV rights. When you see no top-line growth, it doesn't matter how well you do managing expenses. We kind of bled to death."

Hostetter says he lost about $20 million on the Boston Breakers alone over the three seasons, and $30 million overall because he half-owned the Bay Area CyberRays.

After the third season of the WUSA commenced, everyone knew the league was out of money and they might not see one another again, so when the league held its end-of-the-season banquet in 2003, there was a somber feeling.

"We went through 36 months of this torture of trying to get the economics together to make this a viable long-term proposition, and everybody knew this was probably going to be the last event of the WUSA because we couldn't continue," John Hendricks says. "The players were thanking everybody for the effort. Tears were aplenty in the room."

On September 16, 2003, during the offseason, the situation reached its conclusion. The national team players were at camp for the 2003 World Cup when everything they feared became official. Hendricks made the call to pull the plug on the WUSA. The 2003 Women's World Cup was just five days away.

In all, 375 people—players and staff—lost their jobs. After investors poured more than $100 million into the league all told, the league folded in the face of a $17 million shortfall that figured to grow if the league continued.

"If only we had six or seven CEOs in America that had stepped forward in the past year," Hendricks told reporters when the league's suspension was announced. "An independent women's professional league can survive—if it has corporate support."

The reasons for the WUSA's demise are varied, but some of its supporters can't help but think its challenges weren't all that different than what MLS has overcome.

Perhaps what the WUSA never found was their Philip Anschutz or Robert Kraft or Lamar Hunt. When MLS was on the brink of failure in 2001 after losing $250 million, the three billionaires agreed to take control of a handful of teams each to keep the league afloat. While two teams folded, the 10 remaining teams were all owned by those three men. It was a massive investment that eventually paid off—today, MLS commands $200 million expansion fees and is financially stronger than it's ever been.

"MLS survived because a billionaire man decided it was worth it to give his money and continued to give his millions and millions to fund the league," Tiffeny Milbrett says. "That's a really big reason that league never folded. I just feel like the women never had that—that person who was willing to do it because the women deserved it."

CHAPTER 9

"It Was Their *Team"*

Heather O'Reilly, just 17 years old, was up in her room when the phone rang at her family's house in New Jersey. Her mom answered and then called up the stairs in a way that made O'Reilly curious as to who was on the phone.

It was April Heinrichs, the coach of the national team. Mia Hamm was injured, leaving an open spot in camp, and Heinrichs wanted to bring O'Reilly in for the 2002 Algarve Cup.

"It was surreal," O'Reilly says. "We thought that somebody was playing a trick on us."

If the phone call was surreal, O'Reilly's first training camp was even more so. She admits that if a veteran like Brandi Chastain or Julie Foudy or Kristine Lilly called for the ball, she just immediately passed it because, well, why wouldn't she?

"I wanted them to like me and I wanted to fit in," O'Reilly says. "So, it took a little while for me to feel like I truly belonged. Like, no, I didn't just win a contest to train with the team for a day."

Nicknamed HAO for her initials—pronounced "hey-oh"—Heather Ann O'Reilly grew up in East Brunswick, a suburban town outside New York City that happened to be what she calls "a soccer-savvy community." She knew more about the Women's World Cup than most kids her age—her dad happened to be in Sweden for a business trip during the 1995 tournament and brought her back a T-shirt when she was 10.

Unlike the veterans—players who admit they knew nothing of the national team when they first joined—O'Reilly grew up keenly aware of the U.S. team's significance. At the opening game of the 1999 World Cup, she was there at Giants Stadium in the crowd with her youth soccer team. She jokes that she was more excited to see *NSYNC, who performed during the opening ceremony, but then she saw Mia Hamm score the tournament's first goal, and it inspired her.

"I remember being in the supermarket after they won and seeing the magazine covers and thinking that was so cool and I want to do that one day," O'Reilly says. "The '99 World Cup solidified that it was my dream."

Now, she was there with the national team at training camp and feeling like she was out of her depth. But what O'Reilly had going for her was an intensity and mental toughness that would eventually carry her to a 14-year career with the national team. Her friends teased her for being Mia Hamm's replacement on the roster—how could O'Reilly possibly replace a legend like Hamm?—but she started to belong soon enough.

The way it worked was that respect was earned and not given on the national team. That was a culture set by the earliest members, and it endured even as players came and went.

When Cat Whitehill, a native of Birmingham, Alabama, first arrived as a teenager, she knew she made a bad first impression. She had a poster of the 1991 World Cup–winning team on her wall growing up, and she was more than a little starstruck when she walked onto the team bus for the first time and saw Mia Hamm, Julie Foudy, and Kristine Lilly seated in front. Whitehill had a pillow in her hand because she hated the thick pillows hotels used—and it came in handy when that moment on the bus overwhelmed her.

"All I remember is ducking my head into my pillow and running to the back of the bus before even saying anything to them," Whitehill says, laughing. "I was so scared because these were my idols and I was going to play with them."

It wasn't until she had a few caps under her belt that Whitehill won over the veterans. She thinks the turning point was a crunching tackle she delivered in an exhibition rivalry game versus Canada.

"That was the first time I earned respect from them," says Whitehill, who first played under her maiden name, Cat Reddick. "Slowly but surely they welcomed me in because they liked my attitude and that I was a hard worker."

O'Reilly will never forget learning what it meant to be competitive in the national team environment. The veterans—including Mia Hamm, Julie Foudy, Brandi Chastain, and Kristine Lilly—all lived together in a house in Manhattan Beach, California, during residency camp. The team would split up into groups to play small-sided five-on-five games, and O'Reilly would watch them scrap and fight like they were playing in a World Cup final.

"I remember this one day during training, they were all on opposing teams, and some people won and went home happy, and some went home pissed off," says O'Reilly, a University of North Carolina graduate. "The next day, they were laughing about how some of them didn't speak until that evening."

Everything demanded 100 percent effort. That's why this team was so good.

That, in a nutshell, was the culture: If you played hard and could keep up, you were one of *them*. People may have thought you were on the national team once you got a call-up, but that's not what it *really* took to be part of the national team.

"One of the things that was really special about the veteran players was the way they were able to stay competitive but at the same time find a way to welcome younger players into the squad," Danielle Slaton says. "The culture they established, that was a gift I didn't really appreciate at the time. The culture really came from the players because they, quite frankly, outlasted all the coaches. They were the ones who were the guiding force. It really was their team."

As much as the arrival of new players sparked alarm among the veterans early on, finding a pipeline of young talent was something April Heinrichs had to do. It was at the core of her coaching philosophy—that every player had to keep fighting for her spot—and it's ostensibly what U.S. Soccer wanted when they hired her.

Even if Heinrichs would not be the coach to eventually enjoy the career primes of some of the raw, young talent she brought into the program and reap the full benefits, players like Heather O'Reilly, Hope Solo, Shannon Boxx, and Abby Wambach would go on to have massively influential runs with the team. The crop of skillful players Heinrichs was bringing into the team, perhaps more than anything else, would be her lasting stamp on the program, even as it cycled through coaches.

But first, the 2003 World Cup was around the corner, and she needed her best players to be ready right away. Many of them were veterans—and that raised a lot of questions.

Could the USA's biggest stars still compete, or should they have retired as World Cup champions after 1999? Was the American squad simply past its prime? Media outlets doubted "the Americans' aging back line" anchored by Brandi Chastain and Joy Fawcett. Long think pieces were written about Mia Hamm and whether, at age 31, she could still lead the attack.

As one columnist put it: "This is an experienced U.S. team. Alas, by women's soccer standards, it's also an aging one. You won't hear Heinrichs bragging about team speed. If you watched four years ago, you know these women. Hamm is 31. Joy Fawcett is 35, just a few months older than Chastain. Julie Foudy and Kristine Lilly are both 32. Why are they still here? A good question." The column concluded without an answer.

The American squad would be the oldest one at the World Cup with an average age of 27.6 years.

It wasn't that Heinrichs was resting on her laurels or shied away from spotting new talent. But when she named Torrance, California, native Shannon Boxx to the team's pre–World Cup camp, she told her on the phone before it started: "I want to see how well you do, but you don't have a chance to make the World Cup team."

Boxx, a disruptive and fierce midfield presence, much like the retired Michelle Akers, remembers: "It was like a dagger right into my heart. *I don't even have a chance for this?* I was still excited, but that kind of blew the wind out of my sails. Then it actually ended up being a great thing because I was super free in the way I played."

Heinrichs, realizing that Boxx's physical play and ability to lock down the midfield would be an asset, named the new player to the 2003 World Cup roster before she even earned her first national team cap. Newer talents like Abby Wambach, Aly Wagner, and Cat Whitehill made it, too. But Heinrichs was also counting on veteran experience to guide those younger players.

"I would say this is a perfect blend of wisdom and composure, energy and enthusiasm, young professionals and some great stories within this roster," Heinrichs told reporters once the roster was announced "People ask me, *Who can step up?* Anyone can move up to be a heroine."

* * *

If the Americans were primed to win in 1999, the 2003 World Cup felt very different.

The tournament was supposed to be held in China, but four months before it was set to start, FIFA moved the event due to fears over the SARS virus, which had killed more than 100 people and had no known cure. The United States was deemed the best option to host the tournament on short notice, but the timing of the event planned for China—September and October—was the busiest season in American sports. Not only would scheduling games in busy venues be tougher, the games would never match the attention and excitement from the 1999 World Cup four years prior.

Then, there was the news in the middle of the national team's World Cup camp that the WUSA was folding. Julie Foudy was in her hotel room getting ready to head to practice when she got word the league was officially being shut down. She delivered the news to her teammates, who were devastated but still had to train.

"There will be a few days that we will have to deal with the black cloud, and then we will have to put it behind them," coach April Heinrichs told reporters. "I have great faith in these women and know they will be able to handle it during the World Cup."

"I wish we would not have this distraction, absolutely," Julie Foudy said from training camp days before the World Cup was set to begin. "But the reality of the situation and our team is that we are not genetically predisposed to giving up."

And so, when the Americans stepped out onto the field for their opening group game of the 2003 World Cup, versus Sweden, it was a bit like sharks smelling blood in the water. Their resolve to win was as strong as ever.

The national team played a ruthless game at RFK Stadium in Washington, D.C.—it was evident from the 13th minute, when goalkeeper Briana Scurry flattened Swedish striker Hanna Ljungberg in the box, earning a yellow card in the process. The Americans would top Sweden, 3–1, with Hamm assisting on all three goals.

"It's the World Cup," Scurry said of the physical nature of the match. "You've gotta bring it, and if you don't, you'll go home early."

In the next match, against Nigeria in Philadelphia four days later, Hamm played like a woman who wanted to prove her doubters wrong.

Over her career, she had always been the most reluctant of stars. When reporters shoved microphones in her face and pushed her to talk about herself, she heaped praise onto her teammates. She rarely took penalty kicks and famously tried to get out of the shootout at the 1999 World Cup. But in the 2003, it was as if she was tired of being questioned about whether or not she could still lead the team.

When the Americans got an early penalty kick against Nigeria, Hamm announced that she was going to take it and then emphatically buried it. When she followed that up minutes later with a screaming free kick that sailed some 35 yards into the Nigerian net, it was a statement all its own. It was as if she was telling the world: "Hey, I'm still Mia Hamm."

But then, with the Americans having already secured their spot in the knockout round, Heinrichs rested Hamm for the third group-stage match, versus North Korea, three days later in Columbus, Ohio. It was a controversial decision, not least because Heinrichs had told reporters herself: "If you take Mia out, you run the risk of turning the faucet off."

It was a risk, to be sure.

The reason the Americans dominated so thoroughly over their first two matches was largely due to do Hamm's efforts. Though the Americans sailed past North Korea, 3–0, without her, that didn't necessarily mean anything—the Americans should have beaten North Korea, no matter the lineup. Now the knockout round was about to start, and there would be no easy games.

Heinrichs, for her part, was keenly aware that her every decision would be scrutinized.

"In coaching, you're either a jackass or a genius," Heinrichs said at one point during the tournament.

Mia Hamm wouldn't score again for the rest of the tournament. While Abby Wambach stepped up to score the only goal of the match in the quarterfinal versus Norway, there were no goals for the Americans to be found in the 2003 World Cup semifinal versus Germany. The Americans lost in a crushing 3–0 defeat, and Germany advanced to the final, where they beat Sweden to win the tournament.

"A lot of us played in the WUSA, so we knew that they were not better than we are," German forward Birgit Prinz told reporters afterward. "In '99, their pressure scared us. Everybody was like, *Oh, my god, don't give me the ball!* This time it was different. We knew we could play one-on-one and beat them."

The Americans were thoroughly outplayed. They looked hesitant on the ball. They looked like they lacked confidence and weren't sure of what to do. The rigid, direct tactical approach the team took under Heinrichs wasn't working. The German team was just better all around.

As Grant Wahl of *Sports Illustrated* put it: "Against the more skillful Germans, Heinrichs never deviated from the curious strategy of sending all-time-leading scorer Hamm out wide, where she air-mailed harmless crossing passes at the goalkeeper. It was like asking Barry Bonds to bunt in a World Series game."

For the veterans near retirement, it was a bitter pill to swallow. Their last World Cup had ended in failure. Their only opportunity to end their careers on top was at the next summer's 2004 Olympics in Athens.

"Right now, you want another chance, there's no question," Foudy said after the Germany loss when asked about the Olympics. "But at the same time, I want to let this sink in. I want to feel that this is the shittiest way to go out."

* * *

For whatever April Heinrichs was doing right, too much was going wrong for the veterans of the national team. They had now lost back-to-back major tournaments they had expected to win.

Worse still, Heinrichs's strict coaching style had been wearing on some of the veterans, both on and off the field. It would be tolerable, maybe, if they had some results to show for it. But these veteran players had already proved they were winners—they didn't need Heinrichs imposing harsh restrictions on what they could and couldn't do.

Some players recall bed checks with stringent curfews and limits on how many times they could touch the ball before passing. Others remember that they went to a Garrett Game for Mia Hamm—the charity event in memory of her brother—and Heinrichs fined them for missing a team practice.

The training sessions became brutal as Heinrichs increased the difficulty of fitness tests to push the players to their limits. Only about a quarter of the team was able to even pass the grueling new tests, shaking some players' confidence in the process. Many team practices didn't even involve soccer—the players just ran the entire time. Whatever Heinrichs was trying to do with the change in fitness regime, she didn't communicate it to the players.

Some level of dissatisfaction with how things were going wasn't necessarily a secret. Brandi Chastain and April Heinrichs were known to disagree and spar during team meetings.

"I remember going to seven o'clock meetings and people would be like, *Brandi, don't ask any questions because* Friends *starts at 8*," Shannon MacMillan says. "But Brandi was very cerebral and liked to ask questions. It wasn't disrespect on Brandi's part, but they'd get into these conversations and the whole team would be like, *Ugh.*"

As put by another former player anonymously because of Heinrichs's connections to U.S. Soccer: "Brandi is a smart soccer player and April wasn't a smart coach, and that was their biggest issue. April was more, *Try hard, be competitive, run a lot,* and Brandi was more, *Let's pass the ball around and let's play good soccer with the ball.*"

Whatever clashes were happening philosophically, it all seemed to come to a head in December 2003. In a meeting that seemed designed to get Heinrichs fired, Chastain spoke with U.S. Soccer president Robert Contiguglia and Dan Flynn, who had replaced Hank Steinbrecher as the federation's secretary general. (Details of the meeting would leak to the press months later, but Chastain and Heinrichs never publicly commented on it.)

Asked about it now, Chastain admits she did talk to Contiguglia and Flynn about the state of the locker room, but it wasn't a formal or planned meeting—they happened to be at the men's World Cup draw in Germany. And it wasn't specifically about trying to oust Heinrichs—Chastain wanted to make sure both Contiguglia and Flynn knew the team was unhappy.

"It was about what the overall sentiment at the time was and how something clearly was not going well," Chastain says. "I felt that it was need-to-know information for the president of U.S. Soccer. I didn't want to hear any more complaining—I was done complaining."

The meeting didn't have the effect she probably hoped it would. Contiguglia stood firm in his support of Heinrichs, and the relationship between the veterans and Heinrichs frayed further.

Contiguglia says now that he doesn't remember the meeting, but he had been keenly aware of problems between the players and their coach. From his perspective, however, it was the players who were the problem.

"There was a lot of feedback to me that there was disrespect from the players to the coach," he says. "There were instances where players didn't come to team meetings because they were watching *Friends* on TV or times where players would openly say, *We're going to win this game despite the coach.* You had leaders on the team walking around the locker room saying the federation is the enemy."

"Part of it had to do with their mentality," Contiguglia adds. "Their mentality was to fight to the end and make everything a combat sport. Part of that was reflected in their attitudes toward April."

Tiffeny Milbrett, who was for a spell the most dangerous attacking weapon in the world, decided she'd rather retire than keep playing under Heinrichs. The authoritarian methods of Heinrichs didn't sit well with the outspoken and creative striker.

"I'm an adult. I'm 31 years old," Milbrett told reporters after she announced her decision. "I've played maybe a thousand more games in the modern era of the women's game than April has, and I feel like there's things that need to happen in order to facilitate an environment for professional women soccer players."

"If that environment isn't going to be professional and if that environment isn't going to allow me to be the player that I am, then it's not worth it. Soccer's not a game that you can restrict players, especially creative players and players who have proven themselves at that level."

With the 2004 Olympics on the horizon, the veterans were desperate to get the situation under control.

A group of about seven senior players planned to stage an "intervention" of sorts with their coach to lay out their grievances. One of the younger players on the team remembers the veterans told the team about the plan and it was welcome news. It wasn't just the veterans who were fed up—many other players shared similar concerns.

"In the locker room, we were suffering," says the player, declining to speak on the record. "The locker room was the place where we were always together and where people complained. Players were breaking down in tears."

When the veterans met with Heinrichs, they put it all on the table. Overworking the players, not communicating decisions, enforcing such strict rules both on and off the field—everything. The message was clear: "You need to back off because we are miserable."

Heinrichs sat back and listened. She didn't argue. She also didn't make any promises. But she did cut back on the training regime that players felt was driving them into the ground. She did make an effort to find the middle ground between what she believed as a coach and what the players were demanding.

For the veterans behind the intervention, their resolve was as strong as ever to band together and figure out how to win in Athens. They told one another: *The best thing we can do is to find a way to win, regardless of who our coach is.*

For the younger players, they had to balance their loyalty to the coach who brought them into the fold and the veteran players they revered. But as the 2004 Olympics approached, there was a keen awareness that the veterans would retire after the tournament. All the players felt they owed it to the veterans to succeed in Athens, and sending them off the right way became a theme.

"There was this overall sense of: We need to figure out a way to do this and to honor their legacy," says Angela Hucles. "When you talk about mentality and figuring out ways to get what you want in life, all of it starts with your *why*. It all starts with having a good enough *why* because it is the driving force of the actions that will take place after that. For many of us, honoring the veterans was a big enough *why*."

* * *

With the veterans determined to finish their careers as champions and the rest of the team committed to the same goal, the Americans started the 2004 Olympics in Greece in the way they were accustomed to: They won and they won and they topped their group. As usual, they headed for the knockout round with momentum on their side.

But conspicuously, Brandi Chastain was the only non-goalkeeper who hadn't yet played a single minute of the tournament. Even when the Americans were comfortably set to advance out of the group stage, no one was rested to give way to Chastain. When *Los Angeles Times* journalist

Grahame L. Jones asked Heinrichs why Chastain hadn't played, he wrote, "Heinrichs went into a long and convoluted explanation."

As the Olympics knockout rounds approached, Grant Wahl from *Sports Illustrated* caught wind of Chastain's meeting with Robert Contiguglia months earlier and started asking both Chastain and Heinrichs about it. Both declined to comment.

Around that same time, Cat Whitehill, the young defender who had been starting in Chastain's place, was asked to meet with Heinrichs before the quarterfinal game. There, Heinrichs told her: "My hand has been forced and I have to start Brandi over you." Whitehill asked Heinrichs what that meant but didn't get an answer.

The U.S. won the quarterfinal versus an on-the-rise Japan team with Chastain playing the full 90 minutes, her first appearance of the tournament. Wahl's article came out three days later, and he reported that Chastain "asked that Heinrichs be fired" and that "Contiguglia told her no." It was the first time details about that meeting had been made public.

Contiguglia confirmed to *Sports Illustrated* the meeting took place, but he declined to discuss specifics. He also vigorously defended Heinrichs, saying: "As our technical director, she has built the youth teams into powerhouses, so our future is incredibly bright. And I can tell you the national team is better today than ever before: tactically, technically, and fitness-wise."

The timing of the news scoop—amid an Olympics—couldn't have been worse. It led to further speculation about why Chastain spent the first three games on the bench. Some players had already known about Chastain's meeting with Contiguglia and were angry it was being rehashed during the Olympics. For others, it was new information, but not surprising—everyone knew Chastain and Heinrichs had differences of opinion.

But the team didn't dwell on it because looming in the semifinals was Germany. It was the same team that had so thoroughly dismantled the Americans the year before at the 2003 World Cup, and it was the exact same stage of the tournament when that defeat had happened. Would the Americans be able to topple the Germans in what was practically a do-over?

Mia Hamm was determined. Heading into the semifinal match, she studied clips of her performance a year earlier in the 3–0 loss. Watching herself, she was frustrated.

"I wasn't as aggressive as I should have been," Hamm later said. "If it's an organized back line, the way you beat it is to try and tear it apart."

She wanted to make up for her performance last time around. This time, she wanted to be relentless and smother Germany. That's exactly what she did, slicing her way through Germany's back line and being so threatening that the Germans could never feel too settled.

The U.S. went up 1–0 in the 33rd minute, but moments before the match was about to end, Germany equalized in stoppage time. Now, with the score tied, the match had to go into extra time.

The stakes couldn't be higher, and Heinrichs turned to 19-year-old Heather O'Reilly, who only a few years prior had posters of Hamm on her wall. This was O'Reilly's first major tournament.

Almost immediately after extra time began, O'Reilly got past the charging goalkeeper but scuffed her shot on the open goal. It hit the outside of the post and trickled out of bounds.

"I remember that play like it was yesterday, and it was a really defining moment in my career because it was almost so bad that it was embarrassing," O'Reilly says. "The team was relying on me to come in and be poised enough to make an impact, and I blew it. And I remember looking over at Abby, who was my strike partner at the time, and I was looking for her to say, *No problem, HAO, you'll get the next one!* But she was so tired and the team was so tired that she didn't say anything— she just kind of shook her head in disbelief."

"It was a defining moment because it was something where I definitely could've crumbled. I was 19 years old. I could've let it impact me. But I was able to shake it off, and just a couple minutes later, Mia got in behind and cut it back to me."

In the 99th minute, Hamm fed a ball to O'Reilly, and the youngster made no mistake this time—she tapped it in for a heart-stopping finish. It was perhaps the best hint yet of the national team's upcoming transition. From old to new—from the player on the brink of retirement to the player competing in her first major event—the Americans found their winning combination.

The golden-goal rule had ended months earlier, and Germany could still wage a comeback before the clock ran out, but the Americans defended well through the end of extra time. After 120 minutes, the U.S. beat Germany, 2–1. The Americans were moving on to the gold-medal match.

This was the moment. This was the chance for the national team to reclaim its first world title in five years. The team could win a gold medal here in Athens and send the veterans out in the right way. Nothing less than winning would do.

The only team standing in the way of gold was Brazil—the same Brazil team the Americans had already beaten 2–0 in the group stage. There should be no reason the Americans couldn't beat them again.

But things are always different in a tournament final. The players only had to look back four years to the 2000 Olympics—they beat Norway in the group stage, 2–0, and then lost to them in the gold-medal match. They beat Brazil 2–0 in the group stage this time around— would the gold-medal match end up like last time, too?

The final in Athens quickly stirred up feelings of déjà vu.

The U.S., just like four years before, scored first. In the 39th minute, Lindsay Tarpley collected the ball in the midfield, turned, and fired a gorgeous shot from about 25 yards out. Goalkeeper Andréia couldn't reach the ball, even with her arms at full stretch as she dived toward the ball.

But Brazil would eventually return fire after some spectacular saves from goalkeeper Briana Scurry. In the 73rd minute, Cristiane ran onto a long ball and raced up the field. She crossed the ball, hoping to find a yellow shirt, but Scurry came off her line and cut it out. Scurry couldn't hold on to the ball, however—it was just too far out of her reach—and Pretinha was there to tap the ball in.

With the score locked at 1–1 at the end of 90 minutes, the match went into extra time. The last time a gold-medal match went into extra time for the Americans, it hadn't gone so well.

But this time, the Americans had Abby Wambach. They also had Wambach's head, which would eventually be responsible for 77 goals for the national team alone, almost as many as she'd score with her feet. The 5-foot-11 Wambach tended to tower over everyone else on the field, and she had a brawny build that made her difficult for defenders to outmuscle.

In the 112th minute, with penalty kicks looming, Kristine Lilly lined up to take a corner kick. Her left-footed kick was a powerful one that sailed high and toward the back post. Wambach lunged into the air, drove her head toward the goal, and connected perfectly. The ball made the back of the net rattle.

The Americans had to hold on to their lead for another eight minutes, plus stoppage time, and they defended in numbers to prevent Brazil from equalizing.

The whistle blew and the Americans ran into a huddle together, laughing and crying. The final score was 2–1, and the USA won gold in Athens.

Mia Hamm, tears streaming down her face, ran to the crowd to get some American flags for her and her teammates.

It was the end of an era. The players who had been the face of this national team were going out on top.

"There was closure," Julie Foudy said afterward. "I can go away and feel good about it."

* * *

On a cool December 2004 evening in Los Angeles, the national team gathered into a huddle before a friendly versus Mexico. Julie Foudy gave the pregame pep talk: "Let's have a ball out there tonight, huh?"

Her teammates whooped and called out, "Yeah!" Foudy continued: "Let's have fun. That's what this team has been about for 18 years. Let's do it!"

With that, the players put their hands together for their final chant before running onto the field. It was the last time Mia Hamm, Julie Foudy, or Joy Fawcett would be part of a pre-match huddle, and they knew it. This was their farewell game. The match was the last stop of a 10-game victory tour—the very victory tour they helped engineer six years earlier after the 1999 World Cup.

Young girls held up signs that said things like "I dream big—thanks Mia" and "Thanks Mia, I ♥ you." Another one said: "1987–2004—I was born . . . so was a legacy . . . Thanks for a lifetime of memories."

It was the end of an era with the team's veteran leaders stepping away, but for the players who remained on the national team, there was another big change they wanted.

By this point, four years into April Heinrichs's tenure as head coach, many players continued to feel disenchanted with the direction of the team. The intervention before the Olympics had been only marginally successful at improving the way Heinrichs related to the players.

Players who decline to speak on the record say Heinrichs often didn't read the room well and failed to communicate her decisions. She was also so inflexible and strict that it felt like disrespect for the players' input as longtime professionals. Some players share off-the-record anecdotes about alternative career plans they had lined up in case they had to follow Tiffeny Milbrett's lead and quit.

After the Olympics, a group of players went to U.S. Soccer president Robert Contiguglia and demanded that Heinrichs be let go as coach. Contiguglia says now: "I do remember them threatening to retire based on who they had as coach, but I'm not going to go into that."

Again, just as he had with Chastain a year earlier, Contiguglia rejected the players' pleas and continued to support Heinrichs. The players threatened to go public with their complaints, but he refused to act. As one player puts it: "It was time for a change, but U.S.

Soccer didn't think it was time for a change. We definitely made our viewpoints known."

So, instead, the players went to Heinrichs directly and brought her a letter formally asking for her resignation. The letter was blunt and ruthless: The players said they didn't think they could win with her, and they didn't feel she was qualified for the job she had. She was a poor leader, and she had alienated too many players, the players added.

The letter offered strength in numbers and Heinrichs eventually agreed to leave her post. She had almost a year left on her contract, but she stayed with U.S. Soccer as a consultant.

"I think so highly of April Heinrichs that it was not easy for me to accept her resignation," Contiguglia said in the U.S. Soccer press release announcing her exit. "Through her five years on the job, the program has grown tremendously."

With its coach gone and its core of veteran leadership retired, the team was about to go through some severe growing pains.

CHAPTER 10

"Why Do We Have to Deal with This Discrimination?"

The national team had just finally won another major tournament. Five years after the 1999 World Cup, which was a turning point for the players, they had won the Olympics in Athens.

The timing, it seemed, couldn't be better. The team's contract was about to expire at the end of 2004 and, again, they had proved their worth, giving them leverage heading into negotiations. Or so they thought.

In actuality, the team winning a gold medal triggered bonuses from their 2000 contract that didn't come cheap for U.S. Soccer. The team got a shared $720,000 bonus for winning gold, on top of smaller bonuses each player got for making the roster, plus a payout for a victory tour. If anything, winning the gold medal must have reminded the federation just how much was at stake in these contract negotiations.

"They were so mad about what we had done—the independence we had created," says John Langel, the team's lawyer. "In the previous contract, the women got a huge Olympic-gold bonus and then a tour bonus. U.S. Soccer had to do a 10-game outdoor tour—it was a payday of $2.5 million for the players, and the federation didn't like it."

With a quiet post-Olympics year ahead, U.S. Soccer secretary general Dan Flynn informed the players that the national team would "go dark" for 2005 and play between four and six games total that year. Rather than schedule the usual slate of games, the federation would instead focus on scouting new players.

"If there are no games, where will the women play?" Langel asked.

"The W-League," replied Flynn.

"Are you kidding me?" Langel said.

The W-League wasn't a professional league. It was a development league that included amateur, unpaid players. There was no comparison between playing international opponents with the national team and competing in the W-League.

"We told them we don't necessarily need a residency camp, but we don't have anywhere to play at all," says Cat Whitehill, who graduated from the University of North Carolina with a degree in communications. "They wanted nothing to do with us."

U.S. Soccer argued the next World Cup wasn't for another three years and there were no major events the team needed to prepare for. It would be similar to the team's schedule in 2001, when U.S. Soccer hosted just two home games for the national team.

But for the players who had now made soccer their living and didn't have the WUSA anymore, that was unacceptable. It's not as if U.S. Soccer was simply scaling back friendlies. The federation said it had no plans to send the team to the annual Algarve Cup in Portugal, which the team always competed in. A team wouldn't be sent to the Four Nations Tournament in China either, despite the competition being a usual fixture on the team's calendar.

The players demanded to know how U.S. Soccer could justify skipping the tournaments. Flynn replied that it was "the technical director's recommendation" to play a lighter schedule. The technical director? April Heinrichs.

The players wanted to figure out if Heinrichs really believed the team should play so few games in 2005, so Julie Foudy reached out to her.

"Is that true? Did you tell U.S. Soccer we should only pay five games?" Foudy asked.

"I never said anything like that," Heinrichs told her. "I told them you should play 20 games."

If Heinrichs hadn't recommended such a sparse schedule and, in fact, recommended around 20 games, it seemed that U.S. Soccer was making a decision that went against what was best for the players. The players saw a clear double standard—the men's team hadn't played so few games since 1987, almost two decades earlier.

They concluded U.S. Soccer's real reason was the same one behind most disputes between the players and the federation: money. The federation, it appeared, did not want to spend the money for training camps, player stipends, and travel for overseas competitions, even as it was sitting on a $30 million surplus at the time.

"In 2005, they had no plans for us and wanted us to go quiet so they didn't have to pay us the entire year," says defender Kate Markgraf.

As it turned out, the players didn't have much leverage at all. There were no games to boycott. No World Cup draws in California to threaten to skip. The tactics the team had used successfully in years prior weren't going to work here. They needed another way to force U.S. Soccer to come to the table.

* * *

While the U.S. Soccer Federation may have had the ultimate authority over soccer in the United States, there was an organization that had authority over U.S. Soccer: the U.S. Olympic Committee.

The USOC was comprised of national governing body members from all Olympic sports, including soccer, which was represented by the U.S. Soccer Federation. The Olympic and Amateur Sports Act—the law that created the U.S. Olympic Committee—explicitly stated that all national governing bodies must offer the opportunity for athletes to compete "without discrimination on the basis of race, color, religion, sex, age, or national origin."

On November 15, 2004, John Langel wrote a letter to Jim Scherr, the CEO of the USOC, and he CC'd Dan Flynn, U.S. Soccer's secretary general. It was a scathing rebuke of not just U.S. Soccer's decision to cut the national team's schedule in 2005, but the federation's treatment of the team over the years up to that point.

"These recent events are shocking," Langel wrote, after summarizing the back-and-forth over the 2005 schedule. "It is unethical and violates the USSF's obligations of transparency to misrepresent to United States Olympic athletes about the reason they will be denied the right to compete in protected competitions."

"Unfortunately, over the years, there have been a number of other telling illustrations of discrimination," the letter continued.

Then, Langel launched into a laundry list of allegations of how U.S. Soccer discriminated against the women:

- *USSF's statements in the 1990s to the effect that they would not have a women's national team if they were not required to do so;*
- *USSF has attempted to persuade the Men's National Team Players' Association to structure its contracts in a way that would not result in any payments to the women under the same matrix;*
- *USSF's unwillingness to pay the women anywhere near equal compensation for successes comparable to the men's (indeed, USSF is committed to paying the women less than the men even though the women have been far more successful on the playing field);*
- *Unequal support with respect to items such as equipment managers, trainers, massage therapists, meals, hotel accommodations, and transportation;*
- *The commitment of funds to pay for 14-year-old boys and not girls to live and train in Bradenton, Florida, while attending a private soccer academy;*
- *The commitment of $10 million to build soccer stadiums for a for-profit professional league for men, Major League Soccer ("MLS");*
- *The commitment to loan or give millions to assist in the start-up of MLS. Correspondingly, when repeatedly asked by the Women's United Soccer Association ("WUSA") for start-up funding to help relaunch a league, US Soccer has repeatedly claimed "it is not in the business of building leagues";*
- *The commitment of funds to pay Major League Soccer reserve players, again using not-for-profit funds to support a for-profit league that is at no current risk of failure;*
- *The recent decision to avoid scheduling events at or near certain MLS cities so as not to adversely affect the MLS while conducting the Women's Post Olympic Victory Tour;*
- *The decision to assign the USSF's marketing rights to the marketing*

arm of Major League Soccer, thereby benefiting the MLS and ending any attempt to appeal to sponsors of women's sports;

- *The recent and repeated refusal to even provide dates to meet with the women to negotiate a new Uniform Player Agreement even though the current agreement requires the parties to meet to negotiate in good faith at least sixty days before the expiration date of December 31, 2004; and*

- *The refusal to even discuss a plan for the Team for the next four years, knowing the women stop getting paid on December 8, 2004.*

The letter went on for another five pages after that. It mentioned that U.S. Soccer's board of directors appeared to be below the mandatory 20 percent threshold of women. It mentioned that U.S. Soccer had no official policy on ethics. It cited a report that claimed U.S. Soccer engaged in "back room politics" and was "an old boys club." It was an all-out assault on the federation.

"In the short run, the women are asking that USSF be directed to take the steps necessary to ensure that the women play in the upcoming protected competition in Portugal," the letter concluded, referring to the Algarve Cup. "In the long run, the women are asking that USSF be directed to remediate the effects of its discrimination."

The goal of the letter, as brutal as it was, wasn't really to convince the USOC to reprimand U.S. Soccer or revoke its national governing body status. Its aim was to get U.S. Soccer to cooperate with the national team and back off the plan to gut the 2005 schedule.

The USOC told U.S. Soccer officials they had to cooperate with the team, and after some back-and-forth, the federation agreed to send the team to the 2005 Algarve Cup.

"They were incredibly reluctant to cooperate until the USOC told them they had to cooperate," Langel says.

Tiffeny Milbrett, who returned to the team after April Heinrichs left, says the ordeal reinforced a second-class status for the women's national team with the federation.

"U.S. Soccer had to be threatened by the Olympic Committee that they weren't managing their governing status toward the women appropriately," she says. "It was like, *Why do we have to deal with this discrimination and these attitudes?* It was the Olympic Committee that changed things, not these men at the federation saying, *Yes, the women deserve it.*"

Amid the fight over whether the team would play a real schedule in 2005, the team's contract expired, bringing both issues to a head. Contract negotiations were ongoing throughout the back-and-forth over the schedule, and they were highly contentious.

In the end, the national team ended up playing only nine games in 2005, which included the Algarve Cup and a few friendlies in the United States. That was better than what had been initially proposed by the federation, but it still fell well short of what had, by now, become the team's usual schedule. As part of the contract negotiations, the federation gave the players a retroactive payment of around $50,000 each to make up for the quiet schedule they played. It was tantamount to an admission that the federation was wrong to "go dark" in 2005.

But there were bigger financial concerns. For all the gains the national team had made in their previous contract, the deal didn't look as good once the WUSA folded. The players were guaranteed a monthly stipend ranging between $3,500 and $6,500 per month, but only for eight months out of the year. On the low end, that was a salary of less than $30,000 per year, and there were no protections if a player got injured.

The players still didn't have enough financial stability—they weren't earning actual salaries. Playing soccer for the federation was their job, and they needed to know they could be paid year-round. The negotiations to make that a reality would end up being the lengthiest and most difficult ones by that point. Negotiations started in mid-2003 and would go all the way to the end of 2005.

In the end, U.S. Soccer and the national team agreed to a contract structure that was a pivotal step forward: finally, soccer became a full-time, year-round job for the players. The deal established three different tiers for players, all of whom would receive contracts that paid salaries.

It wasn't a stipend, it didn't depend on whether U.S. Soccer held any games, and it wasn't for a few months out of the year—it was an actual annual salary.

The first-tier players who competed in the highest-profile competitions would earn $70,000, mid-tier would earn $50,000, and bottom tier $30,000. It was hardly a windfall for the players, but it allowed them to make a stable living playing soccer, and that's all they had ever wanted.

"The 2005 contract was really the contract that secured them without regard to residency," Langel says. "That's when they earned a true salary and injury protection."

Robert Contiguglia says the idea for guaranteed income for the players was his. Langel vehemently denies that. Regardless of how it came about, however, it was a historic step forward for the players.

"All the other soccer federations and in all the other sports, the women had to have outside jobs, working as secretaries or as coaches or other employment, because the pay for playing for the national team wasn't adequate," Contiguglia says. "So, we were the first as far as I know in the world to do that, giving them a guaranteed income. They got paid whether they played or not."

* * *

The most vocal players on the national team got what they wanted when they pushed out April Heinrichs as coach. The only problem? They wouldn't get to decide who took her place.

While U.S. Soccer interviewed several candidates for the job, Greg Ryan, who was Heinrichs's assistant, took over in the interim. Ryan was among those being interviewed, but he wasn't a frontrunner—at least not among the players.

As Hope Solo later put it in her book, *Solo: A Memoir of Hope*: "Of all the candidates, the one who seemed the least qualified was Greg Ryan. Before coming to the national team, he had coached at Colorado College, never earning an NCAA berth there before becoming April's vanilla assistant. The consensus on the team was that we needed a fresh start, and Greg was a leftover from the past."

Other candidates reportedly being considered for the job included former coach Tony DiCicco and University of Santa Clara coach Jerry Smith, who was Brandi Chastain's husband. But this was a new generation of players—Mia Hamm, Julie Foudy, and Joy Fawcett had all retired—and the remaining national team wanted an outsider. They wanted someone new, like Sweden's Pia Sundhage. But the federation, which was in the middle of the contentious 2005 contract negotiations with the national team, wasn't exactly keen to follow the team's wishes.

The players unwittingly helped Ryan's case for the job with a string of dominant wins at the March 2005 Algarve Cup, beating France, Finland, Denmark, and Germany without conceding a goal.

On April 8, 2005, the federation announced that Greg Ryan would become the new head coach and dropped the interim tag. Players suspected it was a power play by U.S. Soccer. When the hire was announced, one player anonymously told the *San Diego Union-Tribune*'s Mark Zeigler: "The federation wants to show us who's running the show." Hope Solo later said: "It seemed to me that Greg was a pawn in a power struggle."

Robert Contiguglia admits he hired Ryan on April Heinrichs's recommendation. Some players, declining to speak on the record, long suspected that was the case—they are convinced that Heinrichs knew the players didn't want Ryan for the job and that he wouldn't be a good fit. Recommending him was a final dig, they believe, in the back-and-forth between the players and the coach they had butted heads with for nearly five years.

Whether the players favored Greg Ryan to be their new coach didn't matter now. He got the job, and the players had to abide by whatever decisions he made.

PART II

CHAPTER 11

"If There Isn't a Goalkeeper Controversy, Why Make One?"

One of Greg Ryan's first acts as coach was to cut Brandi Chastain from the team.

There was no last call-up as a courtesy or the opportunity to let her try to earn a spot. One day, shortly after he took over, Chastain's national team career was suddenly over.

Chastain asked to have a meeting to talk through it. She told him: "Look, I'm not assuming I should be on the team. But I do think the fair thing to do is to give me a chance. Put me on the field with the players you believe belong, and then everyone will know."

She was 36 and not in her prime, to be sure. But it's also not unheard of for a top defender to keep playing at a high level at that age. Maintaining a veteran presence on the team would also have its benefits.

Chastain, who had 192 caps for the national team, just wanted a tryout. Ryan met with her in person, where he told her, to her face, that he had no plans to call her into the national team ever again.

"He flew up to San Jose and we had a meeting at the hotel where he was staying," Chastain remembers. "I can't say I begged, but I asked very strongly to be given the opportunity, and I was denied that."

Chastain had watched teammates like Mia Hamm and Julie Foudy end their careers with testimonial matches—the special farewell games that important players earn—but she was never going to get one. Her last game was the final stop of the post-Olympics victory tour in 2004, the same last game as Hamm and Foudy, only Chastain didn't know it at the time.

"It wasn't on my radar—it wasn't supposed to happen like that," Chastain says. "He was the assistant coach. I'm not sure how he became coach of the national team, to be honest, and there was no discussion."

Shannon MacMillan, another veteran, tells a similar story. She, too, was surprised to find herself left off rosters, but in her case, it was because Greg Ryan had reassured her that she was in his plans. As time went on and she still hadn't gotten a call, at age 31 she gave up hope of ever returning to the team. Her career ended at 176 caps.

"I was like, *Enough's enough*," she says. "That's kind of what forced my hand into retiring. I just got sick and tired of the politics and the B.S."

Briana Scurry took some time off after the Olympics before she returned to the fold, but the team under Ryan largely skewed toward new players. Tiffeny Milbrett returned to the team with April Heinrichs gone but was quickly cut, ending her career at 32 years old. With some of the veterans pushed out of the way, there was room for up-and-coming talent.

Ryan's new roster had a dozen players 23 years or younger and a dozen players with five or fewer caps under their belt. One of them was a midfielder named Carli Lloyd. Ryan gave Lloyd her first cap on July 10, 2005, during a friendly in Portland, Oregon, versus Ukraine just before her 23rd birthday.

At the time, Lloyd wasn't a well-rounded player. She wasn't strong defensively. She wasn't consistent. But she had lofty ambitions and allowed her wildest dreams to produce special, unexpected moments.

A native of Delran, New Jersey, a suburban town near Philadelphia, Lloyd had risen through the youth ranks of U.S. Soccer on her natural abilities as an attacker with a nose for the goal. When she had gotten cut from the under-21 national team in 2003, the coach, Chris Petrucelli, told her it wasn't for lack of talent—she just hadn't worked hard enough.

Lloyd eventually hired a personal trainer, James Galanis, whose role morphed into something of a life coach, mentor, and spiritual advisor. Together, they set a course to make Lloyd the greatest soccer player in the world, which started with having Lloyd earn back her spot on the U-21 team. She did that, and in 2005, with her first cap, Lloyd took another major step toward her goal.

Though Lloyd would describe an up-and-down relationship with Greg Ryan in her memoir, *When Nobody Was Watching*, he ultimately became the one who gave her the chance to develop into a core national team player.

As a coach, Ryan emphasized letting players make their own decisions on the field and expressing themselves how they wanted—a stark contrast to April Heinrichs.

"For a long time—and I think this may be with American coaching—we want to be the ones to tell the players what to do," Ryan told reporters. "But soccer isn't a game where that works very well at the highest level, not unless you're a lot better than everybody else. I'm giving some of the responsibility and freedom back to the players."

In another one of his first moves, Ryan quickly anointed Hope Solo the team's new No. 1 goalkeeper. Solo was a dominant force in goal. Her natural athleticism was one reason for that, but another one was her fearlessness. Nothing seemed to rattle her between the posts.

Many of the players on the national team had similar middle-class, suburban upbringings—they were, in some ways, the personification of the so-called American dream. But Solo's background was different. She was conceived during a conjugal visit when her mother had visited her father in prison. When she was 7, her father was arrested for kidnapping her and her brother—police with guns drawn surrounded her father as he took Solo to run an errand at the bank.

She grew up hoping soccer would help her escape her hometown, Richland, Washington, which happened to be where plutonium was created for Fat Man, the atomic bomb dropped on Nagasaki, Japan, during World War II. Locals embraced the city's uneasy place in history—Richland High School's logo features a mushroom cloud and its mascot is the Bombers. A popular cheer when Solo was in school was: "Nuke 'em, nuke 'em, nuke 'em 'til they glow!"

Solo had always been a forward growing up—she scored 109 goals for the Bombers and reached a state championship her senior year. But when her academy team had a goalkeeper shortage, she stepped in, even as she continued as a forward for her school. It was as a goalkeeper that she caught the attention of the youth national team.

Solo's tall, muscular stature and far-reaching wingspan were ideal physical attributes for a goalkeeper, and her aggressive style in net made her difficult to beat. From the point Ryan named Solo the No. 1 goalkeeper, she would go on to record a stunning 55-game unbeaten streak.

But that streak wouldn't come easily. First, Greg Ryan had to make the worst coaching mistake in the history of the national team—a miscalculation that fractured the team and tested the culture built by the players who came before.

* * *

The national team was two days from the 2007 World Cup semifinal versus Brazil when an assistant coach leaned over to Hope Solo. Solo was sitting at a table in the team's meal room at their hotel in China when the assistant told her Greg Ryan wanted to talk to her once she was finished eating dinner.

That struck her as unusual, and she immediately had a bad feeling about it. Through the group stage and the quarterfinal, the national team was unbeaten, and Solo was getting better with every game.

She *did* open the tournament with a mistake—a wet ball slipped through her hands and into the back of the net, forcing a 2–2 draw with North Korea in the opening match. But it was a strange game—North Korea's two goals came during the 10 minutes striker Abby Wambach spent on the sideline getting 11 stitches on her scalp after a collision and Ryan opted not to sub her out—a risky decision. Solo followed up that draw with three consecutive shutouts, all wins, against Sweden, Nigeria, and England.

When Solo went up to her coach's room to talk with him, she found out she was right to be worried. Ryan was going to start Briana Scurry in goal for the semifinal instead of Solo.

"Bri has a winning record against Brazil," he told her. "Her style just matches up better with Brazil's style."

Scurry had been a fantastic goalkeeper for the national team, to be sure, and some of her best performances had indeed come against Brazil. In 12 career matches versus Brazil, Scurry averaged just .41

goals conceded per game. Only three months earlier, Scurry recorded a shutout versus Brazil in a friendly when Solo was away dealing with the death of her father.

The problem, however, was that friendly versus Brazil in June was the last time Scurry started for the national team. By now it was September and in the middle of the knockout round of a World Cup. There was no way Scurry could be at her sharpest. If Ryan's decision wasn't fair to Solo, who had done nothing to lose her spot, it really wasn't fair to Scurry, who didn't have the proper preparation to perform at her best.

The decision—as stunning as it was—was bad enough. But making it worse was that Ryan admitted he made it with input from Abby Wambach and Kristine Lilly.

In defending his decision, he later said: "My veteran players told me over and over again that they felt much more comfortable with Briana and less so with Hope because Briana communicated well with the defense."

Solo was furious, and as soon as she left her meeting with Ryan, she set out to confront her teammates. Lilly didn't want to be involved, but Solo says that Wambach didn't flinch when asked about it, telling her: "Hope, I think Bri is the better goalkeeper."

When Solo got back to her own hotel room, all her emotions were unleashed. As one player puts it now: "All the sudden, we were seeing furniture fly into the hallway." Several players who decline to speak on the record say Solo trashed her room and punched a hole in the wall. Nicole Barnhart, the backup goalkeeper who was her roommate at the time, picked up the furniture and put the room back together.

Later, Aly Wagner, Cat Whitehill, and Angela Hucles went to Solo's room to check on her. She was crying.

The trio understood why Solo was so upset. The decision to change a goalkeeper in the middle of a World Cup was unprecedented, and everyone knew it. The players tried to support her and give her a pep talk to be ready, just in case.

"We get it," the players told her one by one. "This is an awful thing to go through. We've all been there. But you are still part of this team, and we still need you. You never know what's going to happen in the game."

The press corps in China was small, but once reporters there learned about Ryan's decision, it was all they could ask about.

Would it shake Solo's confidence?

"That's not our concern," Ryan said. "We came here trying to win a world championship and put the players on the field that we thought could win each game."

Was Ryan concerned that Scurry would be rusty?

"She'll be ready—wait and see," he said.

Julie Foudy and Tony DiCicco were now both working as broadcast analysts for ESPN. On air, they expressed astonishment at Ryan's decision and both said, in no uncertain terms, that it was a bad move.

"If there isn't a goalkeeper controversy, why make one?" DiCicco asked rhetorically. "It's not just those two players—every player is affected."

* * *

Once the semifinal versus Brazil began, the national team looked to be in trouble immediately, struggling from the first whistle.

In the seventh minute, Scurry got her first test. She reached out to pluck a floating free kick out of the air, but the ball slipped through her hands. A Brazilian player shot the loose ball, but it went over the bar.

Julie Foudy, who was ESPN's color commentator, told play-by-play announcer JP Dellacamera on the live broadcast: "This is precisely what we've been talking about. Briana Scurry has only started in seven games since 2005. The problem with that is you just aren't in a rhythm—you aren't used to handling balls with pressure like that."

But the first goal the Americans conceded would come on a miscommunication and an own goal. On a Brazil corner kick, Formiga played a relatively harmless ball into the box. There wasn't a yellow shirt nearby, and the Americans had it covered. Scurry called out, "Mine!"

but Leslie Osborne dived to head the ball clear and accidentally headed it straight into the net.

By the 28th minute, the Brazilians were firmly in control. The world's best player, Marta, was doing what she does best as she danced her way through the box and fired off a low, skipping shot. Scurry read the ball and got a palm on it—but it wasn't strong enough. The ball flicked past her hand and skipped in. It was 2–0. The Americans looked frazzled. At this moment, for the first time in 51 games under Greg Ryan, the Americans trailed by more than one goal.

As if things weren't going poorly enough, Shannon Boxx earned her second yellow card of the night and was thus red-carded out of the game. Her first yellow was deserved, but the second one was a shockingly inept referee decision.

Video replays show the center referee did not even see what happened. Replays also show it was Cristiane who clipped Boxx, not the other way around. It was a terrible call and, just like that, any hopes for an American comeback were all but dashed. Boxx watched the rest of the game through tears from the locker room while the U.S. continued, down a player.

When halftime arrived, Boxx was no longer the only player sitting in the locker room in tears.

"The team had already given up," says Cat Whitehill, who scored 11 goals over her national team career, despite being a defender. "Players were already crying. We had been down before, but I had never seen that. When I saw everyone in the locker room, I thought: *We don't have a chance.*"

In the second half, the Brazilians started toying with the Americans. Marta would let the ball sit in front of her and, as a U.S. defender stood at the ready, trying to anticipate the next move, Marta would feign her hips one way and then the other. She'd go back and forth, like a Brazilian samba dance. She'd bring her favored left foot into the dance, faking like she was about to kick the ball. Finally, she'd catch the defender flat-footed and tap the ball around her.

"It's fair to say that was one of our worst games in the history of the program," says Heather O'Reilly, who started in the match. "There was an own goal, there was a red card, all in the first half, and we were just climbing this enormous mountain with 10 players for the majority of the game. As it got more challenging for us, the Brazilians grew in their momentum and their energy. They were having the time of their lives on the field, and for us it was the game from hell."

For whatever scrutiny Greg Ryan would face for the goalkeeper change and its effect on the back line, the American attack was struggling just as much. The front players couldn't string anything together and played desperate, haphazard soccer.

"It was like watching an accident happen in slow motion and there's nothing you can do about it," says Angela Hucles, who watched the game from the bench. "It didn't matter how hard we were working, it just wasn't syncing up."

In the end, Brazil crushed the Americans, 4–0. It became the team's worst-ever loss in World Cup history. Briana Scurry's 12-game winning streak versus Brazil throughout her career, including eight shutouts, had come to an end.

Afterward, coaches and players alike walked past the mixed zone, which is the wall of reporters trying to get postgame quotes. The Brazilian players, all smiles, formed a conga line and danced through it past the American media.

Greg Ryan, meanwhile, was asked about the goalkeeper decision.

"I don't have any regrets about that," he said. "I think Bri played a great game. The first goal that Marta scored was a great goal. Briana in that situation gives us the best chance to stop that shot because of her quickness and speed. If you look at the rest of the match, there is nothing she could have done about any of the other goals."

A reporter from Canada's CBC asked Solo if she wanted to comment. Aaron Heifetz, the team's longtime press officer, intervened: "She didn't play. You only want to talk to players who played in the game." Solo heard this, spun around on her heels, and snapped, "No, I want to talk!" She gave CBC reporter Erin Paul a blunt, honest assessment of her feelings:

It was the wrong decision, and I think anyone who knows anything about the game knows that. There's no doubt in my mind I would have made those saves. And the fact of the matter is it's not 2004 anymore. It's not 2004. It's now 2007 and you have to live in the present and you can't live by big names. You can't live in the past. It doesn't matter what somebody did in an Olympic gold-medal game three years ago. Now is what matters, and that's what I think.

The CBC had a content-sharing agreement with ESPN, and the video of Solo was quickly all over the channel and the network's website, where Solo's teammates would eventually watch the clip over and over.

Back at the hotel, the turmoil was only getting started. The Americans and the Brazilians, who were staying at the same hotel, ran into each other in the lobby. The Americans cried as the Brazilians danced.

"That was one of the most excruciating postgame hotel moments I can remember," Heather O'Reilly says. "We were with family and friends, sobbing, and they're trying to console us, and the Brazilians show up and are just relentless in their celebrations. I'll confidently use the word *obnoxious,* because it was. It was pretty over-the-top and absurd. I remember them in the turnstile of the door, just going around and around."

* * *

It didn't take long for Solo to get a phone call in her hotel room from Kristine Lilly, the captain of the team. Lilly and some of the veterans had seen her post-game interview and wanted to talk to her.

As described in Solo's book, when she walked into Lilly's room, there was also Briana Scurry, Abby Wambach, Christie Pearce, Shannon Boxx, and Kate Markgraf. They felt she had broken an unwritten rule.

Wambach would later explain it in her own book, *Forward,* like this: "There's an unspoken code in our sport, with a few key tenets: you don't talk shit about your teammates, you don't throw anyone under the bus, and you don't publicly promote yourself at the expense of the team."

One by one, the players expressed their anger and disappointment. They said Solo had torn down what the players before her—players like Julie Foudy and Mia Hamm—had built up. This team had a vitally important culture that Solo was destroying.

Solo argued: "This isn't about Julie Foudy or anyone else from the past." But her pushback only seemed to further upset the veterans.

"I didn't know to handle this betrayal of the team culture," Markgraf says now. "I was tired, I was hurt, I had blown my ankle out after a poor World Cup. We played horrible soccer. And she blasted Bri, who had handled the transition of power at goalkeeper in a very classy way, so when she did that, it became a mess. I wish I had kept my cool, but her actions were the telling sign that the old culture would no longer work."

For the rest of the players outside that leadership group, the situation was viewed with a range of attitudes, but everyone knew it was something that needed to be dealt with. The problem was that there wasn't a consensus on what to do.

"Some people were very upset, some people were moderately upset, and some people were indifferent," says Angela Hucles, "but the general sense was that we need to solve this quickly because if it festers it's going to hurt the team. It was a bit urgent."

The next morning, the team had a players-only meeting. The goal was to get everything out in the open. Players could express what they were feeling, and Solo could say whatever she needed to clear the air, too. There was hope for a moment of reconciliation, but it never came. Solo was asked to leave the room while the team discussed how to proceed. The meeting lasted hours and, in the end, the players didn't get the contrition they wanted from Solo.

The net result was that Solo was essentially kicked off the team. She was banned from practicing with the team before the third-place match against Norway, and Ryan informed her she would not be named to the roster for the game.

Ryan told reporters he sought input from veteran players before taking such drastic steps.

"Obviously, this has been a distraction to the team," Ryan said. "We have moved forward with 20 players who have stood by each other."

Solo was shunned by most of her teammates. She was shut out of team meals, barred from the team's final match of the World Cup, and not welcomed to the medal ceremony to collect the bronzes the team won. Afterward, she had to take a separate shuttle bus to the airport. The veterans were furious, and players who may have felt differently didn't want to go against the team leaders.

"I have felt compelled to clear the air regarding many of my post-game comments on Thursday night," Solo wrote on her MySpace page. "I am not proud or happy the way things have come out. Although I stand strong in everything I said, the true disheartening moment for me was realizing it could look as though I was taking a direct shot at my own teammate. I would never throw such a low blow. Never. Many of this goes way beyond anyone's understanding, and is simply hard to justify. In my eyes there is no justification to put down a teammate. That is not what I was doing."

Her apology did little to quell the controversy, which represented the first fracture in the tight-knit national team that the public had ever seen. Columnists and bloggers openly mocked Solo for saying the situation was beyond the public's comprehension.

But there *was* more to the situation than fans and media knew at the time. The fact that Solo's father had died three months earlier of a heart attack wasn't widely known. A couple of months before that, Solo's longtime best friend had been struck and killed by a car while jogging. Even before she was benched in the most important game of her life and watched her World Cup dreams slip away, Hope Solo's world was already in turmoil. Some players say they had noticed how those recent tragedies affected her.

There were no excuses, though. Just about everyone seemed to think that what Solo said had crossed a line. Except one very important person who didn't: Sunil Gulati, the new president of U.S. Soccer, who had taken over for Robert Contiguglia in March 2006. Gulati met with

Solo in China and told her that if this situation had happened on a men's team, it wouldn't have blown up the way it did.

Ryan defended his decision to bench Solo to U.S. Soccer, telling officials she had missed curfew and a team dinner the night before the team's quarterfinal match. Meanwhile, the team had to embark on a short "victory tour" of three games for coming in third place at the World Cup. Ryan didn't want Solo to be there, but the federation did. She attended the games but wore street clothes because Ryan wouldn't let her play.

After the last game in Albuquerque, Greg Ryan was fired. No coach could lose a World Cup in such chaotic fashion and remain in charge of the U.S. women's national team. He left the job with just one loss on his record, the fewest of any non-interim head coach to hold the job.

The qualifying tournament for the 2008 Olympics was less than four months away, and the national team was a mess. Not only did the team not have a coach, but the No. 1 goalkeeper was in exile. U.S. Soccer would need to move swiftly to fix both problems.

CHAPTER 12
"Whoa, Can We Do This Without Her?"

Pia Sundhage was at the top of the list of candidates to take over as coach of the national team. But she had actually interviewed for the job once before, and had been passed over, when the federation sought to replace April Heinrichs in 2005.

Sundhage, who had done scouting work for Heinrichs, had been invited as one of seven candidates for the job. She'd felt honored to be granted an interview, but she wasn't about to lie just to get the job.

"To be honest, I want half the job. I do not want to be technical director," she said in her 2005 interview. "I'm not American. I don't know the American culture well enough. I know soccer and I have some ideas how I can coach this wonderful team, but I just want half the job."

That's perhaps Sundhage's defining quality: She's unabashedly herself and never pretends otherwise. She's known to break out into song and celebrate goals by leaping exuberantly into the air. She was a forward for the Swedish national team before she retired in 1996 and moved into coaching. Her first head coaching job came in the WUSA with the Boston Breakers, where players recall she was direct and blunt. With natural salt-and-pepper hair, a toothy smile, and a preference for tracksuits, what you see is what you get with Sundhage.

But her admission that she didn't want to be the USA's technical director had been a problem. At the time, U.S. Soccer and Robert Contiguglia were looking for the national team's head coach to oversee the entire women's program, including the youth pipeline into the senior national team. That was a crucial part of the role they'd created for April Heinrichs, and that's what they wanted to continue.

When Greg Ryan got the job over Sundhage, she joined the Chinese national team as an assistant coach. Because China never faced the Americans in the 2007 World Cup, she didn't follow the USA's run through the tournament at all.

When she got a call asking her to interview for the USA job again in late 2007, she was surprised. Winning bronze in a major tournament would've been an honor anywhere else in the world. Greg Ryan's firing was news to her.

Meeting with the new U.S. Soccer president, Sunil Gulati, Sundhage told Gulati what she had told his predecessor: "Just so you know, I don't want to be technical director. One of my strengths is that I know what I'm good at and I know what I'm not so good at."

This time, that was just fine. The federation needed someone who could come in and clean up the mess left in the wake of Ryan's disastrous decision to bench Hope Solo. Sundhage, with her easygoing yet decisive approach, seemed like exactly what the team needed.

The players were eager to turn the page with Sundhage, too. After she was selected for the job, the new coach held a conference call with the players.

"She really wanted a camp in December, and that was usually our break, but we were all willing to do it because we all wanted to start fresh," Shannon Boxx remembers.

When the players arrived for their first meeting with their new coach in Carson, California, they were greeted by Sundhage with her guitar in hand. She opened the meeting by singing Bob Dylan's "The Times They Are a-Changin'." Though Sundhage was fluent in English, it wasn't her first language, and the song said it better than she could've otherwise: Things were going to be different now.

Hope Solo was at that camp. The first thing Sundhage set out to do was bring her back into the fold and patch up whatever divides had emerged within the team. For Sundhage, there was never even a question that Solo would be the team's starting goalkeeper.

In her first meeting as national team head coach, after she finishing playing guitar, she said to all the players: "I want to win. Do you want to win?" The response was a resounding "Yeah!" Sundhage knew it would be because, as she says now, "Americans, they are winners."

That settled the matter. "Well, to win, you need a goalkeeper," she told the team. "I don't expect you to forget, but I do expect you to forgive."

That four-day camp was less about the team playing together than it was about patching up rifts. Between training sessions, it was a marathon of meetings for Sundhage. She spoke to Solo privately and to the leaders on the team, and before the camp started, she'd spoken with Greg Ryan on the phone.

"He had his story. I talked to the players. I got about five different stories about the state of the team. But I got an idea of what happened," Sundhage says. "For me it was good, and my mission was: We need to take the next step."

Sundhage went out of her way to make sure everyone felt heard. But she already knew what she was going to do, regardless of what anyone said, and she wasn't open to any suggestions to the contrary. If Ryan's downfall was being too easily swayed by his own players and their whims, Sundhage wasn't going to have that problem.

Luckily for the national team, there wasn't much time to let any bad feelings fester. The Olympics were right around the corner. The Beijing games would become the team's sole focus.

* * *

The 2008 Olympic Games were 21 days away. The national team was in San Diego for one final send-off game before departing for China. On the field for this friendly versus Brazil was the lineup Pia Sundhage hoped would win a gold medal.

The atmosphere was festive. The national team's popularity and attention had waned significantly since 2004, when stars like Mia Hamm retired, but a sellout crowd of 7,502 fans came to see the team they would support during the Olympics.

In the 32nd minute, Abby Wambach slipped the ball to Amy Rodriguez, who knocked it back in Wambach's path for a give-and-go. Defender Andréia Rosa, reading the play, stepped up to the ball to clear it away. At the exact same moment, Wambach took a full swing at the ball to shoot. Wambach got to the ball first, but on the follow-through, her shin smacked against the Brazilian's shin.

The moment Wambach went down, she knew it was bad. She quickly looked over to the bench and signaled that she needed to come out of the game.

"I still remember the sound of it and seeing Abby on the ground," Shannon Boxx says. "I remember being concerned for my teammate, thinking: *Is she going to be able to play soccer again?*"

Christie Pearce, who played under the last name Rampone for much of her career, ran over to Wambach and squatted down to check on her.

"I broke my leg. My tib and fib are both broken," Wambach said, referring to the tibia and fibula, the shin bone and its counterpart.

"Are you sure?" Pearce asked.

"Yeah. Tell Pia to get a sub ready," Wambach replied.

It was a jarring sight to see Wambach on the ground, helpless. She was often the player throwing her height and weight advantages around—going into hard challenges as defenders bounced off her. She had grown up in Rochester, New York, as the youngest of seven children, and it showed—she wasn't afraid to speak up for herself, and she was tough as nails. She could seemingly play through anything and was known to shout at her teammates to pump them up, too. Her communication style straddled the line between leadership and bossiness, but she was an incredibly effective messenger.

More important, however, she was the national team's most productive player. At that point, Wambach led the team in scoring for 2008 with an impressive 13 goals and 10 assists in 21 games.

The players on the field huddled and put their arms around one another in a circle as Wambach's leg was put in a splint by trainers on the field. They told each other there was nothing they could do about Wambach now and there was still a game to finish.

"I remember looking around at everybody's faces," says Heather O'Reilly. "You're of course devastated for Abby. But it was also kind of like: *Whoa, can we do this without her?* Abby at that juncture was our everything—she was our goal-scoring leader."

Wambach was wheeled off the field and into the back of an ambulance, where she called out, asking if anyone would lend their phone to her. A medic handed Wambach his phone, probably expecting the player to call a loved one. Instead, she dialed Lauren Cheney.

"Cheney!" Wambach blurted out after Cheney, who would later play under the married name Holiday, picked up. "I hope you've been working out. I'm injured, and if they replace me with another forward, it's going to be you."

"Shut up," Cheney said, laughing. "You're being dramatic. You're fine. You're always fine."

"I'm serious," Wambach insisted. "I can't run. So you need to get fit because you're going to the Olympics."

Scans at the hospital would confirm Wambach had suffered a mid-oblique fracture of her tibia and fibula, and Cheney would eventually take Wambach's place on the roster—but Cheney wasn't a replacement for what Wambach did on the field. Pia Sundhage needed to decide who could take over Wambach's vital attacking role, not just in this game but as a starter at the Olympics.

As Wambach lay on the field waiting to be stretchered off, Sundhage and assistant coach Jill Ellis had plenty of time to discuss their options. Natasha Kai, who had been a frequent starter with Wambach, seemed to be the obvious choice. Ellis tossed out Angela Hucles's name. By that point, Hucles wasn't starting games—she was a late substitute.

"I had other players in mind, but Jill Ellis was smart enough to say we need someone to keep the ball," Sundhage says. "Angela Hucles took her place, and that was a crucial moment—a winning move because I listened to Jill Ellis."

Hucles was an unlikely choice to replace Wambach. It wasn't just that she was a very different player than Wambach, lacking the same physical bite or pushy communication style on the field. It was that Hucles and Sundhage had a history—when Sundhage was Hucles's coach at the Boston Breakers, she thought so little of the player that she traded her away. Sundhage later said that Hucles wasn't dynamic enough. When Sundhage took over as national team coach, Hucles thought maybe her career in red, white, and blue was over.

"We butted heads at the Breakers," Hucles says. "I had never butted heads with another coach like that. So when she came onto the national team, I was like, *Huh, I know I have to prove myself every time, but we'll see if I make the team again under Pia.*"

But Sundhage needed to change tactics without Wambach. No, Hucles didn't have the aerial presence that Wambach did, but no one else on the team did. She also didn't have the speed that Rodriguez or Kai did, but she could hold on to possession. The skills she *did* have would allow her to be a fulcrum for the attack and provide service to speedier players around her.

After the send-off game, which the U.S. won, Sundhage met with Hucles and told her that she was going to be starting during the Olympics—with Wambach out, Hucles would take her place. Though she had been a backup midfielder for the team, Hucles was now going to be starting as a forward.

Meanwhile, Wambach was in a hospital undergoing a four-hour surgery that involved a titanium rod and a bunch of screws to put her leg bones back together. Afterward, as she was recovering, a small group of players went to visit her before they left for China: Christie Pearce, Kate Markgraf, Angela Hucles, Heather O'Reilly, and Leslie Osborne.

Wambach, ever the leader and motivator, told her teammates to go get 'em and win the Olympics without her. No one expected anything less from her. But the visit in the hospital was still quiet and uncomfortable—a feeling of sadness hung over everyone like a fog.

"It was definitely a bit somber," Hucles says. "I wonder now if I could have done more? It's one of those situations where that had to have been one of the hardest experiences for her to go through."

If the players had somehow forgotten that Wambach, their best player, wasn't joining them in Beijing, the constant peppering of questions from the media would remind them.

No one was talking about Hope Solo or Greg Ryan anymore. How could this team possibly win without Wambach?

* * *

When the national team got to China, it was time to try out the plan Pia Sundhage and Jill Ellis had devised.

The team stuck to the 4–4–2 formation that Sundhage preferred, but the way it worked had to change. No longer could the team pump the ball into the box and hope Abby Wambach got a head to it. No longer could Sundhage put players like Amy Rodriguez and Natasha Kai on the field to link up and feed the ball to Wambach. The team had to readjust its focus.

"When we got there, we played China in a scrimmage, and you could tell we were just flustered," says Shannon Boxx. "We had no real idea how we wanted to play now without Abby up there. It was like, *Oh my gosh, the games start in a week, so what are we going to do?*"

After that scrimmage, it was time for the real games of the 2008 Olympics to start and the team wasn't feeling confident at all. It showed in the opening match. The U.S. lost to Norway, 2–0.

They looked sluggish and out of ideas in the attack. Norway looked comfortable. It was the team's first loss under Sundhage.

"I just remember being at the hotel the next morning to do recovery work and Norway was there in the workout room," Boxx says. "I was like *Ugh, why do I have to be in the same room with you guys right now?* It was the worst feeling."

Sundhage had to figure out how to move forward from the loss, and she sought input from April Heinrichs, who was then a consultant for the U.S. Olympic Committee.

"You know what?" Heinrichs told her. "You can do something the U.S. team has never done before."

"Oh, what's that?" Sundhage asked.

"You can lose a game and still win the Olympics," Heinrichs said.

"Well, shoot," Sundhage chirped. "That's a great way to look at it."

Sundhage credits that little pep talk with getting her through that moment.

"She helped me out with that kind of thinking," Sundhage says. "Winners, they come back and make it work."

That's exactly what Sundhage and the national team did. Sundhage adjusted her personnel slightly so the new pairing up top would be Angela Hucles with Amy Rodriguez, who would start over Natasha Kai. Something clicked. Hucles was able to hold the ball up and feed it to the other speedier attackers racing in behind. It was at this Olympics that Heather O'Reilly made the permanent switch from striker to outside midfield, where she would spend the rest of her national team career, racing up and down the right flank.

After that Norway loss, the U.S. went on a five-game winning tear to land in the gold-medal match. Waiting for them was Brazil, the team that had humiliated them only one year before and the same team Wambach had broken her leg going up against. The Norway rivalry seemed to be slowly fading away as the Marta-led Brazilian team turned into the most constant thorn in the USA's side.

If the American attack—the masterstroke of putting Hucles in Wambach's spot—was the catalyst for the five straight wins, the defense was going to get the Americans through the gold-medal match. The back line was full of experience—Christie Pearce, Kate Markgraf, Heather Mitts, and Lori Chalupny—while goalkeeper Hope Solo was growing in confidence with every game.

By then, 22-year-old Marta was well on her way to winning a third straight FIFA World Player of the Year award, but neither she nor goal-scoring partner Cristiane could find a way to score on the USA.

The Americans had trouble, too—it was a tight, chippy affair—and the match moved into extra time after a scoreless 90 minutes.

Six minutes into the extra-time period, Lloyd pounced on a loose ball, darted into the box, and fired a left-footed shot that skipped under the hand of goalkeeper Bárbara. The Americans finally had a lead.

The Americans had to hold on for another excruciating 24 minutes. But the defensive unit drilled in and the U.S. won, 1–0. Lloyd's goal was the game-winner.

"It brings chills to my body," Lloyd said afterward. "It was the most memorable moment in my career. I hope that I have more memories like that."

The Americans were gold medalists again. They finished the tournament with six different goal-scorers in six games.

"That was probably the greatest team victory of a team I was ever part of," says O'Reilly. "We didn't have Abby—we didn't have our superstar—but everybody stepped up."

At one point amid the celebration in the locker room, the players decided to call Wambach to share the joyous occasion with her.

The equipment manager for the national team dialed Wambach, and after she answered, he said, "Hold on," and pointed his cell phone toward the players. Then Wambach, on the other end, sitting in the diner where she watched the game, was hit with a rush of screaming and cheers.

She would later admit that the thought of the team winning without her terrified her. Did the team really need her? A resounding answer would come soon enough.

* * *

There had been no guarantee Pia Sundhage would continue with the national team after the 2008 Olympics.

Sunil Gulati, the president of U.S. Soccer, had probably seen how tumultuous Robert Contiguglia's choices of April Heinrichs and Greg Ryan turned out to be. He had only given Sundhage a contract through the end of the Olympics with a promise to reassess after the tournament.

Once the team won gold, Gulati quickly awarded Sundhage a contract extension through the next World Cup–Olympics cycle. At the team's party in Beijing to celebrate winning gold, Gulati got down on one knee and jokingly proposed that Sundhage stay on as head coach.

An economist who was born in India but came to the United States as a child, Gulati seemed to put in more effort with the women's national team than his predecessors at U.S. Soccer. He had been involved with the federation since the late 1980s and came into the job with a clear understanding of the women's program. That included a grasp of how important the women's team was for the landscape of soccer in America.

He had not only seen the 1999 World Cup and the explosion of growth in women's soccer since but he had been rooting for the women's team since its earliest days. Chat with Gulati long enough about his involvement with U.S. Soccer and he'll eventually talk about a phone call he made to the women's team in 1991.

He just wanted to wish them good luck at the first-ever Women's World Cup in China, but it wasn't so simple in an era before everyone had a cell phone. Gulati was in Russia for his job at World Bank, the team was in the meal room at their hotel in China, and he was patched through via the U.S. Soccer Federation headquarters in Colorado Springs. It was a collect call.

"It was Russia to Colorado Springs to China, and it was Thanksgiving Day," Gulati says. "I remember saying words to the effect of, *Be thankful you're playing for the United States and be thankful you're at least one goal better than Norway.*"

The sorts of very public fights that Contiguglia and his second-in-command, Hank Steinbrecher, got into with the women's team would stop under Gulati—at least for the time being—and the Gulati era would usher in a friendlier relationship with the team. John Langel, the team's lawyer, would eventually become something closer to friends than adversaries with Gulati. Disputes still arose—travel accommodations and using the players' likenesses for sponsorships were frequent issues over the years—but compromises came more easily.

"With John, we would have our screaming matches and then we'd walk out and shake hands," Gulati says. "We got to a point where if it was really important, either one of us could call the other, even if it wasn't in the contract, and say, *Hey, we need to get this done.* With a commercial appearance, he'd say, *Can we take care of this?* Or, *You need to get these players different flights.* When you get to point of trust, regardless of what was in the contract, he could rely on me to be fair."

But that didn't mean serious problems never came up.

In 2009, Kate Markgraf got a phone call from Pia Sundhage. As head coach of the national team, Sundhage had to call players twice a year to let them know if their contract with U.S. Soccer would be renewed and whether the player would stay on the same salary tier.

Sundhage called to tell Markgraf that her contract wasn't going to be renewed. Markgraf had just given birth to twins three weeks earlier, and Sundhage didn't think the defender would be able to return to form after that. The best Sundhage could offer her was a "floater" contract—a small stipend instead of a salary, which was usually reserved for newer players trying to break into the team. It was a huge drop-off from the Tier 1 contract Markgraf had been on.

Markgraf knew that players like Amy LePeilbet and Rachel Buehler were playing well and she'd have a tough time earning her centerback spot back. Christie Pearce was pregnant at the time, but she had returned from having children to being a starter before, so the competition for a spot figured to get even harder for Markgraf when Pearce returned.

But being cut solely because she had given birth? That sounded like pregnancy discrimination to Markgraf. So, she called up John Langel.

"There was a back-and-forth for four to six weeks about whether it was okay for them to cut me," Markgraf says. "I had the chance to sue them if I wanted, but I was like, *I just don't want this to happen to anyone else again.*"

The issue had never come up before. Markgraf had her first child in 2006 and rejoined the team afterward under Greg Ryan. When Joy Fawcett, Carla Overbeck, and Christie Pearce had children, they were never cut from the team and always had the chance to fight to win their spots back, too. Markgraf wondered if the fact that she had twins was the reason it was treated differently—no player had ever done that. To

Langel, it seemed the difference was that players were now paid guaranteed year-round salaries.

Langel thought Markgraf could win if she were willing to file a claim. But Markgraf didn't want to turn it into an ordeal—she just wanted to prove she could win her spot back.

"I thought Kate had a clear case for pregnancy discrimination and she decided not to bring the case," Langel says. "She decided to suck it up and earn a spot on the team, which she did."

Once Markgraf worked her way back into the team and proved she could do it, she happily walked away from the game.

"I played well, and Pia was like, *I'm going to offer you a contract*, and I said, *No, I'm retiring*," Markgraf remembers. She finished her career at 201 caps for the national team.

Because of the dispute, however, the national team's contract with U.S. Soccer started to contain a new clause going forward—it was nicknamed "The Markgraf Rule." It guaranteed that if a player left the team for pregnancy, once she was fit enough to return, she would be put back on the same contract and continue to be called up for at least three months—enough time to try to prove she still deserved her spot.

That rule went on to benefit a number of players over the years. Amy Rodriguez has been perhaps the best example. She gave birth in 2013, and through repeated call-ups after she recovered, she discovered arguably the best form of her career. She led her club team to two National Women's Soccer League championships and helped the U.S. win a World Cup. Shannon Boxx is another player who earned her spot back after giving birth and won a World Cup.

But by 2009, all anyone knew was that a woman should never be kicked off the team for having a child again. Little by little, even if it didn't happen in the public, acrimonious ways of the past, the national team was continuing to stand up for itself.

CHAPTER 13
"You Wouldn't Be on the Field If It Was Up to Me"

By the time the national team won gold at the 2008 Olympics, plans for a new women's soccer league were already afoot.

After the WUSA folded, club owners like John Hendricks and players like Julie Foudy formed the WUSA Reorganization Committee in hopes of reviving the league. The group was led by Tonya Antonucci, a businesswoman who played soccer while attending Stanford.

It would take years to come together, but the group would eventually put together a new league: Women's Professional Soccer, or WPS.

The plan was to learn from the mistakes of the WUSA and take a more conservative approach. Player salaries would average around just $32,000, well below the WUSA averages, which hit a high of $46,000. The stadiums would be smaller to reflect lower expectations for ticket sales.

The league also scrapped the single-entity model of the WUSA. In that league, one team's loss was everyone's loss. But in WPS, an individual team's struggles wouldn't burden other teams. No longer could one bad apple spoil the bunch.

But before WPS launched, it was already up against some factors the league had no control over. One of them was the worst global recession since the Great Depression. Everyone ended up feeling the financial squeeze of the sputtering economy, from the kinds of investors the league would need to run the expensive franchises to average working Americans, whom the league needed to buy tickets and show up to games.

Even the NFL, the powerhouse sports league in the U.S., laid off 150 employees, or 13 percent of its workforce, in response to the recession. The NBA cut 80 jobs. A new football league, the Arena Football League, suspended operations, citing the shrinking economy as part of the reason.

"The idea of postponing was not even on the table," Tonya Anto-nucci told reporters as the WPS launch neared. "Is this the right model? Yes. Are the conditions ideal? No."

The other problem WPS encountered was that the popularity of women's soccer in the U.S. had been on a long backslide. The stars of the sport—most notably Mia Hamm—had retired. Consider this: A national poll in 2007 found that 48 percent of Americans knew who Hamm was, yet only 9 percent could identify Landon Donovan, the greatest male soccer star the U.S. had ever produced. Hamm's retire-ment was a huge blow to the women's game.

The last time the national team had a culturally important moment—one that broke through the soccer bubble and into the mainstream—was still back in 1999. As big as that moment was, it couldn't sustain the entire sport of women's soccer for years. The Amer-ican public had fallen out of touch with the sport and its players. The federation's decision to "go dark" in 2005 couldn't have helped.

The national team returned from winning a gold medal in China to paltry crowds. On September 17, 2008, less than a month after the Olympic final, just 4,227 fans showed up to Giants Stadium to see the 2008 gold medalists. That was about 5 percent of the crowd that showed up to the same stadium for the 1999 Women's World Cup. Weeks later, the team played in front of just 3,387 people at the University of Rich-mond Stadium in Virginia, which could've fit a crowd more than double that size. If the national team couldn't draw large crowds, how could club teams?

WPS may have learned lessons from the WUSA about how to approach ticket sales, but there was little the league could do about a lack of enthusiasm for women's soccer at the time. When the inaugural match of WPS rolled around on March 29, 2008, the enthusiasm gap was evident—the announced crowd of 14,832 was less than half of what the WUSA's opening match drew. By the end of WPS's first season, the trend continued and the average attendance across the league was just 4,684, half the average attendance in the first year of the WUSA.

There was no Mia vs. Brandi matchup to promote, but there was at least one very big star: Marta, the Brazilian who had just won her third straight FIFA World Player of the Year award.

"When we got a new league, WPS, you had international players wanting to come over to play, and that was when Marta came over," says Shannon Boxx. "Overall, you were seeing that the women's game was improving, and you started seeing so many countries starting to get better."

The league unquestionably helped its players develop. That's because, like the WUSA, the new league sought to attract the best talent in the world. Marta's addition to the Los Angeles Sol especially was seen as a way to bolster the WPS's goal of being the best women's league in the world, but her salary would later be revealed to be a staggering $500,000 per year.

The Sol were owned by Anschutz Entertainment Group—Philip Anschutz's company that invested so much in MLS clubs—so if any team could afford to pay a high price for Marta, it was the Sol. But the club lost about $2 million within its first season, despite leading the league in attendance and winning the championship.

Again, as was the case in the WUSA, it wasn't so much the spending that was the problem—it was the lack of revenue.

As Arnim Whisler, the owner of the Chicago Red Stars, puts it now: "You can't cost-save your way to success. You couldn't cut enough costs to keep every WPS team going. That's because it starts with: What are your league standards?"

Operating a team in a league that sought to be the best in the world was going to cost a certain amount. Unless the league was willing to sacrifice its quality, cost cutting could only do so much. Thus, the Sol ownership group didn't see a path to profitability. When a buyer for the Sol couldn't be found, the team folded after just one season.

At the time, it was shocking. In retrospect, it was an early warning. Across the league, teams were finding that neither investors nor fans were showing up in the numbers they had hoped.

"The end of WPS was easily predicted by almost the third or fourth game in the inaugural season, when it was clear we didn't have a path to get things right side up," Whisler says. "The first few games after a year of announcements and planning and trying to build excitement in the market should be your strongest, so if you couldn't even hit your goal in the hysteria of a new team launch, you weren't going to find it midseason."

The loss of the Sol had a chilling effect on potential investors and sponsors who didn't want to board a sinking ship. The following season, the St. Louis Athletica became the next team to fold. After losing $1 million, the team's overseas investors simply stopped funding the team and walked away. The WPS front office tried to take over the franchise but couldn't afford the team's debts.

It was like a set of dominos. First it was the LA Sol. Then, the St. Louis Athletica. After that, FC Gold Pride. Then, the Chicago Red Stars opted to leave the league rather than choose between going bankrupt or dropping standards to a sub-par level. The Washington Freedom were evaluating an exit strategy, too.

But the fate of those teams shouldn't have taken anyone by surprise. Within the first year, board meetings with the league's franchise owners were already contentious. Everyone was struggling but there was little agreement on how to proceed.

At one point, Arnim Whisler proposed dramatically reducing the salary cap, which would cut player salaries, one of the only areas where the league could find significant savings. Another owner in the room was furious and shouted back at Whisler: "I am *not* going to be part of a glorified W-League! There's no way that is going to happen!"

After all, WPS was a Division I professional league, and it sought to be considered the best in the world. But Whisler knew the revenues weren't there to match the costs. Some standards had to be downgraded—otherwise, revenues and expenditures would never line up.

"I left that meeting wondering how much longer we had," Whisler says.

* * *

Becky Sauerbrunn remembers the moment she really broke into the national team. Or at least the moment she had the chance to try.

She played every minute of every game with the Washington Freedom in 2010 and was quickly developing a reputation as one of the league's top centerbacks. A University of Virginia graduate, Sauerbrunn wasn't the fastest or strongest defender, but she seemed to read the game a step ahead of players around her. That had always been apparent to reporters who interviewed her, too—when they asked questions, she spoke too rapidly for them to keep up with writing down quotes.

The Freedom were knocked out of the semifinals in a brutal extra-time loss to the Philadelphia Independence. A few days later, she was about to step into a movie theater with her boyfriend to see the Ben Affleck film *The Town* when she noticed a missed call from a California area code on her cell phone. It was a voicemail from Cheryl Bailey, the national team's general manager. She told Sauerbrunn to call her back because Pia Sundhage wanted to speak with her.

A callback couldn't wait, so there was Sauerbrunn, outside the theater, quickly making a round of calls to find out what Sundhage wanted.

"Hi, Becky. Joanna Lohman has picked up an injury and she's not coming to camp anymore," Sundhage told her. "Would you like to come as an alternate? We can fly you out tomorrow."

Sauerbrunn, who had been trying to figure out where she'd play soccer in the WPS offseason, didn't hesitate. She left the movie theater immediately to go pack—she could see the movie another time.

While WPS was going through its share of struggles behind the scenes, everything between the lines on the field—the actual soccer—was going well. New national team stars were emerging.

In the days of WUSA, it was players like Shannon Boxx and Angela Hucles who probably would've quit soccer and never made it onto the national team radar without a league. In WPS, it was a player like Becky Sauerbrunn, who had come up through the youth national team ranks but needed a league like WPS to prove she could cut it at the highest level.

"It was instrumental for me to be able to prove myself against the best players, day in and day out," Sauerbrunn says. "I don't think I would've ever gotten that shot if it wasn't for the league."

The roster that Sauerbrunn ended up making in 2010 was a very important one, but a seemingly routine one. The national team had to go to Cancun, Mexico, in November 2010 to qualify for the 2011 World Cup, a step that was more a technicality than anything. The national team had not only qualified for every Women's World Cup but had made it to at least the semifinal every time.

The qualifying tournament for the region that includes North America, known as CONCACAF, got off to a rip-roaring start in Mexico. The U.S. bulldozed their way past Haiti, 5–0, and then followed up with a 9–0 dismantling of Guatemala. By the time they beat Costa Rica, 4–0, in the next game, it looked like the Americans' momentum would carry them straight to the final.

Heading into the semifinal versus Mexico, the Americans felt confident. In 25 prior meetings with Mexico, the U.S. had never lost, and they had conceded just nine goals.

But on November 5, 2010, it took only two minutes for a surprise twist. Lydia Rangel headed a ball into the path of Maribel Domínguez, who toe-poked the ball on the bounce past goalkeeper Nicole Barnhart, the backup behind Hope Solo, who was recovering from shoulder surgery. The U.S. was already down, 1–0, and the game had just started.

The Americans quickly fought back. In the 25th minute, a U.S. corner kick fell into the box, and Carli Lloyd turned her hips and fired, slotting the ball perfectly inside the opposite post of where goalkeeper Erika Venegas stood. The score was even at 1–1.

But only two minutes after that, it was a shocker again. A long, somewhat desperate cross floated into the USA's box, and Verónica Pérez got her head to the ball, knocking it past Barnhart. The Americans, down 2–1, were at risk of being knocked out of the qualifying tournament.

In the 93rd minute, with the whistle about to blow at any moment, Amy Rodriguez chipped a ball over Venegas, and the American players threw their arms in the air in celebration. They had equalized and taken back control of their qualification campaign—or so they thought until they saw the fourth official with her flag up. Offside.

Seconds later, the match was over. The U.S. lost.

The players didn't immediately understand what it meant, but Sundhage did. With the loss, the U.S. couldn't automatically qualify for the 2011 Women's World Cup anymore. Now, they had to take a detour and try to qualify via playoff, something they had never needed to do before.

"I remember the referee blew the whistle and I knew we had to go through a playoff to qualify," Pia Sundhage says. "That was crazy. I looked around and it seemed like no one understood what happened—nobody. I looked at players and coaches and it was just an unusual situation."

It was certainly uncharted territory for the national team. If they could beat Costa Rica in the next match and finish third overall in the qualifying tournament, they would be eligible for a playoff against Italy, a home-and-away two-leg series that would decide who advanced to the World Cup.

Now the Americans were at risk of not even qualifying for a tournament that they were the favorites to win. Suddenly, the media that hadn't paid attention to Women's World Cup qualifying became interested.

"The irony of the whole thing is that when the U.S. men win, they get the coverage, but when the U.S. women lose, we get the coverage," striker Abby Wambach said.

The U.S. went on to dominate Costa Rica, and with third place secured, an unforeseen trip was set for Italy. No one expected to have to pack up and play an extra two games, but now a spot in the 2011 World Cup would go to either the USA or Italy.

Sundhage admits everyone—the players and herself included—took it for granted that the U.S. would find the goals they needed to beat Mexico and earn one of the automatic qualifying spots.

"Everybody was thinking, *Shoot, we can't go for vacation now,*" she says. "Everybody planned vacations. So they had to tell their boyfriends and girlfriends and husbands that they had to change plans because we had to go to Italy."

When the national team got to Italy, a slog awaited them. Stadio Euganeo in Padua, near Venice, had a damp, heavy field, and Italian fans disrupted the match by lighting firecrackers in the stands. The circumstances weren't going to make it easy.

The Americans were able to control possession and get into dangerous positions but struggled with the final ball in front of goal. The clock ticked past the 90th-minute mark and well into stoppage time and neither side had scored a goal. The Americans didn't want to return to the U.S. with a 0–0 draw—that would leave them no margin for error.

As the clock entered the 94th minute and the waning seconds ticked by, Abby Wambach flicked a long ball from Carli Lloyd into the path of Alex Morgan, a second-half substitute. Morgan ran onto the ball, settled it, and slotted it past the Italian goalkeeper in the dying seconds of the match.

It was the fourth international goal for 21-year-old Morgan, the national team's youngest player, and her most important one to date. She leapt into the arms of Wambach, who caught her. The U.S. ran out the clock to victory and returned to Chicago for the second leg with some of the pressure off.

The return leg was another close one, but an early goal from Amy Rodriguez was enough to book a spot in Germany the following summer. They almost hadn't made it, but the U.S. was off to the 2011 World Cup.

"That was a really good lesson," Sundhage says now. "Don't take anything for granted."

* * *

Mike Lyons, the first head coach of the new WPS franchise in Boca Raton, Florida, knew immediately there was something unusual about his new boss, Dan Borislow.

TOP · The first-ever U.S. women's national team in Jesolo, Italy, in August 1985.

BOTTOM LEFT · The 1991 Women's World Cup–winning team and coach Anson Dorrance with President George H. W. Bush in January 1992 in Washington, D.C.

BOTTOM RIGHT · The veterans with the team's sport psychology consultant, Dr. Colleen Hacker. Players from left to right: Brandi Chastain, Mia Hamm, Kristine Lilly, Julie Foudy, and Joy Fawcett.

TOP · Briana Scurry dives during a drill at Tony DiCicco's SoccerPlus goalkeeper camp in Simsbury, Connecticut.

BOTTOM LEFT · Michelle Akers carries a bag of balls at training during the 1995 Women's World Cup in Sweden.

BOTTOM RIGHT · Tony DiCicco with backup goalkeepers Jen Mead, Kim Wyant, and Saskia Webber in the mid-1990s.

PHOTOS COURTESY OF THE DICICCO FAMILY.

TOP · Mia Hamm versus Fan Yunjie of China during the final of the 1999 Women's World Cup.

BOTTOM · The coaches celebrate at the Rose Bowl after winning the World Cup in 1999.

TOP · The players watch as Brandi Chastain steps up for her penalty kick at the 1999 Women's World Cup. From left to right: Carla Overbeck, Kristine Lilly, Joy Fawcett, Kate Markgraf, Tisha Venturini, Shannon MacMillan, Mia Hamm, Sara Whalen, Julie Foudy.

BOTTOM · Brandi Chastain celebrates after scoring the game-winning penalty kick versus China.

TOP · Mia Hamm with President Bill Clinton, First Lady Hillary Clinton, and their daughter Chelsea.
BOTTOM · Kristine Lilly, Carla Overbeck, and Julie Foudy with the 1999 Women's World Cup trophy.

TOP · The veterans with coach April Heinrichs in San Jose, California, in August 2003. From left to right: Mia Hamm, Kristine Lilly, Brandi Chastain, April Heinrichs, Julie Foudy, and Joy Fawcett.

BOTTOM LEFT · The national team after winning gold at the 2004 Olympics in Greece.

BOTTOM RIGHT · The players in the locker room, circa 2004. From left to right: Christie Pearce Rampone, Tiffeny Milbrett, Cat Whitehill, Aly Wagner, and Tiffany Roberts.

TOP LEFT · Carli Lloyd during the 2010 Algarve Cup in Olhao, Portugal.

TOP RIGHT · Angela Hucles, Kate Markgraf, and Shannon Boxx at the 2008 gold medal ceremony in Beijing, China.

BOTTOM LEFT · Heather O'Reilly and Lindsay Tarpley with their 2004 gold medals on the team bus.

BOTTOM RIGHT · Sunil Gulati with Carli Lloyd in Zurich, Switzerland, at a friendly scrimmage organized by FIFA featuring legendary players and members of the FIFA Council.

PHOTOS COURTESY OF HEATHER O'REILLY (BOTTOM LEFT), SUNIL GULATI (BOTTOM RIGHT), AND FROM ISI PHOTOS (TOP).

ɔP · Ali Krieger defends against Marta of Brazil during the 2011 Women's World Cup.

ɔTTOM · Abby Wambach celebrates a goal in 2011 as Megan Rapinoe chases.

TOP · During the 2012 Olympic qualifying tournament, the players write "Liebe" on their arms in honor of injured teammate Ali Krieger.

BOTTOM LEFT · Alex Morgan races past New Zealand's Abby Erceg during the 2012 Olympics.

BOTTOM RIGHT · The national team sings "The Star-Spangled Banner" atop the gold medal podium at the 2012 Olympics. From left to right: Carli Lloyd, Sydney Leroux, Lauren Holiday, Alex Morgan, Abby Wambach, Megan Rapinoe, and Rachel Buehler.

PHOTOS COURTESY OF HEATHER O'REILLY (TOP) AND FROM ISI PHOTOS (BOTTOM).

TOP LEFT · Hope Solo prepares for a friendly match in October 2013.

TOP RIGHT · Alex Morgan signs autographs and takes selfies with fans in 2013 after an open practice in Columbus.

BOTTOM · Heather O'Reilly fights for the ball in a friendly versus New Zealand at Columbus Crew Stadium on October 30, 2013.

TOP · Carli Lloyd celebrates scoring a goal during the 2015 Women's World Cup final in Canada.

BOTTOM LEFT · Becky Sauerbrunn and Meghan Klingenberg circle BC Place with an American flag after becoming World Cup champions.

BOTTOM RIGHT · Fans hold up signs at the 2015 Women's World Cup final in Vancouver, Canada.

TOP · Christie Pearce Rampone, left, and Hope Solo land in the United States on July 6, 2015, after winning the 2015 Women's World Cup.

BOTTOM · The players take selfies together during their 2015 Women's World Cup campaign.

The players celebrate winning the 2015 Women's World Cup in the locker room right after the game and the next morning with Fox Sports.

P · Julie Ertz and other players ride a float for the ticker tape parade in New York City on July 10, 2015.

)TTOM LEFT · The players and one of their lawyers prepare for their final negotiation session with
S. Soccer for a new collective bargaining agreement in April 2017.

)TTOM RIGHT · The players are honored at the White House after winning the 2015 World Cup and
ve President Barack Obama a jersey in October 2015.

The national team during the 2015 victory tour in Pittsburgh, Pennsylvania.

After going back and forth on a salary, Lyons agreed to take the job to coach the new WPS franchise that was starting in 2011. As the conversation was wrapping up, he realized they hadn't discussed the exchange of paperwork.

"What about a contract?" Lyons asked.

"You don't need a contract," Borislow responded.

"How do I know I'm going to get paid?"

"You'll get paid. You don't need to worry about that. I don't deal in contracts—I deal in handshakes."

Lyons thought that was odd. Borislow ran a huge company. The company was built around a device Borislow invented that could connect people's phone lines to their computers to make unlimited free calls. The device, which made him hundreds of millions of dollars, was called magicJack.

When Borislow took over the Washington Freedom and moved the team to South Florida, in a strange decision, he renamed the team magicJack. But Lyons went ahead with the offer to coach magicJack since the $80,000 salary he negotiated was more than any other team in WPS could pay him.

Before Lyons ever arrived in Florida or met Dan Borislow, he went straight from his hometown in New Jersey to the 2011 college draft in Baltimore. He called Borislow to talk about the plan for the draft, which included star players like Alex Morgan and Christen Press. As Lyons remembers it, Borislow immediately started screaming at him.

"You need to get the players I want! Don't fuck this up!" Borislow shouted.

"I'll get any players you want, but don't you think they should tell me who they are first?" Lyons asked. He hadn't been given a list, even though Borislow was acting as if he had.

"I thought, *This guy's wacky*," Lyons says. "He's screaming at me to get specific players and he's never told me who they were."

At first, no one at the draft realized Lyons was there on behalf of magicJack. There had been no announcement or press release about the coaching hire, and Lyons was prohibited by Borislow from talking to the media.

If those were the first hints that Dan Borislow and his money weren't going to save WPS, they certainly weren't the last. But the league had little choice but to take a chance on the eccentric business-man. Hopes were high for the 2011 season of WPS—it was a Women's World Cup year and a national spotlight could help. But, with teams folding left and right, it needed someone with deep pockets to provide some stability.

The Washington Freedom, which had been owned by John Hen-dricks for a decade since the WUSA launched, had been struggling. By 2011, it was time for the franchise to be sold or fold. The Chicago Red Stars were on their way out and, if the Freedom folded too, WPS couldn't survive having just five teams.

There was urgency to find a new team owner to buy the Freedom. Dan Borislow, who had a daughter who played soccer, had the deep pockets to commit, and there weren't any other options. With a reces-sion afoot and poor optics from other vanished WPS teams, interest from quality investors was thin, but Borislow seemed credible—at least on paper.

"When someone comes to you out of the blue and he has more than enough money to commit and he has a daughter playing soccer—the usual story that sounds like it makes sense—I think people were just thrilled," says Arnim Whisler, owner of the Chicago Red Stars.

Borislow promised to keep the team in Washington, D.C., and call the team the Freedom. But as the league moved forward and the tran-sition went into motion, Borislow began to chip away at the terms of the agreement. One day he might want to move the team to Florida, he said—not right now, but he'd like the right to move the team. Once the league agreed, he immediately moved the team to Boca Raton. That's how the Washington Freedom disappeared and magicJack took over.

From there, the situation unraveled quickly.

First, it was small things—the team had no website, didn't issue any press releases, and conducted no marketing. MagicJack played their games at a stadium with only a few hundred seats, well under the minimum 5,000 capacity that WPS required.

MagicJack's home field was also too narrow, according to WPS rules. FAU Soccer Stadium, where the team played, had plenty of space to be regulation size, but Borislow wanted it narrower to help his team's attack. In preseason, Lyons had spent eight weeks working with the team, but two days before the opening match of the season, Borislow told Lyons to switch formations because he thought it would be better for striker Abby Wambach. Lyons argued with him but eventually obliged. The narrow field apparently worked, and magicJack won their first few games.

Borislow would even have the magicJack players scrimmage his daughter's under-13 team on a regular basis.

"The players would say to me, *What are we doing this for?*" Mike Lyons says. "I said, *He's standing right there, go ask him.* If he said we're playing his daughter's team, we were playing his daughter's team. It didn't matter—we had to do it."

Lyons, meanwhile, was fired after just three games—three straight wins—after a confrontation with Wambach. They disagreed about an injury substitution and Lyons lashed out at Wambach, whom Borislow had an affinity for.

"You wouldn't be on the field if it was up to me!" Lyons told her.

"So why don't you bench me?" he says Wambach responded.

Lyons pointed to Dan Borislow: "He won't let me."

After the game, a 2–0 win over the Atlanta Beat, Lyons was fired. Borislow kept paying him for eight weeks anyway and never replaced him. Instead, Borislow said magicJack would be collectively coached by the players themselves and Wambach was named player-coach.

But there were also the big things—the sorts of things no one could let go and ignore.

There were no medical staff or supplies to take care of players. At times, magicJack players would have to ask for treatment from the opposing team's medical staff. One player, Ella Masar, said after she broke her nose, Borislow wouldn't let her go to the hospital. When she protested, he offered to take her, and then he took her to dinner with his friends instead. Weeks later, an MRI scan found her left nostril had collapsed.

Some players alleged he made sexually inappropriate comments toward them. Others say he was just rude and abusive, telling them they were "fucking idiots." The WPS Players Union eventually filed a grievance with the front office over his comments toward players, including allegations that Borislow had told the players to call him "Daddy."

The WPS front office's own interactions with Borislow hadn't exactly been cordial, either. At one point, he emailed Melanie Fitzgerald, the league's operations manager:

I don't ask for a worthless speech from you. Have somebody else respond to my requests and inquiries.
Your Boss,
Dan

Some of the people who dealt with Borislow say he reminded them of Donald Trump. As it turns out, the two were friends.

Borislow brought the team to Mar-a-Lago for Easter Sunday in 2011—back when it was still just Trump's golf club for rich people and not a place where the president of the United States held meetings with world leaders. There, the players of magicJack mingled with Trump and Rudy Giuliani, who were there eating caviar and lobster.

But for all of Borislow's money and the promise it would save the cash-strapped league, all it did was make things worse. When the league sanctioned magicJack for failing to meet basic requirements, he ignored it. That happened over and over until the league finally took points away from the team, affecting their place in the standings. He still ignored it.

Finally, WPS board members voted to terminate his ownership rights, but Borislow—who once gave Lyons a motorcycle because Lyons noticed it was sitting in the magicJack warehouse untouched—had no qualms about pouring money into a legal battle. The league, on the other hand, couldn't afford the same. The legal mess surrounding the dispute turned into a black hole that threatened to suck up the entire league.

There, of course, were still all of the league's other problems, but the legal battle between Borislow and the WPS front office added strain the league couldn't withstand. On January 30, 2012, Women's Professional Soccer announced that the 2012 season was canceled while they figured out how to deal with the escalating fight with Borislow.

"Everyone has been trying so hard to keep things going—considering settlement options, discussing union legal action to intervene in the lawsuit, etc., but we just couldn't manage to make things work," league commissioner Jennifer O'Sullivan told players in an email.

The plan was for the league to come back. It never did.

CHAPTER 14

"The Americans? They Just Go for It"

With the 2011 Women's World Cup in Germany around the corner, coach Pia Sundhage was faced with the very difficult decision of choosing which players would make the roster.

Alex Morgan was a bright young forward, but she played a very specific and narrow role for the team. She was a "super sub"—she came off the bench late in games and did her best to exploit tired defenses.

When Sundhage would send Morgan onto the field, she never gave her any instructions. She'd tell her: "Just go for it and have fun. Go out there and score some goals."

It was the kind of message a youth soccer coach might tell a 10-year-old kid, and it was a deliberate decision by Sundhage. Morgan had been scoring goals all her life and Sundhage didn't want to over-complicate it. If Morgan had a simple job—to come on for the last 15 minutes of a game and score a goal—her instincts and her physical ability were all she needed.

Morgan, like any hungry young player, wanted more than that. She wanted to be a starter. She wanted Sundhage to trust her to do more than "just go out there and score goals."

So one day, Sundhage explained to her: "Listen, I'm not coaching you." (Remembering that moment, Sundhage says now: "She looked at me like I had come from another planet.")

"But I want to learn and grow," Morgan told her.

Sundhage shook her head. "You just go out there," she said. "You have no problem coming off the bench."

That approach had been working. It was Morgan who had bailed the team out of missing the World Cup altogether with an all-important goal in Italy. By following her instincts, she took advantage of a combination of speed, strength, and agility that no one else on the team had. Over a 20-meter distance, Morgan was as fast as male players, and Dawn Scott, the national team's fitness coach, once said of her physical prowess: "Alex is a freak in a positive way."

Still, Morgan was inexperienced. Before that Italy game where she scored, Morgan had appeared for the U.S. only eight times. Granted, she scored in four of those appearances, but at 21 years old, she was the youngest player on the team.

Was there a spot on the World Cup roster for a player like her? That was the question Sundhage had to answer before the 2011 World Cup.

Once Sundhage made her decision—before she announced the final roster—she met with Morgan, who was eager to learn whether she'd made the cut.

"You know what?" Sundhage told Morgan. "There will probably be journalists coming up to you and saying, *Hey, you scored a goal again— don't you think you should be in the starting lineup?* What would you answer to that journalist?"

"Well, I would tell them that I just want to help the team and do my best and I'll do whatever the coach asks of me," Morgan replied.

Sundhage smiled. That was what she wanted to hear.

"Well, that's a very good answer because that's what's going to happen in Germany," Sundhage said. "I don't want to ruin you—you're smarter than I am coming off the bench. The only thing I want is for you to do your very best. Use your speed and, if you have a chance, take a shot."

And that was how Alex Morgan found out she was going to play in a Women's World Cup. It wasn't going to be as a starter, but she was going to her first major tournament.

Half of Sundhage's roster featured players making their World Cup debuts with Morgan, including Ali Krieger, Becky Sauerbrunn, Tobin Heath, and Amy Rodriguez. But it was balanced by veterans Sundhage liked to count on, such as Abby Wambach, Shannon Boxx, and Christie Pearce.

"We have people that organize defensively, people that can step up when it really matters, people that are good in the air, people that are fighters, and tricky ones as well," Sundhage said of her roster.

The 2011 tournament started for the U.S. in familiar fashion: They won comfortably over North Korea, 2–0, in Dresden. Then they rolled past Colombia, 3–0, in Sinsheim.

They had enough confidence that they had planned out goal celebrations. The first, after a screamer from Heather O'Reilly, saw all the players line up on the center circle and salute the American servicemen and servicewomen stationed in Germany.

After Megan Rapinoe, the flashy midfielder with bleached-blonde short hair, scored an emphatic goal next, she ran over to the corner, picked up the large fuzzy microphone used for capturing ambient sound for the TV broadcast, and belted out the chorus of "Born in the U.S.A." by Bruce Springsteen.

By the time the players were set for their last group-stage match versus Sweden—the team from Sundhage's homeland—they were already guaranteed a spot in the quarterfinal. The Americans still wanted to win, though, so they could top their group and face an easier opponent in the quarterfinal round.

Instead, the Americans lost. An early penalty gave Sweden the edge, and they went on to win, 2–1. With that, instead of facing Australia, a team that had never beaten the U.S., the Americans now had to face Brazil, the team that had humiliated them in the semifinal of the previous World Cup.

* * *

The quarterfinal match of the 2011 Women's World Cup seemed to be off to a dream start. In just the second minute, Brazil's Daiane accidentally knocked the ball into her own net when trying to clear out a dangerous cross.

The Americans held that lead going into halftime, and it appeared they were well in position to beat a Brazil team that was every bit as good and as talented as they had been in 2007. Marta was still the best player in the world, having just won the FIFA World Player of the Year honor again. The Brazilian team wasn't giving the Americans many chances to score on their own.

In the second half, the USA's fortunes quickly changed.

At one point, Marta did something only Marta could do. She flicked the ball into the air from her left foot, over defender Rachel Buehler's head, and to her right foot. As Marta made a lunging effort to shoot the ball on the bounce, Buehler stayed with her the whole time. Buehler lunged at the same time as Marta to block the shot, and both players crashed to the ground.

Referee Jacqui Melksham blew her whistle. She held up a red card to Buehler and then pointed to the penalty spot for Brazil. It was a double-whammy nightmare. Buehler, who was nicknamed the Buehldozer, had to leave the game, forcing the U.S. to play a woman down, and Brazil had a golden chance to equalize.

For a moment, Buehler couldn't believe it. She had never received a red card in her life—not in college, not in club play, not with the national team.

"She was kind of wandering around on the field," Heather O'Reilly says. "I remember putting my hand on her shoulder, being like, *Rachel, you've got to get off. You need to go.*"

It was a shocking decision from the referee. Replays showed Marta lunged into the air before Buehler made contact and was responsible for herself falling down in the box. Whether Buehler's challenge deserved a red card was controversial.

"To be honest, when Buehler was sent off, for a couple seconds, I thought Marta was sent off because she just fell over in the box," coach Pia Sundhage says. "When I saw Buehler coming at me, I thought: *Where is she going?*"

Cristiane stepped up to the spot to take her penalty kick. Luckily, Hope Solo had been carefully studying Brazil's penalties, and she knew which side Cristiane favored. When Cristiane struck, Solo was in position to comfortably bat it away. The Americans celebrated Solo's save furiously.

That is, until the referee blew her whistle again. She judged the Americans to have encroached the penalty box before Cristiane's foot struck the ball. Again, it was a shockingly harsh decision. The Americans angrily protested, and Solo was given a yellow card for dissent.

Brazil switched kick-takers for the do-over, and Marta stepped up. Solo couldn't save two in a row. Brazil equalized, and the Americans were incensed . . . furious . . . outraged. But it seemed only to fuel the Americans' desire to win.

For Sundhage, the red card presented a situation she hadn't prepared for. She initially told Shannon Boxx to drop back as a centerback to keep the Americans in a four-back defensive shape. But as the game stretched on, it was clear the U.S. needed Boxx in the midfield, so Sundhage pushed Boxx back up and the Americans played in a 3–4–2 formation.

"That's one of my proudest moments as a coach," Sundhage says. "It was brave, and it was smart."

The Americans, reeling and determined after the referee's harsh calls, battled on, but after 90 minutes, the whistle blew with the score deadlocked at 1–1.

The match was headed for extra time. But the Brazilians looked gassed—they used the short break between full time and extra time to sit down and rest their legs while they sipped water. The Americans, meanwhile, stayed on their feet, pacing around furiously and pumping one another up.

When they noticed the Brazilians trying to catch their breath and relax before the start of 30-minute overtime, the Americans knew they had a mental edge.

"For me, that was an emotional up-lifter," Abby Wambach said. "I thought, *Even with 10 men, we're still fitter, we're still stronger.*"

But it didn't take long for Marta to again do Marta-esque things. Just two minutes into extra time, she scored again. In a splendid flash of individual brilliance, she flicked a ball behind her off the far post and into the net. The Brazilians now led, 2–1. Unless the Americans could fire back, Brazil would win as soon as the whistle blew.

The Americans had their chances. Alex Morgan had a shot deflected away. Carli Lloyd fired a shot over the bar. But they weren't finding their equalizer, and the clock ticked past the 120 minutes that marked the end of extra time.

It looked like the Americans were going to suffer their earliest exit ever in a major tournament. The referee's decisions, Marta's skills, the soccer gods—everything was just conspiring against the Americans.

The clock ticked ahead into the 122nd minute—the match was now into the stoppage time of extra time, and the whistle would blow any second. Cristiane dribbled the ball into the corner, trying to waste precious seconds off the clock. When Christie Pearce contested for the ball, Cristiane went down like she had been zapped by an electric shock—a dive in a cynical attempt to stop play, which the referee ignored.

Carli Lloyd collected the ball and took a few touches in the USA's half, muscling off a Brazilian player before spraying the ball out wide to Megan Rapinoe. The clock kept ticking.

"I was like, *What are you doing?*" Wambach later recalled thinking. "*Why are you passing it wide? In my mind I was like, Just kick it straight direct north towards the goal as possible because that's where I am.*"

Rapinoe, running into Brazil's half, took a touch to settle the ball, looked up at the back post where Wambach was waving her arm, and then launched the ball off her left foot. Or as Rapinoe would later tell reporters: "I just took a touch and friggin' smacked it."

The ball sailed through the air—it must've gone 50 yards—and as it dangled in the air, moving toward the box, it lingered just long enough to build a gasp of anticipation. Americans who were hunched around their TVs had enough time to clutch hands or hold their breath.

For Wambach, who was ready at the back post, her eye never left the ball as it dropped toward her. She was waiting . . . waiting . . . waiting.

The anticipation must've gotten to Brazilian goalkeeper Andréia, who erroneously thought she had enough time to come off her line and punch the ball away. Instead, Wambach planted her feet and jumped straight up into the air, thrusting her head toward the ball. She beat

Andréia to the ball and snapped it toward the goal. Wambach's eyes were closed, but the sound of the ball rattling the back of the net was unmistakable. Goal, USA. The score: 2–2.

"OH, CAN YOU BELIEVE THIS?!" ESPN announcer Ian Darke shouted at the top of his lungs to American viewers through their TV sets. "ABBY WAMBACH HAS SAVED THE USA'S LIFE IN THIS WORLD CUP!"

Wambach ran over to the corner flag and slid, releasing a primal scream. The players closest to her—Tobin Heath and Alex Morgan—hugged her first. Kelley O'Hara leapt off the bench and raced over to Wambach, and everyone else soon followed. Rapinoe fist-pumped furiously and pounded on her chest.

It was perhaps the most exhilarating moment in the national team's history—perhaps it could rival the 1999 World Cup win, which had fittingly happened exactly 12 years earlier. Either way, coming after 121 minutes and 19 seconds, it was the latest goal in World Cup history—men's or women's—and it was a thrilling boost for the Americans. There was no way they were going to lose to Brazil on penalty kicks now.

"No doubt whatsoever," Rapinoe said.

In the shootout that followed, Hope Solo saved one of Brazil's penalty kicks, while the Americans buried all theirs. The Americans were advancing to the semifinal.

The stunning last-second goal—Rapinoe's cross and Wambach's header—would captivate the nation back home. Suddenly a country that hadn't been particularly attuned to this Women's World Cup fell back in love with its national team. A team that had fallen off the radar since 2005 was thrust back into the spotlight again.

If Abby Wambach worried in 2008 about the team not needing her, she proved her fears wrong at the perfect time.

"The power of that goal is amazing," Wambach later said. "People tell me all the time how they remember where they were when that happened. It's cool that I was a part of it, but I think it's more cool to kind of look at it from an evolutionary aspect, to see where the game was and where the game has gone. That's kind of the pivotal turning point . . .

We really felt there was a huge shift in the popularity of women's soccer in 2011."

To this day, Wambach's goal is widely considered one of the best and most important goals in American soccer history. It felt like a miracle, but it was actually by design. It was the result of relentless training every day and a team culture that demanded preparation.

"What sticks for me with that goal is that we trained that," Heather O'Reilly says. "It wasn't something that was just lucky. Certainly, we didn't plan that exact play, but with Pia, when we played in a conventional 4–4–2 with Abby up top, we worked on crosses so much. Pretty much every training session was changing the point of attack and putting lethal crosses in the box."

"Training pays off and hard work pays off and repetition pays off," O'Reilly adds. "When you do those things with purpose year-in and year-out, then when these big moments come, people think it's so incredible and such a miracle, but in reality, it was just practice and, in the biggest moment, being able to execute."

At the same time, the performance said something else about what the Americans had—something that couldn't come simply from training. The national team never gave up, even in the face of what seemed liked insurmountable odds. They kept their heads in the match and believed they could win, even with their backs against the wall, down to the very last possession.

That never-say-die mentality, Sundhage says, was something she found in the American players when she took over as the USA coach. She certainly didn't teach it to them.

"In Sweden, we talk about attacking, defending, positioning, this and that," Sundhage says. "I think we are fairly smart when it comes to tactics. But here, the Americans have another component: They just go for it."

Marta was once asked by a reporter why the Americans were so hard to beat. She pointed to her head, and the reporter thought she was saying they had a strong aerial presence. "No, no," Marta interjected. "It's the mentality."

* * *

After that dramatic thriller versus Brazil, the Americans had still only advanced to the semifinal. They had two more games to play if they wanted to be World Cup champions, and recovering from an emotional roller coaster like they just experienced wasn't easy.

"It's been such an emotional experience that talking about it has helped," Abby Wambach said the next day. "When you talk through some of these crazy emotional things, it allows you to not only feel them, but to have experienced them and be able to put them somewhere you can hold them for a while so you can move on."

When the semifinal versus France arrived, the Americans approached it with the same dogged determination as the previous match.

In truth, France outplayed the USA at times. They knocked the ball around and held on to possession, which frustrated the Americans. But the Americans looked determined and well-organized as a unit. With an early goal from Lauren Cheney, a game-winner from Abby Wambach, and an insurance goal from Alex Morgan, the U.S. beat France, 3–1.

With that, the national team was set to appear in its first World Cup final since they won in 1999. Their opponent? Japan, a team that had never beaten the U.S. in 25 prior meetings.

There was a bigger sense of purpose for the Japanese team, though. Before they'd embarked on their 2011 World Cup campaign, they'd left a country in devastation. Just 75 days before the tournament started, one of the strongest earthquakes ever recorded struck off the coast of Japan, triggering a tsunami that killed around 16,000 people and obliterated the country's infrastructure, causing damage worth $360 billion.

The people of Japan rallied around the team's run through the tournament, finding joy and respite from the tragedy at home. For the players, there was a belief that they weren't just competing for themselves. Indeed, the Japanese weren't considered favorites coming into the tournament. Even as they got through to the final, they didn't do it in dominating fashion. But something propelled them forward.

"Every game we won was something of a surprise for us," Japanese forward Mana Iwabuchi later said. "We didn't expect success after success. Beating Germany in the quarterfinals was something very special. That is when we realized that we were actually pretty good."

The Americans were used to being the favorite in major tournaments. If anything, they seemed to relish the chance to prove how good they were. Now, they had to do it against an opponent that was the clear easy-to-root-for underdog.

On July 17, 2011, the Americans walked onto the field at Waldstadion in Frankfurt. They were finally back in a World Cup final for the first time in 12 years.

The Americans started strong and dominant, creating dangerous chance after dangerous chance. Lauren Cheney tapped a onetime shot inches wide. Then Abby Wambach smashed a rocket off the crossbar. Later, an Alex Morgan shot went off the post. After that, a Wambach header was tipped just over the bar. Nothing was going in, and the frustration of the Americans was palpable.

Finally, in the 69th minute, the USA broke through. Rapinoe ran onto a ball poked away from a Japanese player, saw Morgan racing up the field, and launched a pass. Morgan took a touch with her right foot to set the ball in front of her favored left and smashed it into the back of the net.

But a defensive mistake 12 minutes later would erase the USA's lead. A Christie Pearce pass up the field was cut out, and Japan moved into counterattack mode. Yūki Nagasato crossed the ball into the box and Rachel Buehler stopped it, but when she went to clear it out, she cleared it past the face of the goal. Aya Miyama was right there for an easy tap-in. It was 1–1 with the 90 minutes nearly over—the match would have to stretch into extra time.

With another 30 minutes added to the clock, the Americans continued to battle. In the 104th minute, it was Alex Morgan, the youngster, yet again. This time, she picked out Abby Wambach in the middle of the box and crossed a pinpoint ball to Wambach's head. All Wambach had to do was tip her forehead down and let the ball knock into the back of the net. The Americans were up now, 2–1, and victory felt close.

It wasn't close enough, though. Ten minutes later, Japan came roaring back. This time it was a corner kick. Aya Miyama launched the ball toward the near post, and Homare Sawa, the team's captain, faced the sideline but stuck her foot out. With the outside of her foot, her body not even facing the goal, she flicked the ball past Hope Solo. Her finish was as unexpected as it was crafty.

Japan had equalized and, once time ran out, the Americans again had to win a back-and-forth thriller on penalty kicks.

Shannon Boxx took the first kick, firing to the right. Goalkeeper Ayumi Kaihori guessed correctly but lunged well ahead of the ball—she would never be able to get a hand on it. Instead, she kicked her trailing leg out and blocked the ball.

"No matter what, I'll always question whether I should have gone the other way when I hit that PK against Japan," Boxx says now. "That will never go away. When I start to think about it, it upsets me again."

Next was Aya Miyama, who calmly fired past Hope Solo. It was then Carli Lloyd's turn. She ran up to the ball like she was sprinting through the last steps of a 100-meter dash, and her shot sailed over the bar.

The World Cup trophy was slipping away. But Solo blocked Yūki Nagasato's shot, giving the U.S. a lifeline, if only Tobin Heath could bury her chance. She placed the ball down, and her body language showed some obvious nerves. On the run up, Heath's body position gave away that she was shooting to her left, and Kaihori dived that way to make the save.

The Americans had missed three straight penalty kicks. It didn't matter that Abby Wambach was next in the rotation and that she scored. When Saki Kumagai, Japan's fourth kicker, buried her shot, it was over. Japan had won the 2011 World Cup.

The Americans walked away crestfallen as the Japanese players jumped into a dogpile of celebration. Once the Japanese players recovered from the celebrations, they unfurled a sign that read: "To our friends around the world—thank you for your support."

"Who knows—maybe it was fate," Boxx says now. "Maybe they needed that more than we did at that time. Maybe I say that to make myself feel better. But I think it really was good for their country to take that home and have some happiness."

The U.S. team's equipment manager had covered the players' belongings in plastic wrap so celebratory champagne wouldn't get all over their stuff in the locker room. But when the U.S. lost in penalty kicks, he had gotten only partially through removing it by the time the players returned.

"I remember going into the locker room and we were so upset. We saw the plastic laying around, kind of half on our stuff," Heather O'Reilly says with a laugh. "That was really tough."

Pia Sundhage, the coach who was normally so effervescent, became stoic. Normally, she'd offer up some sort of speech to the players after a game, but she had nothing to say. When the team went back to the hotel ballroom U.S. Soccer had rented out for the players and their loved ones, Sundhage didn't stick around for long.

"Afterward, I wasn't able to enjoy that moment after the final," Sundhage says now. "I'm a little bit ashamed of that because I should've been very happy because of the way we played. That was a lesson to learn."

The Americans had played their best, most complete game of the 2011 World Cup. They had looked dominant, and they were better than Japan. But they lost.

CHAPTER 15

"Okay, This Is Our Payback"

When the national team returned to the U.S. from losing the 2011 Women's World Cup, they returned as, well, losers—at least in the most literal sense of the word. The players had just lost the World Cup, and they were disconsolate about it.

But when they arrived in New York City and stepped off the team bus into Times Square, they were shocked by what they saw. A throng of people was cheering for them as if they were the world champions. For the players, who were still devastated, the heroes' welcome had a strange dissonance.

"The streets of Times Square were just absolutely packed," says Heather O'Reilly. "It was a very bizarre feeling—it was this atmosphere as if we won, but we didn't. We were being celebrated, but nothing less than winning was acceptable to us. It was an interesting thing for us to cope with."

The American public, it seemed, had been reminded of the national team's existence and wanted to talk to the players. In New York, they did the media rounds, appearing on the *Today* show, *Good Morning America*, *The Daily Show*, CNN, and *Late Show with David Letterman*, among others. Fans wanted to shake the players' hands and take pictures with them.

"We'd be walking down the street and hear people screaming *Great job!* and we'd look at each other like, *But we didn't win*," Shannon Boxx says. "It was really weird."

Even in defeat, the 2011 World Cup final was huge for the national team's popularity. It was watched on ESPN by 13.5 million Americans, a soccer record for the channel. Getting people to watch was one thing, but the national team won over the hearts of Americans with their attacking style of play and their gutsy, relentless never-say-die mentality.

The final lit social media abuzz and set a new record on Twitter for the number of tweets per second.

Other than Christie Pearce, who was on the 1999 World Cup team as a depth piece, none of the players had experienced anything like what they saw when they returned from Germany. The team surged back into the American mainstream practically overnight. Hope Solo, a breakout star, appeared on the cover of *Sports Illustrated* and was asked to compete on ABC's *Dancing with the Stars*. Everyone on the team was more famous than they had ever been.

At one point in New York City as the players looked out from their bus onto the crowd of fans who had gathered to catch a glimpse of the team, a scream came from Abby Wambach.

"Fuck!" she shouted. Those around her—startled and worried that something bad had just happened—turned to her and asked her what was wrong.

Wambach, with resignation in her voice, responded: "We didn't win."

It hit Wambach like a ton of bricks. She saw the response the team had gotten—a massive surge of fan support—and she saw the missed opportunity. If the national team had actually won the World Cup, how much bigger could it have been for the sport?

The 2012 London Olympics were around the corner, and the national team had a chance to keep the momentum going. If they could play well and win gold, maybe they could even build off of what they started in Germany.

They would have to qualify for the Olympics first, though. With the memory of losing to Mexico in the 2011 World Cup qualifiers still fresh, they knew this tournament needed to be treated like it was its own Olympic Games.

* * *

Alex Morgan had enjoyed a very good World Cup as a super sub. She scored two goals, one of them in the final, and looked suited for the highest level of the international game.

Fans of the national team saw it too and were clamoring for more of the youngster on the field. With her distinctive pink headband that kept her ponytail in place, it was hard to miss the Los Angeles–area native as she galloped toward goal. She earned a nickname, Baby Horse, and started being covered in the media as the next big thing.

With her strong showing in Germany behind her, Morgan met with her coach, Pia Sundhage.

"Do you remember the conversation we had before the World Cup?" Morgan asked. That was the conversation where Sundhage told Morgan she wasn't going to coach her into a starting role— she just wanted Morgan to come off the bench and score goals with minimal instruction.

"Yes, I do," Sundhage responded. "Of course."

"Well, I would like to have the conversation again," Morgan told her. "I want you to coach me."

Sundhage smiled and nodded. "Of course I will," she said, "because you will soon be in the starting lineup."

When the CONCACAF Olympic qualifying tournament arrived in January 2012, Sundhage wasn't ready to put Morgan in the starting lineup immediately. She started the qualifying tournament conservatively, sticking with what had worked for her previously, and Morgan continued the super-sub role.

The U.S. opened the tournament in Vancouver, Canada, by demolishing the Dominican Republic, 14–0. Despite the strong start, it included a setback, as Ali Krieger, arguably the best right back in the world at the time, was recklessly tackled, tearing her ACL and ruling her out for the Olympics if the U.S. did qualify.

The U.S. followed that by beating Guatemala, 13–0. Sydney Leroux, a young Canadian-born striker with American citizenship, scored five goals as a second-half substitute. Leroux did not make the 2011 World Cup roster, but she was proving she belonged at London 2012.

Next loomed Mexico, the team that had nearly prevented the U.S. from making it into the World Cup less than a year before.

"We all remember what happened in the qualifiers for the World Cup," Shannon Boxx said at the time. "Now we're all looking at this like, *Okay, this is our payback*. This definitely has been marked on my calendar for a long time as the game I want to win."

The match wasn't even close. The Americans dominated from the first whistle to the last, netting a convincing 4–0 result over Mexico. They followed that up with a 3–0 win over Costa Rica and qualified for the Olympics.

The final match of the tournament, versus Canada, didn't actually matter—both teams had qualified for the Olympics—but the Americans wanted to issue a statement of intent for London. Canada was the toughest opponent in this qualifying tournament.

This was the moment for Pia Sundhage to give Alex Morgan the starting spot they had discussed. While the stakes were low, the competition was high. Morgan finally had the chance to prove she belonged in the starting lineup.

It took Morgan just four minutes to give the Americans the lead. Abby Wambach flicked a ball up to Morgan with her head, and Morgan ran onto it to get the shot off. Her finish on the ball was superb.

Morgan ended up playing a role in all of the USA's goals in a 4–0 win over Canada. She scored two and Wambach scored two, with Morgan assisting on both of them. The pairing of Morgan and Wambach together up top in a 4–4–2 pulled apart the Canadian back line and offered a varied attacking threat.

From that moment on, Alex Morgan was a starter for the national team. No matter how super, she was no longer considered a sub.

For Canadian coach John Herdman, who'd hyped the match beforehand and said "the sleeves are off," the loss seemed humbling. He said he'd gotten his tactics wrong and told reporters: "I apologize for not doing what we could have done tonight."

The U.S. and Canadian national teams had already been rivals due to proximity, but the qualifying tournament ratcheted up the tension. On the Canadian broadcast of the tournament, the announcers openly and repeatedly criticized coach Pia Sundhage for celebrating all of the USA's goals as the scorelines grew increasingly lopsided.

Leroux, who switched national team allegiance from Canada to the U.S. in 2008 as a teenager, became a focal point of the growing rivalry. She was booed by Canadian fans every time she touched the ball. Some Canadian fans called her "Judas" in chants and sent racially charged messages at her on social media. Leroux, who was a dual-national, was also mixed race—she had a white Canadian mother and a black American father.

The USA-Canada rivalry hadn't been much of a soccer rivalry—the U.S. hadn't lost to Canada in 11 years by that point—but it was fast growing into a rivalry of raw emotion.

* * *

When the national team arrived in the United Kingdom for the 2012 Olympics, confidence was at a high. If all went well, the Americans would start off in Scotland and take a winding road through England before they could finally get to London for the gold-medal match.

But quickly in their tournament opener versus France in Glasgow, it looked like the Americans might never get that far. Within 12 minutes, Gaëtane Thiney fired an absolute rocket past Hope Solo. A minute later, France doubled their lead to 2–0—it was another rocket, this time from Élodie Thomis.

When Shannon Boxx went down a couple of minutes later with a hamstring pull, the situation had gone from bad to worse. Coach Pia Sundhage looked down the bench and asked Carli Lloyd to take Boxx's place.

By that point, Sundhage didn't have much confidence in Lloyd. Lloyd had lost her starting spot in the central midfield to Boxx and Lauren Cheney because of her inconsistency. She would sometimes have breakout moments—like scoring the game-winner in the gold-medal match of the 2008 Olympics—but she would also have long stretches where she was a turnover machine.

"If you look at the way she plays in the midfield, she takes a lot of risks," Sundhage says now. "Sometimes, that's beautiful. Look at 2008—she scored the winning goal. She can do certain things in the midfield, but she's always playing on a fine line, so to speak. When she's not successful, something happens not only to her but to her teammates."

"As a coach, I think, *Keep on going because sooner or later you will be successful. You'll beat that player*," Sundhage adds. "Meanwhile, you have players around her thinking, *Oh no, she's losing the ball again* or, *She's taking a shot when she shouldn't*. So, it's such a complex situation."

Sundhage was left with no choice in that France game. There wasn't another central midfielder on the bench—she had to turn to Lloyd. After being told she wasn't good enough, now the team was counting on her.

Fortunately for the national team, when the biggest games arrived, Lloyd seemed to find another level. Any poor performances she had in friendlies or minor tournaments seemed to vanish from memory. She relished the moments where she could prove herself to the world.

It took one minute after Lloyd came on for the Americans to score and start a stunning comeback. They went on to score four unanswered goals, with Lloyd scoring the goal that ended up as the game-winner. The U.S. moved past France, 4–2.

From there, the Americans were on a roll. They beat Colombia, 3–0, and Megan Rapinoe unveiled a planned goal celebration for the cameras—she pulled a tiny banner from her sock that read, "Happy B-Day Kreigy, we liebe you." Krieger was out of the tournament after tearing her ACL, and the Colombia match fell on her birthday. *Liebe* was German for love, a word Krieger had tattooed on her arm.

Next up was the match with North Korea, where the national team showed off another choreographed goal celebration in a 1–0 win. After Abby Wambach's first goal, the team lined up and held hands, raising their arms in succession to create a rolling wave—a break dancing–type move. When it reached the last player in the line, the players turned and pointed to the midfield, where Hope Solo and Christie Pearce were doing the dance move known as "the Worm."

"Sometimes Hope doesn't get involved in our celebrations, and she said before the game that the Worm is the only thing she can do," Wambach said afterward. "So we just tried to set her up for something."

In the quarterfinals, the national team's confidence rolled on. After their first goal against New Zealand en route to a 2–0 win, they again celebrated with a planned display, this time with the team breaking out into cartwheels.

The predetermined celebrations clearly rubbed some opponents the wrong way.

"I wouldn't like it if our team did that," New Zealand coach Tony Readings said afterward. "When teams concede, they're disappointed, and they want to get on with the game. But it's obviously something the Americans do. It's something I guess they work on in training. We try to work on scoring goals."

But Sundhage, the coach who was rebuked so harshly by commentators and fans in Canada for her jubilant celebrations during qualifying, even amid double-digit leads, didn't care. She was just glad the players were having fun.

"We score goals and you're happy," she said. "What the players want to do, whatever they do, it has to be fun. If they come up with ideas, that's perfectly fine."

But Canada, the bitter rival that was still smarting from the loss during qualifiers, was next in the semifinal round of the 2012 Olympics. The fun was about to stop.

* * *

Before the semifinal match at Old Trafford even started, John Herdman, the coach of the Canadian team, tried to get in the heads of the American players.

"One of the big threats we've got to take care of, and what we've paid attention to, is the illegal marking in the box on their corners and free kicks," Herdman told media the day before the game, adding that he wanted to "raise awareness" with the referees. "Some of the blocking tactics, which are highly illegal—we'll keep an eye on them in the game."

It took about 20 seconds from the opening whistle for it to become clear what kind of match this was going to be. As Lauren Cheney went for the ball, Melissa Tancredi—nicknamed "Tank" for a reason—shoved her to the ground and was called for a foul. Another 30 seconds later, Christine Sinclair shoved Alex Morgan from behind, sending her face-first into the grass for another whistled foul.

But the Canadians hit the Americans where it hurt first— Tancredi dished a slick pass to Sinclair in the box, and Canada's all-time leading goal-scorer coolly slotted it past Hope Solo. USA 0, Canada 1: 23rd minute.

The match was growing increasingly chippy, with each side wanting to disrupt the other's rhythm. A pair of Canadian players sandwiched Abby Wambach on a set piece, using their elbows to knock her down. Arlo White, the play-by-play announcer for NBC, called it a "Wambach sand-wich" and remarked: "Isn't it interesting that John Herdman, unprompted yesterday—he brought it up, didn't he, this 'highly illegal' activity, and it's his team that is getting very physical on these corner kicks."

One minute after that moment, Megan Rapinoe stood at the corner flag for a corner kick. She launched an in-swinging ball toward the goal and no one touched it. It curled straight into the net—a type of goal that is fittingly known as an "Olimpico." It was the first-ever Olimpico scored in an Olympic Games. USA 1, Canada 1: 54th minute.

The Canadians responded by becoming even more physical. One minute after Rapinoe's goal came a shocking display of bad sportsman-ship. With Carli Lloyd down in the box, Melissa Tancredi seemingly went out of her way to step on Lloyd's head with her left cleat. The ref-eree didn't see it, or else it would've surely been a red card.

Lloyd stayed down for a minute but played on. She later told report-ers she was shocked when she saw the replay and noticed Tancredi looked to have done it intentionally.

Soon after, the duo of Tancredi and Sinclair returned to revive Can-ada's lead. From a wide channel, Tancredi cut around a defender and lofted a ball into the box. Sinclair rose up and headed it off the inside of the post and past Solo. USA 1, Canada 2: 67th minute.

The Americans returned fire just three minutes later, again on a splendid individual effort from Megan Rapinoe. Kelley O'Hara switched the point of attack with a long ball from the left flank over to Rapinoe on the right. From well outside the box, Rapinoe pushed the ball wide, pulled her right foot back and fired a rocket. It bounced off the far post and into the net. USA 2, Canada 2: 70th minute.

But Christine Sinclair was unstoppable. Barely two minutes had passed until Sinclair scored again. She rose up over all the Americans on a corner kick and headed the ball inside the near post. USA 2, Canada 3: 72nd minute.

By this point, John Herdman, Canada's coach, had taken to taunting the Americans who sat on the bench about 20 feet from where he stood. Coaches weren't supposed to leave technical box they were designated to stand in, but Herdman made sure he could get close enough to the USA bench that the players wouldn't be able to miss him. Then, he shouted at them.

"I vividly remember John Herdman coming over to our bench and aggressively celebrating, to put it mildly," says Heather O'Reilly. "We all thought it was completely absurd."

"He would get excited and he'd turn and say something to us," remembers Shannon Boxx. "I remember being so mad, like, *Go away!* It was so intense. It pissed me off, but hey, that's what he wanted, to piss us off, and it worked."

Pia Sundhage had to stand next to him. There was about three feet between her technical box and his. She tried to ignore him. She hadn't read or watched his taunting comments before the game. She didn't plan to pay attention to what he said afterward. But during the game, there he was, shouting at her, and there was nothing she could do about it.

"I would have expected him to behave a little more respectful," Sundhage says now. "The fact that he tried to have a bad impact on the game, I'm not proud of that—I want every one of us to be proud of the women's game . . . We've gotten the chance to compete at the highest level and show everybody this is something good for the women's game. Why on earth would you try to break that down or destroy it?

"He is the only one of all coaches—and I've met a lot of coaches, a lot of coaches. I think they're all pretty much okay, most of them are very good, some are great. But in that particular game, he didn't behave in the right way."

As the match went on and stretched into the 77th minute, the Americans grew increasingly desperate to get an equalizer. Abby Wambach did what she always did in situations like this where the U.S. was playing from behind: She tried to get the referee to clamp down on time-wasting.

Time-wasting is arguably the most frustrating and most cynical aspect of soccer. Once a team gets a lead and there's not a lot of time left, they do everything they can to burn precious time off the clock. The theory is that whatever time is wasted won't be added back onto the clock as stoppage time after the 90-minute point.

Many times, it works. A player fakes a leg cramp here, a player is indecisive on a throw-in there—it all adds up. Many games in the history of soccer have been won on such shrewd time-management and gamesmanship.

But sometimes it backfires. In the World Cup only a year before, Brazilian player Érika had fallen down in the box after not being touched and pretended she had injured her back, forcing trainers to come out and use a stretcher to carry her off the field. Once she was carried to the sideline, she ran straight back onto the field, making her ploy obvious. The ref made sure the wasted time would be added onto the clock. It was in the injury time tacked onto extra time that Abby Wambach scored the stunning goal that captured the hearts of Americans and put the national team through in the 2011 World Cup.

Here at the Olympics, the Canadians wanted to settle down the pace of the game. They had the lead, and there were only 13 minutes left in regulation. If the Canadians could kill vital seconds from the clock, they would do it. Time-wasting, after all, was part of the sport.

So, Wambach started loudly counting every time Canadian goal-keeper Erin McLeod held on to the ball. Wambach held her hand up and counted with her fingers to make sure referee Christina Pedersen could see.

The official "Laws of the Game" that govern soccer say a goalkeeper cannot hold on to the ball with her hands for more than six seconds. Goalkeepers routinely hold it longer, and it's almost never called by referees—it's soccer's version of jaywalking. And yet, it *is* the rule. McLeod had been warned already at halftime by an assistant referee about taking too long with the ball.

"I wasn't yelling. I was just counting," Wambach later explained. "I probably did it five to seven times."

When McLeod prepared to kick the ball away in the 77th minute, Wambach counted. One . . . Two . . . Three . . . She got to 10 seconds, and then Pedersen blew her whistle.

The referee awarded the U.S. an indirect free kick from the spot where McLeod was standing inside the penalty box. It was a bizarre decision. It was to the letter of the law, sure, but no one had ever seen such a call. Yet, it meant that the Americans had a lifeline.

Seven Canadian players stood holding hands in front of the goal to form a wall as Megan Rapinoe stood behind the ball and assessed the situation. Because it was an indirect kick, Tobin Heath poked the ball forward with her toe at the whistle, and then Rapinoe ran onto it and fired. The shot was headed straight for the face of Marie-Eve Nault. She turned her body and put her arm up in front of her head, and the ball bounced off her arm.

Pedersen blew her whistle again. This time it was for a handball in the box on Nault. The Americans had been awarded a penalty kick under highly controversial circumstances. The crowd at Old Trafford buzzed with a mix of boos and cheers. The Canadians were furious.

Wambach stepped up to the spot and, when the whistle blew, she didn't hit the ball hard, but she tucked it neatly inside the post, making it too far for McLeod to reach. USA 3, Canada 3, and the game moved into extra time.

With another 30 minutes added to the clock to decide a winner and break the 3–3 stalemate, goals were harder to come by. Both sides had chances, but both sides looked fatigued, too. When Heather O'Reilly came onto the field in the 101st minute as a substitute, she offered some fresh legs, but she wasn't getting many touches on the ball.

The match ticked past the end of extra time and into stoppage time. It seemed the referee would blow her whistle at any moment and the game would move on to the crapshoot of penalty kicks. But the Americans had one last chance to mount an offensive in the 123rd minute.

"We don't have to talk about what we need to do in the last five minutes of the game," O'Reilly says now. "It's just sort of ingrained in the training culture—and now we have this rich history of doing it over and over again. It's a powerful thing to have in your back pocket that this team doesn't give up. Teams know they might be winning in the final minute but, with the U.S., it's not over. We'll keep fighting."

O'Reilly ran onto a wide ball and launched a long, floating cross into the box. It would probably be the USA's last chance to score before the whistle blew. Wambach couldn't get to it. But there was Alex Morgan, standing smack-dab in the middle of the box.

She wasn't a player known for her heading ability, but Morgan jumped and whipped her head toward the goal. She didn't hit the ball exactly how she wanted—it didn't get much power—but it looped up over the outstretched hand of Erin McLeod and dropped into the goal, almost as if in slow motion. It ended up being the perfect header in the 123rd minute, just like the one Wambach scored the year prior against Brazil. Morgan threw her arms in the air, laughing as if in disbelief. The Americans closed in on her with hugs. The Canadian players looked as if they could collapse into the grass.

USA 4, Canada 3: the end. The whistle blew, and the match was over. The Americans had just advanced to the gold-medal match of the 2012 Olympics in a thrilling classic.

The Canadians blamed the referee and floated conspiracy theories. Christine Sinclair, who told reporters that the game "was taken from us" and "the ref decided the result before it started," was issued for a fine and a four-game suspension for allegedly calling referee Christina Pedersen a profanity after the game.

Melissa Tancredi told the referee after the match: "I hope you can sleep tonight and put on your American jersey, because that's who you played for today."

But the Americans believed it was their tenacity that got them through that game. They fell behind three separate times, and three separate times, they came back. With that signature never-say-die mentality, the Americans prevailed. Again, it wasn't something Sundhage taught the players. Rather, it was something she caught from them.

"It's contagious," Sundhage says. "The American players are exhausted when we want them to be exhausted. Heather O'Reilly is that kind of player—running up and down, up and down. You say, *Are you okay?* And she says she is, but she can't hardly breathe. That's something you need. It's contagious."

"Every country I've been to, we are all amazed by the way the Americans are," Sundhage adds. "It had nothing to do with me and my coaching. I was lucky to be around them."

* * *

With the gold-medal match around the corner, Shannon Boxx was finally ready to play again after recovering from the hamstring injury she suffered in the opener of the tournament.

That left Pia Sundhage with a difficult roster decision. Should she go back to the starting lineup she wanted before the 2012 Olympics began? Would Carli Lloyd be relegated back to the bench?

After all, it was less than four years before that Sundhage had told Lloyd she was being dropped from the national team. Although Lloyd had scored the game-winner in the 2008 Olympics final, she hadn't held on to that form. So one day, Sundhage called her with bad news.

"Carli, I want to give you a heads-up before the official email goes out," Sundhage had told her. "You don't have a renewed contract for 2009. If you do get a contract, it may not be Tier 1."

Lloyd was shocked. She knew she hadn't played that well for the Chicago Red Stars, but she hadn't seen this coming. She wanted to cry, but she just asked Sundhage why she wasn't being renewed.

"The consensus is that, for whatever reason, you are not the same impact player you were," Sundhage explained. "Now what happens from here is up to you. You will have plenty of chances to show that you have improved your game and get your contract."

Lloyd quickly showed Sundhage she deserved to be part of the coach's plans and got her contract. But by the time this 2012 Olympics came around, Sundhage still had her reservations.

Being demoted before the tournament could have discouraged Lloyd, but defender Heather Mitts remembers it seemed to fuel her.

"I was with her when she got benched—she was devastated but determined," Mitts says. "I saw the amount of work and training she put in. I was actually concerned she was overtraining and wouldn't be able to sustain the level during the Olympics if given the chance. When she got her opportunity due to an injury, I just watched her in awe as she was out to prove Pia wrong."

Lloyd did it even as she was asked to play as a defensive midfielder behind Lauren Cheney, a role that wouldn't let her shine. Although Sundhage wanted the now-recovered Boxx on the field for the gold-medal game, she was convinced Lloyd needed to be there, too.

The coach decided to put Boxx in the defensive midfield role and pushed Lloyd up in front of her as an attacking midfielder. That was the spot where Lloyd could truly play her best soccer, and now she had a chance to do it in another Olympics final.

When the match arrived versus Japan, the Americans felt ready. The U.S. players felt they had been the better team in the World Cup final the previous year and they were eager for another chance against Japan.

At historic Wembley Stadium, in front of more than 80,000 people, the players of the U.S. national team stepped onto the field to try to win their third consecutive Olympic gold medal.

Within eight minutes, the U.S. and Carli Lloyd had already scored. Alex Morgan whipped a ball across the face of goal and Abby Wambach was there, ready to try to get her left foot on it. But before the ball could find Wambach's foot, Lloyd had darted in front of her, head first, driving the ball into the net, as if appearing from nowhere.

The Americans dominated the half, despite the close score, but the Japanese had their chances. Hope Solo was forced to make a lunging save at full stretch on Shinobu Ohno. Solo almost made a similar save later on Aya Miyama, but the shot went off the top of the crossbar.

After halftime, Lloyd wasn't finished. Running up the field with the ball in the 54th minute, she dribbled, dribbled, dribbled . . . and once she got to the top of the box, she unleashed a laser strike. It cut through specks of red shirts and into the corner of the net. It was about as sweet a hit as Lloyd could've hoped for when she struck the ball.

Sundhage was never so happy to be proven wrong about a player.

"We had a conversation before the Olympics, and she wasn't happy about not playing in the starting lineup, of course," Sundhage says of Lloyd. "And she had a good reaction. I told her, *Just show me that I am wrong*, and she did."

Unlike the previous two major tournament finals the U.S. competed in, this one would not have to go to extra time. Lloyd carried the team to a 2–1 win that felt more decisive than it looked on paper.

The Americans were champions again.

* * *

The ends of tournament cycles have often marked coaching changes for the national team, and 2012 was no different.

As the team was about to embark on its 10-game victory tour to celebrate their new gold medals, U.S. Soccer announced that Pia Sundhage was stepping down. Sundhage was going to return to her native Sweden to coach the national team there ahead of the 2013 women's European championship, a tournament that Sweden was hosting.

Before the U.S. team's first victory-tour game on September 1, 2012, in Rochester, New York, the news was announced to the crowd in attendance, and Sundhage, bringing her journey full circle, belted out a few lines of Bob Dylan's "If Not for You" as a thank-you and goodbye.

"It's a fantastic opportunity for me," said Sundhage. "It's just good timing."

But in the national team—an ultracompetitive environment where some players always seem to think they know best—it's rarely that simple.

Players who decline to speak on the record recall the leaders of the team quietly pushing behind the scenes for a coaching change. Carli Lloyd shares a similar account in her 2016 book, *When Nobody Was Watching.*

"Everybody wants to make it sound as if Pia was the one who engineered the change, but I'm not so sure, since that's not usually how things work around the U.S. Women's National Team," Lloyd wrote. "April Heinrichs was forced out by a core of veterans who basically ran the team, and Greg Ryan was too, though he was going to be a goner anyway the moment the terrible 2007 World Cup ended."

Sundhage and U.S. Soccer president Sunil Gulati started to have discussions about Sundhage's contract and, according to Lloyd, that's when the push behind the scenes began.

"When word leaks out on the team about what is going on, I am upset, and so are lots of other people who aren't part of the 'leadership group,'" Lloyd wrote.

That any of the players wanted Sundhage out as coach took the federation by surprise, according to sources who were involved in the situation but decline to speak on the record. After all, the team had been extraordinarily successful under Sundhage: two Olympic gold medals and a close World Cup final decided on penalty kicks. Team sources say some players were still upset with how Sundhage handled the Hope Solo situation and Sundhage's tendency to brush issues with her aside. Another player says Sundhage made the players write essays after every game, whether it was for club or country, and constantly checked up on players. She also wasn't open to feedback from players.

Just because some of the players had pushed for Sundhage's contract not to be renewed doesn't mean that U.S. Soccer's higher-ups necessarily agreed. But as discussions dragged on while the federation decided how to proceed and Sundhage sensed hesitancy, she accepted the job to coach the Swedish team.

Whether it was her choice or whether some players forced her out depends on how you look at it. Asked about it now, Sundhage declines to comment.

After Sundhage's last game on September 19, 2012, in Colorado, the video board at Dick's Sporting Goods Park aired a video package of highlights from Sundhage's time coaching the U.S. team. It featured interview snippets, highlights of her famously exuberant goal celebrations, and footage of the team's biggest wins with Sundhage at the helm.

Sundhage sobbed, and many of the players, including Alex Morgan and Lauren Cheney, openly cried as well.

When asked for a goodbye speech, she belted out lines from a Bonnie Tyler song, "The Best."

The crowd broke out into a chant: "Pia! Pia! Pia!"

PART III

CHAPTER 16

"Let's Give This League a Shot, Let's Go for It"

It was October 23, 2012, in East Hartford, Connecticut. The national team had just played Germany to a friendly 2–2 draw on a rainy, cold night, and now they were meeting with Sunil Gulati, the president of U.S. Soccer, in their small, cramped locker room.

There was only one item on the agenda for the meeting: a new women's league. The players had heard the rumblings that a league was in the works. But details on exactly what the league would look like and how it would work were scarce.

Gulati was there to formally present to the players, for the first time, a new model for a women's league: The federation would pay all the club salaries for the national team players. This new model would ease the financial burden on the individual clubs, increase the likelihood clubs could afford to stick around, and ensure all the players earned similar-but-decent club compensation.

It was an exciting idea—a new league for the players to compete in, day in and day out—but the players were immediately cautious.

"A lot of people in that room had played in WPS or the WUSA," Becky Sauerbrunn says. "We knew what a failed league looked like."

Gulati knew that too and had been thinking a lot about it. A few months earlier, he and Dan Flynn, the secretary general of U.S. Soccer, hosted a meeting at the Chicago Hilton with other people who had been involved in women's club soccer. It included Arnim Whisler of the Chicago Red Stars, Michael Stoller of the Boston Breakers, and Alec Papadakis, who was the head of the USL, a lower-tier men's league, and the W-League, a developmental women's league. The meeting was about one thing: figuring out a way to bring women's club soccer back.

"I threw out this concept, and I hadn't talked about it with Dan in advance, and he probably kicked me under the table," Gulati jokes. "But that concept was that the federation would pay the national team players or hire them, however you want to put it."

The initial idea was for the USL to run the league and fund its operations, but after some pushback from the holdover WPS clubs, it was decided that U.S. Soccer would run it. Along with the Chicago Red Stars and the Boston Breakers, Sky Blue FC's owners, including Thomas Hofstetter, signed on. Bill Lynch was the first new owner to agree to be part of the new league, and he would start a team in Washington, D.C. The Western New York Flash signed on, too. A couple of other brand-new clubs were in the works to join the league, as well.

Once the details started to come together, it was time to bring the players on board.

So now, here the national team players sat in East Hartford, Connecticut, being presented with a league and a group of owners, neither of whom they had never heard of or who had been part of the previous failures of women's club soccer in the United States. On top of that, Gulati had not yet hit the minimum of eight teams that he wanted to launch the league, so not all the owners were known yet.

The players were interested—excited, even. It was only a year earlier that WPS had folded and members of the national team grappled with figuring out where to continue their careers. Some played stateside for semi-pro teams; some went to Europe, where the options for women's club soccer had been steadily growing; and some just didn't play club soccer at all.

But they had a lot of questions.

"Are you confident that the owners can afford to do this for the long haul?" Christie Pearce asked.

"No, I'm not," Gulati said.

"Why not?" Pearce replied.

"Because Warren Buffett wasn't interested," Gulati joked.

There was no Philip Anschutz or Robert Kraft or Lamar Hunt among the bunch. There was no one that could afford to fund a women's team forever if they really wanted. But there *was* a group of owners interested in giving it a go. That was the only reassurance Gulati could give the players.

"Everyone was very concerned," Carli Lloyd says. "Who are these owners? What are the facilities going to be like? Is it going be professional in the sense of locker rooms, travel, hotels, and all that?"

Shannon Boxx asked Gulati how the league would avoid the churn that saw young players come into the league and quickly quit. Boxx, before she made the national team, almost became one of those players who quit the WUSA. She had gotten into graduate school at Pepperdine University and planned to retire from soccer entirely, but she decided to stick with it one more year, and April Heinrichs gave her a shot with the national team.

"Players coming out of college might play for a year or two, but if they can't pay their bills or if the clubs aren't good enough, they are going to want to get a better job," Boxx told Gulati.

Gulati admitted he didn't have an answer for that. The players appreciated his honesty, but they were concerned that the league wouldn't be an economically viable option for non–national team players. If players constantly quit and there was constant turnover, the league would never be full of the sorts of experienced professional players who would make it a high-quality, competitive environment.

Another player asked if national team players had to compete in the league.

"No," Gulati said. "If Christie can convince the national team coach that she can stay fit and be a top world-class player by running around a track in New Jersey, then she can play on the national team."

Although the players expressed concerns, the overall sentiment was that they did want a league to play in and they liked Gulati's idea for the federation to support the league. They just needed to know more.

"That wasn't the day where we said, *Okay, we're all in*. As a team, we needed to have further discussions about our participation," Sauerbrunn says. "But I remember leaving that meeting and I was excited. I was hoping it would somehow be different than the previous leagues, even though I was too young at the time to know how it could be different or why."

With the players generally on board, Gulati left that meeting and continued to look for owners to reach the number of teams needed for a first-division league. But they couldn't be just any owners. They needed to be people who had experience running a professional soccer team. There were no more owners from the WUSA or WPS to ask.

When Merritt Paulson, the owner of the Portland Timbers in MLS, got a call from Gulati about starting a women's team for the new league, he was immediately skeptical.

Two other women's leagues had already failed. Maybe the market just wasn't there for women's soccer, he wondered. If the Timbers fielded a women's team and it folded, it could tarnish the Timbers brand. Besides, he had enough going on with the Timbers, who were finishing up a horrible season in which Paulson had fired their head coach.

"My initial reaction was fairly pessimistic," Paulson says. "I didn't give him a no, but I didn't give him a yes, either."

Gulati pushed the idea of the new model for the league. The selling point was that U.S. Soccer's financial backing and oversight would ensure that the league wouldn't face the same troubles as the previous two leagues. The federations from Canada and Mexico agreed to subsidize some of their own players, too.

Paulson was intrigued enough by the model that he told Gulati: "I'll do it if you can get another MLS team."

Gulati had already been trying to do that. He'd spoken with Adrian Hanauer, the majority owner of the Seattle Sounders, who ultimately didn't commit but recruited Bill Predmore, a local businessman who signed on to start the Seattle Reign. He'd also spoken with Sporting Kansas City's co-owner, Robb Heineman, who was interested but asked if Gulati could hold off for another year. Gulati couldn't wait, but instead the Likens family and Brian Budzinski, who already owned an indoor men's soccer team together, agreed to start FC Kansas City.

Eventually, the Vancouver Whitecaps ended up being the only MLS team to say yes—they were not only interested but were going to join the league. That meant Paulson and the Portland Timbers would join, too.

That is, until the proverbial 11th hour, when issues with the Canadian federation made entry into the league more complicated than the Whitecaps thought. Vancouver backed out and Gulati thought the league would have to be put on hold.

"Merritt was in as long as Vancouver was in, but once Vancouver dropped out—and that was late in the game—I thought we were in trouble," Gulati says. "We weren't going to start the league with only seven teams, so I thought we were out of luck."

Paulson wanted an MLS rival to join—Seattle or Vancouver—but continued to think about the idea anyway, even after both declined. There had never been a professional women's soccer team in Portland, but he knew the team at the University of Portland regularly drew large crowds.

Maybe the issue wasn't the soccer itself—maybe the issue was the people behind the scenes running the previous failed attempts at a women's league? Maybe the Timbers could make it work? His wife, Heather, pushed him to do it.

He already knew what it would cost to run a team. Lodging and travel expenses could be estimated based on the Timbers. The budget cap would be low with national team players subsidized by U.S. Soccer.

The Timbers' more than 100 employees could work for the women's team too, meaning the new team would instantly inherit a large, built-in support staff. That offered a distinct advantage over a club like the Boston Breakers, where the club's general manager was not only doing GM-level duties, like scouting and signing players, but was writing the game-day program and handling logistics for sponsorship signage.

The question was whether the revenues could support the costs of running a women's team, which hadn't happened with the clubs in the previous two leagues.

"If I can get comfortable financially with what a worst-case scenario is, then we can manage any negative PR if it's not successful," Paulson told Mike Golub, the Timbers' head of business. "But if we do this, let's launch this thing and not have it be a second-tier product. Let's put our full weight of the organization behind it and give it every chance to be successful."

Their realistic goal was around 5,000 paying fans per game, but they also considered a worst-case scenario of around just 2,000. Financially, they thought they could make it work. After some soul-searching and number crunching, Portland was officially in. The Timbers were set to start a new women's team: the Portland Thorns.

The league now had eight teams. On November 21, 2012, U.S. Soccer announced it was launching the National Women's Soccer League and play would begin in about five months.

Now, there was officially a league—but what it didn't have quite yet was the players of the national team.

* * *

Coinciding with the planning to launch the NWSL was another round of contract negotiations between the national team and the U.S. Soccer Federation.

The national team's collective bargaining agreement expired at the end of 2012, and now the NWSL became a key piece of the negotiations. If getting a contract done was challenging in normal circumstances, the addition of launching the NWSL added a new wrinkle.

The national team hadn't formally agreed to play in the NWSL—there was no contract in place and negotiations were ongoing—but because of the aggressive timeline to launch the league by spring of 2013, national team players needed to start being allocated to teams immediately. The players, who generally wanted the league and had used the same allocation system in the WUSA and WPS, agreed to start choosing their preferred destinations.

Brian Budzinski was sitting at his desk when he noticed Becky Sauerbrunn had started following FC Kansas City on Twitter. The process of matching up players with teams for allocations was only at the beginning. Sauerbrunn, a skilled veteran centerback, would be a defensive piece the team could build around. So, he turned to his partner, Greg Likens, and said, "I think we should DM her and talk to her about Kansas City."

He hesitated to send the direct message at first. Teams were explicitly forbidden from contacting players and trying to influence their allocation lists. The league commissioner, Cheryl Bailey, sent out a memo warning teams not to contact players. Instead, owners were asked to send a presentation to the league, which would then be distributed to the national team players.

But knowing that most of the players on the national team had already played, at some point, for the Western New York Flash, the Chicago Red Stars, the Boston Breakers, or Sky Blue FC, Budzinski determined that the other franchises were probably already secretly in touch with players. He had no contact information for any players, but now that Sauerbrunn and the FC Kansas City account followed each other, the direct message option was available for Budzinski.

So, he pushed some nerves aside, knowing he was breaking the rule, and he DM'd her: "Hey Becky, this is Brian Budzinski and Greg Likens with FC Kansas City. We just wanted to see if you had any questions or had time to chat about our club."

A lot of players were wary of FC Kansas City—the team had a new coach no one had heard of, Vlatko Andonovski, and little was known about the team's facilities except that home games were going to be played at a high school stadium. Some players, like Ashlyn Harris and Ali Krieger, listed it as their one "veto," where they refused to go.

But that DM started a dialogue, and through phone chats with Sauerbrunn, Budzinski and the owners behind FC Kansas City started to realize the sorts of things they needed to offer players.

"The one thing that stood out to us was she asked a lot of questions," Budzinski says. "Her questions and her feedback is the number one reason we had a training location for the team on grass."

This was the sort of minimum-standard issue the national team players would end up spending every season pushing for—an unofficial part of being an allocated player in the NWSL—and the work had already begun before the league even launched.

The allocation process in Portland, meanwhile, went very differently. Merritt Paulson and the Portland Thorns essentially had their pick of the bunch. But it had been established well before the allocation process that the Thorns would be getting Alex Morgan, the most marketable player on the national team. Her preferred destinations included Portland and Seattle, but Paulson targeted Morgan as soon as he agreed to join the league.

"It wasn't a quid pro quo, but I definitely said to Sunil: *If I'm going to be the one MLS team coming, I certainly want to make sure we get some terrific players to build around*," Paulson says. "We had Hope Solo last on our list. So, we had one player that we didn't want anywhere near the team, and then Alex was the big ask for us."

By January 2013, U.S. Soccer had announced its list of allocated players. After taking into consideration the top choices of each player, the players were matched to clubs. The process was complicated by the fact that many players wanted to go to the same teams, with the Portland Thorns and the Seattle Reign being the two most popular choices. The Western New York Flash and FC Kansas City, meanwhile, had few takers, but lucked out that Abby Wambach, who was from Rochester, New York, agreed to go to the Flash in her hometown and Sauerbrunn, who was from Missouri, agreed to go to Kansas City.

"Allocation was a big issue for the players," says Gulati. "And what we ended up with in terms of the players' preferences was pretty incredible. Around 75 percent of them got their first choice, and 20 percent got their second choice."

The league was moving full steam ahead. But for at least some players, it was moving too fast. They worried that they were being allocated to teams they knew nothing about and they were stuck asking to play for specific teams based on little information.

"With all this new excitement about the NWSL, there was still massive concern amongst the players," says Hope Solo. "We didn't know the ownership groups, we didn't know the cities, we didn't know the venues, we didn't know the trainers—things that are important to players. U.S. Soccer wanted us to choose what cities we want to play for without knowing the coaches and the venues. It was counting our chickens before the eggs, you know? This is our profession."

* * *

Now that the NWSL had become part of collective bargaining agreement negotiations because the players would be contracted by U.S. Soccer to play in the league, there was a new sense of urgency. The players had already been allocated to play in the NWSL and they still needed a contract.

The players needed to feel comfortable with the unknown league. The possibility loomed that they could be locked into playing for these unfamiliar clubs or risk their national team status. There was urgency, too, from the federation, which wanted a firm commitment from the players that they would play in the league.

By the time the national team prepared to compete the 2013 Algarve Cup in late February and early March, collective bargaining agreement negotiations had ramped up considerably. With the team's existing contract having been expired since the end of 2012, the players were also no longer bound by the no-strike clause in their contract and a boycott was on the table.

In February 2013, while the team was in Nashville for their final friendly match before the Algarve Cup started, discussion turned to whether they should go on strike and skip the upcoming tournament in Portugal.

"We decided as a team that we want to go on strike to get more money for our new CBA, and we were going to go on strike until we understood everything about the NWSL, before we were forced to decide which team to play for in allocation," says Hope Solo. "There were a few players in the room that didn't know how to vote, but the rest of the team raised our hands and said it's time to take a stand."

Everyone was on the clock, though. The NWSL's preseason camps were set to start during the Algarve Cup, and if the national team went on strike, it could've cast the entire launch of the NWSL into uncertainty.

Ultimately, the strike never happened. Some players felt, after speaking with the team's attorney, John Langel, that striking before the Algarve Cup didn't offer enough leverage. They were better off going to Portugal and continuing negotiations there with striking as an option after the tournament, before the start of the NWSL. They believed the launch of the new league offered the urgency that could make a strike effective.

For Solo, who pushed for the strike, it was frustrating to see her teammates back off so quickly. Even though the Algarve Cup was a relatively minor tournament, it was the biggest national team event on the calendar until the 2015 World Cup, two and a half years away.

The advice of the team's longtime attorney to forgo the pre–Algarve Cup strike amounted to taking the federation's side, as far as Solo was concerned. By that point, she had already lost faith in Langel's ability to fight for the team and months earlier had started, on her own, looking for someone else who could represent the team.

"It was really empowering for us. We finally were taking a huge stance against U.S. Soccer—we said, *We're putting our foot down, we're going on strike, we mean business*," Solo says. "Well, it took about one phone call from John Langel to scare us into backing down and not going on strike."

"It was a moment where I realized that if we can back down that easily and we can get intimidated, then U.S. Soccer has the upper hand on us at all points in time because it didn't take that much," she adds. "We had the courage to say we were going to go on strike, and then, within a few days, we decided, no, we'll get on the plane and play in Portugal."

During the Algarve Cup, discussions within the team continued and Langel met with U.S. Soccer for negotiations while the players were out of the country. By the time they got back, they were close to a deal with U.S. Soccer that would cover them both in the NWSL and in case the league folded.

Striking was still on the table, but the players no longer felt it was necessary. Asked about a strike, U.S. Soccer president Sunil Gulati says he was never made aware that the team was considering it.

In the end, the contract the two sides agreed to offered large increases in compensation for the national team. If the NWSL couldn't get off the ground, salaries would go up between $13,000 and $31,000, depending on each player's tier. But with the new league in place, salaries would stay almost the same while players would get an extra $50,000 NWSL salary. On top of their guaranteed income, more money than ever was available through performance bonuses and a $1.20 cut of every national team game ticket sold that would be put into a team pool.

In the end, the biggest sticking point, however, wasn't the compensation—it was locking the players into the NWSL. It became a requirement in their national team contract, and there was no backing out if the players didn't like their club teams.

"The issue with the NWSL was commitment," says Langel. "The players had to make a commitment that they essentially would play in the league for two of the four years of the contract. That, in the end, was the big concern."

The final contract left them with one of two options: They could play abroad and then join the NWSL for the 2015 and 2016 seasons, or they could play in the NWSL immediately and have the option to play overseas in 2015 or 2016.

For the national team players who could get offers from European teams owned by wealthy top-tier men's clubs, like Paris Saint-Germain and Olympique Lyonnais, it could be a lucrative option. Megan Rapinoe, for example, signed a contract to play in France before joining the NWSL on a $14,000-per-month salary—far more than she could earn playing for an American club. But the players wanted to grow the game at home in the United States and committed themselves to the NWSL.

It was a bit of a leap of faith on the players' parts—not just to agree to play in this league that they didn't know much about but to tie it so directly with their national team contracts. For the players, who wanted a league and saw it as vital for the growth of the women's game, it was worth taking the chance.

"As with most things in our team, it came down to a vote," Becky Sauerbrunn says. "And the vote was: Let's give this league a shot. Let's go for it."

With the NWSL preseason already underway, the contract the federation and the players agreed to was a memorandum of understanding—a hasty replacement for a full collective bargaining agreement—to speed the process along. That MOU wasn't as complete as maybe it should've been, but at the time, it was seen as the best the two sides could do before the launch of the NWSL. One week after the NWSL's preseason started, the national team players signed their new contract and started to join their new NWSL clubs.

"If we had another six months, could we have gotten more clarity on some of the points? That's always the case," Gulati says now. "Deadlines matter in CBAs—most deals get done in the 11th hour, and it was the case with this one."

As much as the players went out on a limb to help launch the league, the federation did, too. On U.S. Soccer's part, it was a significant investment in the women's game, and the federation spent almost $250,000 just getting the league operations started in 2013. That investment would grow year to year, and with operations and all the national team player salaries combined, U.S. Soccer eventually put $10 million into the league over the course of its first six seasons.

The national team did its part to push the federation to want to invest. The team made back-to-back finals in the World Cup and the Olympics, winning gold in London, and the popularity of women's soccer was on the rise. U.S. Soccer needed to keep that going. After all, the organization's mission statement was "to make soccer, in all its forms, a preeminent sport in the United States and to continue the development of soccer at all recreational and competitive levels."

The league would go on to outlast its architect, Sunil Gulati, who left the federation in 2018 after the men's team failed to qualify for the World Cup. While the WUSA and WPS had lasted just three years each, the NWSL is going strong into its seventh season in 2019. One big reason for that has been U.S. Soccer's investment. Clubs don't need to pay the salaries for their biggest stars, the players of the national team.

The federation could've continued to focus on hosting residency camps for the national team, but that would have benefited only a limited set of players. A league, rather, would have a wide-ranging positive impact on the growth of the women's game—that's why U.S. Soccer had been willing to invest as much as it did in the NWSL.

"The benefits of residency are for a small group of players in preparation for an event. The benefits of a league, if you can make it work, are far beyond that," Gulati says. "You're developing markets, you're developing coaches, you're developing referees, you're developing administrators, you're developing fans across the country for the women's game. For everything other than the short-term technical preparation of the national team for a competition, it's a far better setup."

* * *

On April 21, 2013, when the Portland Thorns prepared to host their first-ever home game, there was a big-game feel at Jeld-Wen Field.

Fans who had experienced the passionate and vibrant supporters' culture of the Timbers brought it to the Thorns and welcomed the players from the stands with a huge red-and-white banner display known as a tifo. They waved flags and chanted "P-T-F-C!" for a women's team that hadn't existed a few months ago.

As the players stood on the field for the national anthem, some of them looked around at the crowd, astonished by how it filled all parts of the stadium. In all, 16,479 people showed up. It was almost triple the crowd of the NWSL's debut match a couple of weeks earlier at FC Kansas City.

Cindy Parlow Cone, a former national team player who played in both the 1999 and 2003 World Cups, was the coach of the Thorns. Rachel Buehler, a national team defender for the Thorns, looked at her coach and said: "This is like a World Cup!" As Parlow Cone told reporters later, she agreed: "That's what it felt like. It felt like that atmosphere we had at the World Cup and the Olympics."

Something special had clearly been born in Portland that day—and it was only the beginning.

The worst-case scenario Merritt Paulson set for his new women's team was around 2,000 paying fans per game. The best-case scenario was about 8,000. Their average attendance in 2013 ended up being 13,320. It went on to grow every season, and in 2017, the average attendance was almost 18,000—a staggering number, especially because it was larger than the average turnout for some MLS teams that had been around for decades.

The Thorns were profitable immediately—a first in women's club soccer in the United States. Gulati, seeing the success of the Thorns, asked Paulson if he'd be open to a profit-sharing arrangement with the rest of the league. Paulson initially scoffed at the idea.

"Should we be throwing safety nets to people who should be doing better on their own?" Paulson asked him. In the spirit of growing the league, however, Paulson eventually agreed to set aside $150,000 to be distributed to the rest of the teams in the league.

But as much as the Thorns' sustained and growing success offered hope for the future of the league, it also created a new dynamic that hadn't existed to such an extreme extent in the previous leagues: On one end sat the Thorns, with plenty of resources and the ambitions to match, but on the other end were independent owners who couldn't come close.

"It was apparent to me that the failures of past efforts were more complicated than a simple product issue," Paulson says. "These weren't operators who were dealing with a lot of resources—they didn't have the facilities. There's also a lot of blocking and tackling that's sports business 101 that a lot of them weren't doing."

When Jeff Plush became the NWSL commissioner in 2015, one of the first things he noticed was that divide. There was a sharp contrast between the owners who had been part of failed women's pro leagues and the owners who hadn't.

"The thing I wasn't as prepared for but learned quickly was that there are scars from the previous two leagues and the people involved in those leagues," Plush says. "They were scared of the future a little bit. Getting people to align on an ambitious vision and knowing it's going to take some time was difficult."

A large part of Plush's job involved fielding multiple daily phone calls from owners around the NWSL about various issues. When it came to the divide between ambitious owners and cautious owners, he admits he "spent a lot of time trying to navigate that."

"Initially the league and the other owners were really grateful we stepped up and that the Thorns had changed the outlook of the entire NWSL," Paulson says. "There weren't the constant questions about the viability of the league. There was a certain appreciation for that, but there was probably a bit of jealousy as well."

Paulson, the most vocal and ambitious owner of the bunch, quickly took on a leadership role of his own making and started recruiting other MLS teams to join the NWSL. First was the Houston Dynamo, who founded the Dash and joined as an expansion team in 2014. Then Orlando City founded the Pride, another expansion team, which joined in 2016. As more MLS teams entered the league, the dynamic began shifting in the NWSL boardroom.

Small independent owners had trouble keeping up and started to fall by the wayside. The Western New York Flash were sold to North Carolina FC, a lower-division men's team, and the Flash relocated to Raleigh as the North Carolina Courage. FC Kansas City, after an ownership change, was taken over by the NWSL for failing to meet minimum standards and acquired by Real Salt Lake, who reestablished the team as the Utah Royals.

The surest sign of that ongoing shift arrived when the Boston Breakers, the longest-running women's soccer club in the United States, folded in 2018. The last remaining team from the WUSA was gone.

Owners around the NWSL who decline to speak on the record say Boston had continually missed payments and relied on the rest of the teams to make up for their budget shortfalls. But there was a concern among the league's other owners about the optics of losing a team so early into the league's history. By the NWSL's sixth season in 2018, the increasingly MLS-heavy board of NWSL owners decided the league could afford the hit of losing the Breakers after efforts failed to convince Robert Kraft of the New England Revolution to take over the team.

"It's painful to know that some of the people that have been the fiercest, longest-term proponents of women's soccer can't afford to be part of this anymore," says Arnim Whisler, owner of the Chicago Red Stars. "They're getting crowded out and pushed out. That's hard to watch."

But for the players of the national team, who committed to the NWSL and may have given up lucrative options at powerhouse clubs in Europe, minimum standards were increasingly becoming an issue.

Sky Blue FC didn't have on-site showers in their locker rooms, lacked an equipment manager, and parked a camping trailer at their practice field to provide bathrooms. FC Kansas City played on carpet-like turf at a high school field their first year. The Washington Spirit didn't have a dedicated training room—instead it was just a section cordoned off with curtains in a big multisport area at the Maryland SoccerPlex where there were vending machines and volleyball courts.

For Ali Krieger, who played at the Washington Spirit until 2017, her job as an allocated player extended well beyond simply playing soccer. She ended up having to confront the team's front office to ensure flights didn't have multiple stops or weird hours that would hurt the team's performance for away games. She had to make sure the hotels were clean and in good locations. Small things, like what kind of meals would be provided or whether the players had raincoats, also became concerns she took on.

"You're just like, this isn't my job and I'm having to speak up for things, and at this level, you shouldn't have to—you should just show up for your job and focus on doing it well," Krieger says. "When you leave a national team camp and come back to the NWSL, it's like: *Wow, we really need to do something here.* Each year, you're chipping away and chipping away."

Krieger's experience wasn't unique among national team players. Becky Sauerbrunn recalls that teams would travel without the league minimum of players. Hope Solo recalls a lack of medical equipment and trainers throughout the league. Ashlyn Harris recalls being given one Spirit training top for the whole season that she had to take home and wash every day.

Across the NWSL, national team players had taken on the extra burden of pushing for better standards that would benefit every player in the league. It was a process that started when Sauerbrunn first got on the phone with the owners of FC Kansas City, and it continues to this day.

"These are little things that we didn't want teams to get away with, because it was affecting all the players," Sauerbrunn says. "So we had to keep pushing the level of professionalism higher and higher."

* * *

As time has gone on, the league has seemed to get stronger.

In 2017, A&E Networks bought a 25 percent stake of the NWSL— a deal that sources say was worth eight figures—and started airing games live on Lifetime. It was a major step for the league—after all, in 2013, clubs had to contribute around $40,000 each to pay Fox Sports to air playoff games on the network's soccer-focused cable channel. The influx of millions of dollars from A&E allowed the league to immediately double its minimum salary for non-allocated players from a paltry $7,200 to $15,000 per season.

But the biggest changes in day-to-day standards for NWSL players have come as the league has welcomed more committed, experienced franchise owners who happen to be very wealthy. The blueprint that started in Portland was spreading, and fewer national team players were forced to speak up against poor treatment.

When Orlando City looked at the NWSL, much of their guidance came from the Timbers organization and Merritt Paulson, who shared their financial figures. Orlando City president Phil Rawlins said the

Pride would follow the Thorns model, which involved treating the women's team like an important part of the overall organization—not a niche, ancillary product or an afterthought. The Pride were immediately profitable.

For players like Ali Krieger and Ashlyn Harris, who moved from the Washington Spirit to the Orlando Pride, the difference in professionalism was huge. The addition of the Pride in 2015 forced the rest of the NWSL to be better.

"They set a standard," Krieger says. "They were like: *Look everyone, this is what we're providing, what are you providing? This is the way they should be treated. This is the way professional atmospheres should look. Here's our model. You guys need to keep up or get out.* That's why it's great if more clubs are resembling our model."

Adds Harris: "The professionalism is night and day. It's run like a professional club should be run. They're just as involved with the women's team and the men's team."

Not every MLS-backed team has managed to have the success of the Portland Thorns or the Orlando Pride. The Houston Dash, backed by the Dynamo, are not yet profitable after joining the league in 2013. They aren't far off, but club president Chris Canetti admits they had hoped they would be there by now.

"We thought the financial picture would be a little bit better than what it has been in our first few years of operation," he says. "It's been a little more challenging than what we thought when we put this together as a concept five years ago."

Still, the NWSL has continued to attract more MLS owners that have strengthened the league.

When it became clear the league needed to oust the struggling FC Kansas City franchise in late 2017, it was Paulson who first called Dell Loy Hansen, the owner of Real Salt Lake in MLS and convinced him to take over the team. Within two weeks, Sauerbrunn, a player who constantly had to worry about whether FC Kansas City was providing a professional environment for her and her club teammates, was in Utah looking at blueprints for a new locker room.

That locker room for the Utah Royals, RSL's new women's team, would be designed as the heart of the team's operations—a place players could get medical treatment, lift weights, watch game film, and have meetings. At FC Kansas City, nothing close to that existed—the players shared their facilities with youth teams in the Kansas City community, and the trainers had to set up and break down their equipment every day.

It may seem like a small thing, but it showed that Hansen was fully committed to following the model Paulson created: The Utah Royals and Real Salt Lake would be placed on equal footing.

Now, clubs that can't provide the same standards risk being left further behind. But at the same time, many of these clubs are run by the people who have supported women's club soccer in the U.S. the longest. The NWSL, which is still young at just seven years, still needs to figure out what kind of league it'll be in the long term. It is already the most competitive in the world and has expanded the national team player pool, but where does it go from here?

"You don't ever want to be the one holding the league back," says Arnim Whisler, owner of the Chicago Red Stars. "You don't want to be the one where players won't play in that market because the facilities are bad or what have you. You can't operate if you're not able to be a core part of the league. That's every year what we continue to look at."

The bigger question for the NWSL, however, may be who will continue to run the league.

Sunil Gulati, the NWSL's chief architect, left as U.S. Soccer president in 2018. U.S. Soccer's current management agreement to operate the NWSL ends at the end of 2019. Such agreements have been set to expire and renewed several times already, but sources at the federation say the plan was never for U.S. Soccer to run the league forever. Eventually, they want the NWSL to put together a viable exit strategy so the management agreement can end.

The NWSL's owners and representatives from A&E want the same thing. They have explored ways to take control from the federation, including meeting with executives from USL and MLS about absorbing the women's league, per sources. For NWSL teams, it has become obvious that the federation prioritizes the national team over what's best for the league. That has created conflicts, particularly when the federation pulls the league's stars out of NWSL games for nonessential international friendly matches.

What the NWSL would look like if U.S. Soccer didn't run it is still unclear. Talks are preliminary enough that it appears, for now, that the federation will have to renew its management agreement into 2020.

For its first several seasons, the focus for the league was merely on surviving and not turning into another WUSA or WPS. But now, with a more stable crop of ownership groups, the focus will begin shifting to a longer-term vision.

CHAPTER 17

"I Cannot Comment Further at This Time"

Tom Sermanni wasn't looking to leave his post as the head of the Australian women's national team in 2012.

The job was an ideal fit—he had full autonomy over the way he managed the team, and he found success folding young talent into the Australian player pool. Under Sermanni, the team flourished and broke into the top 10 of FIFA's world rankings and stayed there.

But when the U.S. hosted Australia for a pair of friendlies for Pia Sundhage's final two games at the helm of the team, U.S. Soccer president Sunil Gulati and secretary general Dan Flynn approached Sermanni. They wanted to speak to him informally about the job that was opening up with the U.S. national team.

That's not something any coach would say no to—the U.S. job was perhaps the most coveted in all of women's soccer. So Sermanni met with the U.S. Soccer higher-ups a few times over the course of the two games, in Los Angeles and then in Denver. After the informal conversations, U.S. Soccer asked the Australian federation for permission to formally interview him for the job.

"The first thing they said was that they wanted to win the World Cup," Sermanni says of the interview process. "That was the blunt part of the discussion."

The part that wasn't so blunt had to do with the style of play of the American team. As far as Sermanni could tell, U.S. Soccer liked the way he had continually regenerated the Australian team and integrated young players to build a fast, "positive" attacking style of play.

The players in Australia also seemed to get on very well with Sermanni, and it was easy to see why. His laid-back attitude and penchant for one-liners delivered with a smile—complete with his salt-and-pepper hair and mustache—called to mind more a lovable father figure than a dictatorial coach.

Sermanni isn't Australian, as his thick Scottish accent gives away, but he finished his own playing career there and turned it into a coaching career, working his way up from coaching boys' youth teams to the Australian women's national team. Somewhere in between, he coached in the WUSA for the New York Power, where Shannon Boxx and Christie Pearce played.

On October 31, 2012, U.S. Soccer announced that Tom Sermanni would take over as coach of the national team.

"He has a tremendous passion for the game, knows the American players, understands our system and knows the process of preparing a team for a World Cup tournament," said U.S. Soccer president Sunil Gulati.

But the national team, which had gotten used to a certain style of leader, was in for an adjustment period. It didn't take long for it to become clear how Sermanni was going to change things within the national team.

* * *

On February 13, 2013, Tom Sermanni named Sydney Leroux to the starting lineup for a friendly versus Scotland. Leroux had 29 caps and 15 goals with the national team already, so he didn't think much of the decision. But Jill Ellis, his assistant coach, noticed something he hadn't.

"You've got to say something to Syd," Ellis told him.

"What do you mean?" Sermanni replied.

"Well, this is her first start," said Ellis.

Sermanni was confused for a moment. "Hasn't she got 30 caps?" he asked incredulously.

"Yeah, but she's never started a game," Ellis told him.

Sermanni admits now he was "gobsmacked" when he realized Leroux had never started. She had set a national team record for the most goals scored by a substitute player, but Pia Sundhage never deviated from using her as an off-the-bench substitute.

At first glance, Sermanni seemed a lot like Sundhage, who had one of the most successful runs of any head coach of the national team. Both were affable characters who were considered players' coaches, and each managed to keep the mood light.

But on the field, their styles were almost opposite. She was headstrong, where he was hands-off. She was rigid, where he was flexible. She clung to a core group of veterans, while he gave new players chances. She liked to use the same lineup over and over, and he was always tinkering.

As the 2014 Algarve Cup arrived, Sermanni had given 12 players their first caps and fielded almost a new lineup every game. Sermanni suggested the player rotation would continue, even when the 2015 World Cup arrived the following year.

"I don't think this World Cup is going to be about a starting 11," Sermanni said. "I think there's been a notion in the U.S. that there is a starting 11, and I think we're very much in a situation where it's a squad game. So, the starting 11 is potentially going to vary even when we get to the World Cup."

If new players were getting minutes, that meant, in some cases, that veterans were not. Abby Wambach saw her playing time diminished in favor of the likes of Christen Press, who got her first cap under Sermanni, and Sydney Leroux. Wambach pushed Sermanni to consider a different attacking formation that would use more forwards, but he refused, she admitted to reporters.

But whatever Sermanni was doing seemed to be working just fine. In 15 months on the job, he was unbeaten. Leading up to the 2014 Algarve Cup, the U.S. nabbed wins against key opponents like Germany, Brazil, Canada, and Mexico, among others. There was every indication the Americans would continue their dominance.

Meanwhile, Sermanni hadn't really talked to U.S. Soccer about the direction of the team since he was interviewed for the job. As far as he knew, they were happy with how the team looked.

He says now: "I didn't have an awful lot of discussions with U.S. Soccer, to be honest. I just did my job. Maybe I should've had more."

But he didn't, and then the 2014 Algarve Cup started. Everything was about to change very quickly.

* * *

The Americans opened the Algarve Cup with a draw to Japan. But in the next match, which happened to be against Sweden and Pia Sundhage, the U.S. lost for the first time under Sermanni. Sweden won 1–0, but only after Abby Wambach failed to convert an early penalty kick.

The loss marked the end of a 43-game unbeaten streak for the Americans, 22 of those games under Sundhage and the next 21 games under Sermanni. A U.S. national team that looked practically invincible had finally been beaten, even if just barely.

But, as it turned out, the loss was only a preview of what was to come.

In the next game, Denmark stunned the Americans by scoring three goals before the half. Whenever it looked like the Americans might come roaring back—Christen Press, Sydney Leroux, and Megan Rapinoe all scored goals—Denmark also came back and scored. The match ended 5–3, and the Americans seemed shell-shocked by the result.

The match was a weird one, to be sure. Still, to this day, Sermanni can't really explain it except to say soccer is susceptible to weird results sometimes.

"Denmark is one of those games you can't explain," he says. "Every time they went up the field, they scored a goal."

The loss to Denmark set some dubious milestones. It was the first time the U.S. had ever given up five goals in a single game. It was also the first time they'd lost by two goals since 2008, when they lost to Norway to open the Olympics but eventually went on to win gold. The match also marked the first time the U.S. had lost two games in a row since 2001.

"It was just one of those tournaments," Sermanni says now. "When you get to a tournament and things start to go wrong, it's sometimes hard to turn them around and get them back on track as quickly as you'd like."

The U.S. rebounded with a win over North Korea in their final match of the tournament, but it was small consolation. The Americans finished the tournament in seventh place, their worst-ever showing in an Algarve Cup.

In the grand scheme of the national team, the poor Algarve Cup performance appeared to be nothing more than a small blip. Minor setbacks were inevitable, and the team had come back from bad games before.

But the players started hinting publicly that maybe the results were part of a larger problem.

"We haven't really been playing the way we normally play," Wambach told *Sports Illustrated*. "I think there's been a lot of factors. I know Tom likes to switch up the lineup quite a bit, which is very different than what we've been used to. So, learning how to play with new players game after game after game, it's harder to get a rhythm. That's why our team has always been so successful—because I always know exactly what Alex Morgan is going to do."

Morgan, who was injured and not in Portugal for the Algarve Cup, said she had spoken to her teammates who were at the tournament and delicately hinted the team wasn't in a good state. Echoing Wambach's comments, she suggested Sermanni's constant rotation could be to blame.

"I think the girls are a little bit down in Portugal right now, but I think Tom and the coaching staff and the players all need to get together and work something out because the lineup changes could be a factor," Morgan said. "I've gotten a lot of texts and calls from them and I really hope to be back with them soon, but they're going through a rough time and so I hope they pick it back up."

After that, it appeared the national team was putting the results behind them. Following the Algarve Cup, they were set to host China for a pair of friendlies the next month. It should be back to business as usual.

*　*　*

It was April 6, 2014, on a sunny afternoon in Denver, Colorado. Tom Sermanni had just led the national team to a convincing 2–0 win over China. So when Sermanni met with U.S. Soccer president Sunil Gulati and secretary general Dan Flynn, the furthest thing from his mind was that he may have just coached his last game at the helm of the U.S. national team.

The meeting was a short one. Gulati and Flynn told Sermanni that the federation needed to go in another direction and he was being relieved of his duties as head coach of the national team. They didn't get into specifics, but they said the team environment wasn't working and they hadn't seen the progress they wanted on the field.

Sermanni was blindsided. At the time, he had no idea there were any concerns with his leadership, and still to this day, he doesn't know how he could've seen it coming. There had been no conversations beforehand outlining concerns. No warnings that the federation expected anything other than what Sermanni was doing.

His wife was out of the country, and he lucked out that when he called her to tell her the news, she answered the phone. If she hadn't gotten his call, she would have found out from someone else— Sermanni said the news of his firing was shared on social media immediately after his meeting with Gulati and Flynn.

"That was the part of it where I felt a distinct lack of respect for the organization, because they did that poorly," he says. "It was poor for the organization to do it the way they did. I have no qualms with what they did, but it could've been done better and more professionally, and there could've been something done prior to that happening rather than it suddenly flying out of the blue."

One by one, after Sermanni got the news, the players came up to his hotel room in Colorado to say goodbye and thank him for his time. Abby Wambach was the first player to come to his room.

Later, U.S. Soccer president Sunil Gulati told reporters he consulted with players before the decision to fire Sermanni. The Algarve Cup results were a factor, but they were not the sole reason or even the main reason—rather, the poor results brought to light other concerns. Gulati declined to reveal how the conversation with players started—whether they approached him about a coaching change or the other way around.

But rumors of a player revolt of sorts had already been spreading. After all, players had pushed out national team coaches before. Even if there were no confirmed reports, Sermanni's constant rotation of new players and the sudden nature of his firing led to such speculation. Wambach vehemently denied it, telling reporters: "Everybody out there who may think the players made this happen, none of it's true."

Alex Morgan later admitted, though: "Many of the experienced players felt they hadn't been pushed enough, and they thought the coaching staff's expectations of them had noticeably dropped. It was as if Tom thought there was enough talent on the team that we didn't need to keep fighting. Being too relaxed and not nurturing that ultracompetitive, hard-driven culture caused us to drop games."

Sources now say some of the players actively pushed for the change and initiated some of those conversations with Gulati. The federation was forced into a decisive action because the World Cup was only a year away. In that sense, Sermanni's exit from the team wasn't all that different than the coaches who had come before him. Pia Sundhage, Greg Ryan, and April Heinrichs all ended up leaving the national team, on some level, because of players who wanted a change.

As the focus switched to who would take the job next, Heather O'Reilly told reporters the team needed a coach who was a better "cultural fit." Gulati, asked about that, said she was "probably referring to someone that can take a very strong leadership position." Julie Foudy, now an analyst for ESPN, reported from player sources that Sermanni's "laissez-faire" style didn't sit well with the team.

Looking back now, Sermanni seems to agree with that.

"I needed to be more forceful in managing my way," Sermanni says. "When I think about it in hindsight and how I believe a team should be managed, I should've been more forceful in what I do best. It wasn't about me changing—it was about me being more decisive."

"I didn't get a handle on some of that stuff until it was too late," he adds.

Although his rotation of players was the root of some consternation at the time, Sermanni's legacy may very well be in all the youth he integrated into the team.

Players like Morgan Brian, Julie Johnston, Crystal Dunn, Christen Press, and Lindsey Horan eventually developed into starting fixtures for the team, and Sermanni had given them all their first caps. In some cases, he seemed to spot something special—Brian, for instance, had been a college player at the University of Virginia and with the U.S. under-20 team before he called her into the senior team and quickly saw a player who could play a big role at the 2015 World Cup. Dunn was an attacking player he'd identified as an outside back, a position she would later reprise long after his exit.

With Sermanni's departure, Jill Ellis, who had held various positions within U.S. Soccer, took over as the interim replacement while U.S. Soccer looked for a permanent coach. Ellis had turned down the job after Pia Sundhage left—Ellis had just adopted her daughter and felt the timing wasn't right. But by now, she wanted it.

So Ellis interviewed for the job with two other finalists who were well-known to U.S. Soccer—the surest sign that the federation wasn't taking any chances on another outsider. Tony DiCicco was interviewed but ultimately eliminated from the running. The federation's final decision came down to Ellis or Tony Gustavsson, a Swede who had been Pia Sundhage's trusted assistant coach when the national team won gold at the 2012 Olympics.

In the end, U.S. Soccer hired both—Ellis was named head coach, and Gustavsson, who wanted to continue to live in Europe, was named an assistant coach with the task of scouting players abroad.

In Ellis, U.S. Soccer had someone who had coached almost every single player on the national team over the course of her previous jobs, which included coaching some of U.S. Soccer's youth national teams and the UCLA Bruins. The players knew Ellis and were comfortable with her, and her style was one that focused heavily on tactics and giving clear roles to players.

"She was a modern coach, utilizing video analysis and statistics in a way Tom hadn't," Alex Morgan later said.

But Ellis didn't get to settle into the job too long before one of the biggest controversies in the national team's history struck.

* * *

On June 19, 2014, the national team had a friendly versus France in East Hartford, Connecticut. It was the second in a two-game series against one of the best teams in the world just one year out from the 2015 World Cup—an ideal tune-up match to see where the national team stood.

Hope Solo normally would've started in net for a game like this. She had 152 national team appearances and, in the game before, she had just tied Briana Scurry for the team's all-time shutout record. But on this day, the starting goalkeeper was Ashlyn Harris, who had appeared in only two other national team matches before.

Solo was officially listed as "unavailable due to a family commitment." She was supposed to be available in time for a Seattle Reign match in Rochester, New York, three days later, but she never made it to that NWSL game.

After an incident the evening of June 20, 2014, Solo was arrested and charged with assaulting her 17-year-old nephew and her half sister.

The media picked up on the sordid details of the police report immediately. It revealed, at best, a drunken fight of sorts. The alleged victims in the case called Solo the instigator, saying she punched her nephew in the head with closed fists. Solo denied hitting anyone and said her half sister hit her over the head with a broomstick. Police observed bruises and scrapes on Solo's relatives, while Solo refused to let police inspect injuries she might have, and Solo was arrested.

The misdemeanor fourth-degree assault charges were given the "domestic violence" tag because the alleged victims were family—even though Solo didn't live with them and they told police they had been estranged until relatively recently. The "domestic violence" label was attention-grabbing fodder for the media, though. Columnists rushed to compare Solo with Ray Rice and Greg Hardy—two male NFL players who had recently been accused of horrific assaults on their female significant others—and demanded that Solo be kicked off the national team.

Once the details of the arrest started to make the rounds, Solo posted a message online apologizing for "an unfortunate incident" but vowing she would be cleared of the charges, even if she couldn't share her side of the story:

Due to pending legal issues, I cannot comment further at this time. However, I am confident in the legal process and believe my name will be cleared.

Sunil Gulati, the president of U.S. Soccer, said he spoke with Solo and read the apology she posted online but the federation would hold off on reprimanding her.

"We have to wait and see what happens with the legal process," he told media before adding: "We would much prefer to have her in the news for great goalkeeping performances than anything else."

Solo promptly went back to starting games for the national team and looking like one of the best goalkeepers the world had ever seen. She even wore the captain's armband on September 18, 2014, in honor of the fact that she had set a new shutout record for the national team. All the while, media outlets slammed U.S. Soccer for it because her assault case was still unresolved.

The case against Solo didn't seem particularly strong—the alleged victims were not cooperating and it looked like it would probably be dismissed. In December 2014, that's exactly what happened, although prosecutors vowed to appeal.

The good news for the national team, at least, was that now the distraction of Solo's legal issues was in the past and the team could focus on the Women's World Cup, which was now only a few months away.

But that didn't quite happen. On January 19, 2015, Solo made headlines again.

She was at the national team's annual January camp outside of Los Angeles when she allowed her visiting husband, Jerramy Stevens, to drive a U.S. Soccer–rented car. Stevens had been drinking and was pulled over after police allegedly saw the car swerving off the road. Stevens was arrested on DUI charges, and Solo, who was the passenger, was reported to have been "belligerent" toward the arresting officers. The federation didn't know about the incident until celebrity tabloid TMZ reported the news.

After the federation had been slammed by the media for not punishing Solo throughout the episode surrounding her arrest, there was little choice this time. Solo was suspended from the team for 30 days. Her suspension was scheduled to end about four months before the World Cup was set to start.

"During our current national team camp, Hope made a poor decision that has resulted in a negative impact on U.S. Soccer and her teammates," coach Jill Ellis said in a statement. "We feel at this time it is best for her to step away from the team."

By this point, Solo was hardly a stranger to controversy within the national team.

The world had seen how she'd criticized Greg Ryan's decision at the 2007 World Cup and was kicked off the team. During the 2012 Olympics, she'd called out Brandi Chastain, who was a commentator for NBC, tweeting: "Lay off commentating about defending and goalkeeping until you get more educated @brandichastain. The game has changed from a decade ago." Now, her arrest and assault charges were front-page news.

But there was a history within the team of things involving Solo that needed to be dealt with, even if they were never made public. Pia Sundhage admits she had to deal with a couple of issues while she coached Solo, but she didn't let it become the focus of what she was doing.

"There were one or two things, but you have to be respectful, you have to be smart, and you have to just talk to people," Sundhage says. "We worked it out. We wanted to train. We wanted to improve the game."

A couple of players who ask not to be identified say Solo had broken team rules about curfew more than once. They remember a specific incident during a tournament where Solo spent the night with her boyfriend instead of in her assigned room. These players say they told Sundhage, who chose not to punish Solo rather than turn it into an ordeal.

On the flip side, Hope Solo was the greatest goalkeeper in the world. Sometimes what makes an athlete so great on the field can be the same thing that causes them problems off the field. Could you have Solo, the top goalkeeper, without Solo, the troublemaker? With a few months until the World Cup, there were more pressing questions at the moment, though. What if prosecutors revived Solo's case and she was convicted? What if she got into trouble again? Would the federation have to suspend her?

Could the USA win a World Cup without Solo?

CHAPTER 18

"I've Dreamed of Scoring a Shot Like That"

Even before the players of the national team knew their opponents for the 2015 World Cup, they were already in a back-and-forth battle.

This time it was with FIFA, the organization that oversees soccer throughout the world and organizes the Women's World Cup. FIFA, along with the Canadian Soccer Association, or CSA, planned to put every game of the 2015 Women's World Cup on artificial turf, something that had never been proposed for a senior World Cup before, including all 20 men's World Cups prior.

Artificial turf has become a necessity in some climates where it's hard to maintain grass or at venues that need to stand up to constant use. Where natural grass isn't a viable option, artificial turf is the next-best alternative. But generally, soccer is supposed to be played on natural grass.

Players report getting injured more and recovery time taking longer when they play on artificial turf. Some studies have supported this perception, while some have been inconclusive. But when Sydney Leroux posted a photo of her legs covered with bloody scrapes from slide tackling on artificial turf, it was a clear example of why there's a consensus among soccer players. Kelley O'Hara responded to Leroux's photo: "You should probs tweet that to FIFA."

It may be less of an issue in other sports, but in soccer, turf can be especially hard on a player's body.

"Not only are they long-lasting injuries, but there are long-term effects of playing on turf," Alex Morgan once explained. "The achiness, taking longer to recover than on natural grass, the tendons and ligaments are, for me at least, I feel more sore after turf. It takes longer to recover from a turf field than natural grass."

For this reason, some players with leverage have refused to play on artificial turf. When superstars Thierry Henry and Didier Drogba joined MLS clubs after careers in Europe, where artificial turf is rare, they refused to play at venues without natural grass. Grass also offers a better quality of ball movement and natural bounces, while artificial turf can negatively affect the flow of the game. In other words, soccer is meant to be played on grass, and that's especially true during a World Cup, the most important tournament in the sport.

When Canada's bid, which included artificial turf fields, was selected by FIFA for the 2015 World Cup, the decision flew under the radar at first.

"You get used to just saying, *Oh, that's kind of messed up*, and you go on with your day," Heather O'Reilly says. "But sometimes it takes people to make a big deal about it."

With the help of attorney Hampton Dellinger, the national team realized they should try to stand up against the decision. They brought in players from other national teams around the world, including Germany, Brazil, Mexico, and others to sign a letter asking FIFA and the CSA to reconsider using artificial turf.

When that didn't work, they filed a complaint with the Human Rights Tribunal of Ontario, arguing the decision to play the tournament on artificial turf was gender discrimination under Canadian law. After all, no men's World Cups had ever been played on artificial turf, and the upcoming men's tournaments had been planned to be on grass through 2022.

"The reality is, the men would never play the World Cup on field turf," Abby Wambach said after the complaint was filed. "So for me, it's a women's rights issue—it's an equality issue."

Of course, FIFA treating the Women's World Cup like it was less important than the men's event wasn't new.

Take, for instance, the prize money that FIFA offered the winners. For whoever won the 2015 World Cup, a $2 million team prize was on the line. If that seems like a lot, it shouldn't—the German men's team won $35 million for winning the 2014 World Cup. That's roughly six cents on the dollar for the women. The last-place men's team at the 2014 World Cup earned $8 million, four times what the winner of the 2015 Women's World Cup would earn.

FIFA may have been a so-called not-for-profit organization that was heading into the 2015 Women's World Cup with around $1.5 billion in cash reserves, but FIFA secretary general Jérôme Valcke argued the women would have to wait 13 more World Cups to see the sort of cash prize the men get.

"We played the 20th men's World Cup in 2014, when we are now playing the seventh Women's World Cup," Valcke said. "We have still another 13 World Cups before potentially women should receive the same amount as men."

In other words, only at the 2067 Women's World Cup would the women be eligible to win as much money as the German men's team did in 2014.

The prize money certainly said something about FIFA's priorities, though. The same week the 2015 Women's World Cup kicked off, *United Passions* debuted in movie theaters. It was a propaganda film that FIFA produced about itself and bankrolled for around $30 million. That's double the total amount of prize money FIFA made available to all teams participating in the 2015 Women's World Cup.

The film earned less than $1,000 in its debut weekend in North America, for the worst box-office opening in history, and it went down as the lowest-grossing film in U.S. history. Almost all the millions of dollars FIFA poured into making the movie was lost. The film has a 0% rating on the popular movie-review-aggregation website Rotten Tomatoes, and a *New York Times* review called it "one of the most unwatchable films in recent memory."

And remember the uncomfortable encounter at the team hotel between the Americans and Brazilians after the 2007 Women's World Cup semifinal? That would never happen in a men's World Cup.

That's because FIFA assigns different hotels and training facilities to each men's team, to serve as a base camp throughout the tournament. The women don't get base camps—they jump from city to city and from hotel to hotel during the World Cup, and they usually end up bumping into their opponents, who are given the same accommodations. American coach Jill Ellis said she almost walked into the German meal room at the World Cup once.

"Sometimes you're in the elevator with your opponent going down to the team buses for a game," Heather O'Reilly says. "It's pretty awkward."

FIFA may have not shown they cared about the Women's World Cup much, but the lawsuit the women filed over artificial turf looked promising. A group of 13 U.S. senators, all Democrats, wrote to FIFA, urging the organization "to begin good faith negotiations with these athletes, free of retaliation and with the equal treatment that they deserve." Celebrities, including Tom Hanks and Kobe Bryant, amplified the cause.

But when the players' request to fast-track the issue was rejected by the Human Rights Tribunal in late 2014, it became clear there probably wouldn't be enough time to resolve the issue before the tournament was set to start. Four months before the kickoff of the World Cup, the players withdrew the case so they could focus on preparing for the tournament.

"We regretted that we didn't step up earlier in the process," O'Reilly says. "But we were glad we brought it to light because hopefully it will never happen again. You could say we lost, but in the grand scheme of sports, it will always be better because we put our foot down and said, *This isn't good enough.*"

The 2019 Women's World Cup in France will be on grass, and the players believe FIFA will think twice before trying to put another tournament on artificial turf.

* * *

On December 6, 2014, the players filed into a meeting room at their hotel in Brasília, Brazil. The World Cup in Canada was still six months away and the team was preparing, but they didn't know who they were preparing for. That's why they were in this room: to watch the 2015 Women's World Cup draw live.

The draw, like always, started by placing the host country, Canada, and the five other best teams into six separate groups. This would ensure that the best teams, plus the host country, wouldn't need to face one another until the knockout rounds. Then, one by one, teams from different regions throughout the world were randomly selected into the groups.

The Americans were seeded into Group D. Then they started learning their opponents.

The first team drawn into Group D with the Americans: Nigeria. The Super Falcons, as Nigeria is known, had proven to be the top team in Africa after having recently won the Women's African Football Championship just a couple of weeks earlier. Most concerning, however, was that the national team was largely unfamiliar with Nigeria, having last played them back in 2007.

"Nigeria was a wild card," Becky Sauerbrunn says. "I had never played Nigeria before."

Then, Australia was called as the next opponent of the group. The national team players looked at one another with some concern. After all, if Nigeria was a mystery, Australia was anything but—the Americans knew how fast and energetic the Australians were and how much effort it took to beat them. The Matildas, as the Australian team is known, was the best non-seeded team in their confederation.

Finally, the players watched on the screen as the last ball for Group D was chosen out of the bin and the little strip of paper was unfurled: Sweden. The entire room erupted with groans and laughter. The Americans shook their heads in disbelief. Sweden was the toughest team that could've been drawn into Group D and, unlike Australia and Nigeria, the Swedes had beaten the Americans many times before. Ashlyn Harris jokes that her reaction was a quick one: *"Oh shit."*

After the initial laughter in the room, then came a smattering of claps and shouts of "All right, let's do this!" The players now knew their fate, and they had to prepare for it.

The coach of the Swedish team was Pia Sundhage, the woman who just three years before had coached the Americans to an Olympic gold medal and knew as well as anyone what their weaknesses were.

Deservedly, Group D was quickly nicknamed "The Group of Death" because it contained the toughest combination of teams in the entire tournament. With the American players knowing their fate, the march toward the Group of Death began—if the national team wanted to win its first Women's World Cup since 1999, this was how they had to do it.

Luckily, the national team knew they had Hope Solo. Prosecutors in Solo's hometown had successfully been granted an appeal—a rare and unusual step for a misdemeanor—and it brought her assault case back to life. But the trial wasn't scheduled to proceed until September, well after the end of the World Cup.

The story stayed in the news, however, as ESPN dug further into the details of the arrest and aired a documentary about it right before the World Cup started. But the legal issues themselves wouldn't keep Solo off the field, and if the Americans wanted to win a World Cup, they were going to need her.

Expectations were certainly high. In Winnipeg, where the national team was set to play its first two group games, the hotel occupancy rate was 100 percent for the dates of their games due to Americans flocking north. Some USA fans were forced into unusual accommodations, like college dorm rooms or sleeping in cars, just to watch the U.S. team in the World Cup.

The pressure was on. American fans expected their team to step up and were about to flood Canada.

* * *

By the time the group stage arrived for the 2015 Women's World Cup, there was one question everyone wanted to answer: Can the USA still dominate?

After all, women's soccer was now the best it had ever been. More federations were investing in their women's programs and the competition was better overall. Being faster or fitter wasn't going to be enough anymore, but the Americans still relied on a direct approach that focused on outpacing and outmuscling opponents. The 2015 World Cup would also be the most grueling iteration of the tournament because it had expanded from 16 teams to 24, adding an extra round of knockout games to the competition.

The group stage in Canada didn't provide any reassuring answers. The Americans did score first in their opening match vs. Australia, but it was a half-chance from Megan Rapinoe that took a lucky deflection. Before that, Hope Solo had been called on to make a spectacularly acrobatic save. They eventually routed Australia, 3–1, but Solo was the hero of the match more than any of the goal-scorers.

"Hope came up absolutely huge for us," Rapinoe said afterward. "I think she had three saves that nobody else in the world could make."

A pair of tight, unconvincing outings next against Nigeria and then Sweden were concerning. The Americans couldn't control the midfield, the possession was sloppy, and the attack wasn't clicking. If they could beat Nigeria by only 1–0, and if they could only settle for a scoreless draw versus a Sweden team that looked out of sorts, how could they possibly advance through the knockout rounds?

"It wasn't clicking at the beginning and we knew that," defender Ali Krieger says. "We're not stupid. You understand how you're playing— you can see it and you can feel it. But we were like, *We still have to win.*"

The Americans may have looked unconvincing, but it didn't matter—they topped Group D anyway. True to the team's identity, they found ways to get results. The Group of Death, however, turned out to be a Group of Disappointment—Sweden, the USA's most-feared opponent, looked underwhelming and missed the right balance of defense and offense.

By winning the group, the Americans headed down a favorable path where they faced a low-ranked Colombia, but again they played poorly. On paper, a 2–0 win in the round of 16 should've looked good, but in truth the match was a slog that turned in the USA's favor only when Colombia's goalkeeper was ejected with a straight red.

A sampling of headlines from news outlets after that match:

- Lackluster Efforts at World Cup Bound to Catch up to Americans (*USA Today*)
- The U.S. Women's National Team Is a Shell of Its Former Self *For the Win* (a *USA Today* blog)
- Clueless Coach Threatens to Torpedo World Cup (*New York Post*)
- USA Faces Flak for Dated Tactics (*Reuters*)
- What's Going on with the USWNT? (Empire of Soccer)
- The US Women's World Cup Team Has a Goal Problem (*Newsweek*)

Jill Ellis maintained a positive attitude in her postgame press conference, saying that she was "pleased" with the win—but that only added fodder for the loudest critics of the team. Michelle Akers, the retired legend who won the Golden Boot in the national team's 1991 World Cup win, told reporters: "If she is pleased with the way we played tonight, then what the hell is she doing coaching our U.S. team?"

It was clear something wasn't working. The Americans were struggling to play the ball through the central midfield to create dangerous scoring chances in front of goal. Luck was turning their way, but luck usually runs out at some point.

Ellis, for her part, never read or followed any of the criticism. Instead, the entire team stayed in what she called a "bubble" where outside forces couldn't affect them.

"I don't read stuff when we win, and I don't read stuff when we lose. Why? Because I was there," Ellis says. "I know how it felt, and I know what it looked like. The only people I worry about and care about is the players."

The questions about their lackluster performances had started to become routine for the players passing through the mixed zones after practices and games in Canada. The players uniformly said the same thing: They know they can play better, they are not worried, and, no, they don't listen to what the critics have to say.

But with Carli Lloyd, who stuck to the same message as her teammates, there was a hint of frustration. Lloyd is the kind of player who wants to take a game by the scruff of the neck and win it all on her own. She hadn't been able to do that.

"We're just following the direction of our coaches, the coaching plan, doing everything they ask of us," Lloyd said after the Colombia game. "At the end of the day, I've got full faith and confidence in everyone that we'll find our rhythm. We're working, we're grinding—the effort's there."

The Americans didn't know it yet, however, but that win over Colombia was serendipitous in an unexpected way. Yellow cards given to both Lauren Holiday (née Cheney) and Megan Rapinoe meant that Jill Ellis would be forced to change her tactics. The team was about to fix all of its midfield problems.

A blessing in disguise was about to save the USA's World Cup. It was about to unleash Carli Lloyd.

Up to that point in the tournament, Lloyd had been asked to play alongside Lauren Holiday in an ill-defined central midfield partnership. Neither one of them was a defensive midfielder, and neither one of them was an attacking midfielder. They were expected to split those duties between them on the fly. That not only led to gaping holes and poor positioning in the midfield, but it restrained Lloyd, who throughout her career was best as a pure attacking player who could push forward without restraint.

With China up next in the quarterfinal and Holiday suspended, Ellis turned to 22-year-old Morgan Brian and asked her to play as a holding midfielder behind Lloyd. It was something Brian had never done before—Brian, like both Holiday and Lloyd, spent her career as an attacking player. The game figured to be decided by how well that roster choice played out.

The first half against China certainly looked better from the Americans, even though China had bunkered as the most defensive team the Americans would face. The U.S. had plenty of scoring chances and China had none, but the match remained scoreless at halftime.

In the huddle before the second half, Abby Wambach shouted loud enough for live television cameras to hear: "We start fast and we keep the faith! In the first 10 minutes, we get a fucking goal!"

It took only five minutes. Lloyd, pushing high toward the goal, put her head on a cross that China's goalkeeper couldn't get a hand on. The player who scored game-winning goals at the 2008 Olympics and the 2012 Olympics finally had her first a goal in the run of play during the 2015 World Cup. She insisted she was far from done.

"I don't want to just be a participant in the World Cup," Lloyd told reporters, almost defiantly, after the win over China. "I want to have a legacy. I want to have people remember me and let my play do the talking."

Morgan Brian credited Lloyd with leading the way in the attack.

"The coaches told me to hold a little more and let her do what she needs to do," Brian said. "That way Carli feels like she can attack more, and that's good because we needed that."

Looking back on it now, years later, players credit the change in the midfield—a change spurred by yellow-card suspensions—as being the turning point.

"Sometimes there are these pairings on the field that work better," says Ashlyn Harris, the backup goalkeeper at the World Cup. "It doesn't matter how great you are. We all know Carli Lloyd is one of the best of all time—every time she's on the field, she's making things happen. But if she's not connecting and pairing with other people there, now you have two players who aren't playing at their best. Sometimes you have to make changes to get those great connections on the field."

Now that Holiday and Rapinoe were eligible to return to the lineup, Jill Ellis would have to find a way to keep a good thing going. Germany, who waited in the semifinal, had dominated the tournament thus far, scoring a whopping 20 goals and allowing only three through five games.

Could Ellis get Lloyd, Holiday, and Brian on the field together? She could, but only by abandoning the 4–4–2 formation she had clung to up to that point. She switched to a 4–2–3–1 formation, which subtracted one striker and replaced her with a central midfielder. That allowed Lloyd to tuck in behind go-to striker Alex Morgan, sit in front of Brian and Holiday, where she could roam wherever she wanted, and prowl for goals.

It mostly worked. Both Morgan and Lloyd were electric in creating chances and testing the German back line. But this was Germany—the No. 1 team in the world after bumping the USA down the FIFA world rankings months earlier—and a breakthrough wasn't coming easily for either side.

By the 59th minute, the match was still scoreless when German striker Alexandra Popp ran down a lofted ball into the box. Julie Johnston, chasing, tugged her from behind. Popp fell, and the whistle blew. Penalty kick for Germany.

This was it. This was the moment, it seemed, the Americans would lose the World Cup. It was a given, of course, that Germany would score this penalty kick. The Germans never missed in moments like this, and a goal would shift the momentum of the match.

Hope Solo did the only thing she could do: stall. As Célia Šašić stepped up to the spot to take the kick, Solo sauntered off to the sideline slowly and got her water bottle. She took a sip. Paused. Scanned the crowd. Another sip. She strolled back slowly toward goal. She still had the water bottle in her hand. She wanted to let this moment linger. She wanted Šašić to think too much about the kick and let the nerves of the moment catch up to her.

Finally, Solo took her spot. The whistle blew, and without even a nanosecond of hesitation, Šašić ran up to the ball and hit it, as if she couldn't bear another moment of waiting. Solo guessed to the right, and Šašić's shot was going left. But it kept going left and skipped wide.

The pro-USA crowd at Olympic Stadium in Montreal erupted into a thunderclap that made the stands shake. The American players cheered as if they had just scored a goal.

"We knew right then and there that we were going to win the World Cup," Ali Krieger says. "That was it. That's when we knew: *This is ours.*"

Johnston, meanwhile, was in tears. She had just almost cost her team the entire tournament, and she was shaking. Her teammates urged her to snap out of it—there was still another 30 minutes left in the game.

"We all went to JJ and told her, you need to get it together and you need to focus," Krieger says. "She was crying, and we were like, *Fucking get it together—let's go!*"

When a similar penalty was called just six minutes later—Annike Krahn fouled Alex Morgan in the box—the Americans had Carli Lloyd step up to the spot.

Lloyd was the exact opposite of Šašić. She didn't break her focus from the ball, staring at the spot where she was going to hit it and ignoring everything else around her. When the whistle blew, a composed Lloyd calmly stepped up and smashed it into the back of the net.

The Americans didn't need their second goal to punch past the Germans, but Lloyd set it up anyway in the 84th minute. She danced her way through the German defense as if they were traffic cones and then slipped the ball across goal, where Kelley O'Hara got a foot to it.

Afterward, when Johnston spoke to reporters in the mixed zone, she was crying again.

"That was probably every defender's worst nightmare. It happened so fast," Johnston said. "The team definitely lifted me up after that moment happened. I really can't thank them enough and I'm sure I'll thank them all the way to the final."

But Lloyd? No longer burdened by a formation and a role that didn't fit her style, she was free to go full throttle and do whatever she damn well pleased.

As she put it herself: "I was a little bit restricted in the beginning games. I wasn't able to express myself."

Now, Carli Lloyd was unleashed.

* * *

The national team was on the precipice of winning their first World Cup trophy since the 1999 team did it 16 years earlier. The '99ers couldn't help but notice how different it was.

The 2015 World Cup was setting new television viewing records even before the final match because people wanted to see the soccer. Tactics and player performances were scrutinized carefully by the media. The coach, Jill Ellis, was being criticized by fans who expected better.

"We're talking about them as athletes, rather than some of the conversations we had in '99: *My god, who are these women? They're kind of hot!*" Julie Foudy said.

After the team won in 1999, the players turned into one-of-a-kind heroes, pioneers, and role models overnight. Many people rooted for them as a larger statement about women in sports. But by 2015, the players of the national team were athletes that America grew to love simply as athletes.

If fans were going to be jubilant about a victory in the 2015 World Cup final, it wouldn't just be because of some deeper meaning or greater impact—it would be because fans knew these players and wanted them to win. It was evidenced by Alex Morgan's almost 2 million followers on Twitter, Hope Solo's autobiography becoming a *New York Times* bestseller, and Abby Wambach appearing in Gatorade television ads on heavy rotation.

No longer did the players need to show up at schools and youth clinics to hand out flyers, like the 1999 team did. The word about the national team was already out. In the team's three May 2015 send-off games, they sold out every match, drawing capacity crowds at Avaya Stadium, the StubHub Center, and Red Bull Arena.

Consider what Foudy told reporters in 1999 after the World Cup win: "It transcends soccer. There's a bigger message out there: When people tell you no, you just smile and tell them, *Yes, I can.*" By 2015? Players like Carli Lloyd were talking about world domination. It was all about the soccer—and that, in and of itself, was something special and powerful.

There was just one more game of soccer left. It was set for a familiar foe: Japan.

The storyline was almost too perfect: It was a do-over—a rematch of the 2011 World Cup. Finally, after four years, the Americans could make it right and shake away the ghosts of 2011 by securing victory over Japan. Vindication was on the line.

In truth, though, the American players didn't feel that way at all. The Americans didn't dwell on the past, and they had a lot of respect for Japan. Going against Japan, if anything, added some comfort to the final. The Americans had been here before—they had played Japan many times and knew their style well.

The Japanese could tiki-taka opponents to death—they were known for quick, short, one-touch passes and an endless supply of patience. If the Americans liked to bulldoze their way up the field with direct long balls and use brute force to score goals like a battering ram, then Japan played the opposite game.

One of the things the Americans knew was that the Japanese weren't strong on set pieces. They didn't have a lot of height or muscle for those kinds of chaotic scrambles in the box. But Tony Gustavsson, an assistant coach to Jill Ellis, saw something else.

For the Nigeria game, Gustavsson had designed some short corners—plays where instead of launching a ball in the air, a short pass is played—that hadn't worked at all, but he had a different idea for the World Cup final versus Japan. He thought the U.S. could spread the Japan defense with an unusual play. The team practiced his new set-piece play just once before the final.

* * *

When game day arrived and the players walked to their team bus, fans had already crowded the outside of the Sheraton in downtown Vancouver and had to part to form a path for the players to walk through. The players held their hands out to give high fives as the fans chanted "U-S-A! U-S-A!"

Meanwhile, fans in USA colors were marching down nearby Robson Street singing the popular American chant, "I believe that we will win!" They held up scarves, waved flags, and danced. Block by block, more fans joined until they all couldn't fit in the middle of the street anymore and took over the curbs and sidewalks, too. By the time the moving mass of red, white, and blue arrived at BC Place, it became apparent that most of the 53,341 fans in the stadium were Americans. Even though the game was in Canada, it *felt* like a home match.

The team huddled up like it normally does, and Abby Wambach, who was participating in her last World Cup, offered some final motivational words, as usual. But she didn't need to say much. As Becky Sauerbrunn puts it: "We all knew what was on the line."

In only the third minute, Tobin Heath won the U.S. their first corner kick. It was time to try that unusual set-piece play they'd practiced once the day before. Lloyd stood just a few steps off of the center circle—well outside the box, seemingly uninvolved in the play—and as Megan Rapinoe got set to strike the ball, Lloyd started sprinting toward the goal. Instead of the usual ball lofted through the air, Rapinoe sent a low skipping ball into the box. It was about to be cleared by Azusa Iwashimizu at the near post, but Lloyd darted in front of her at the last moment and flicked the ball toward the far post with the outside of her foot. Goal, USA!

Lloyd ran over to the American Outlaws, the singing superfans of the U.S. national team, and fist-pumped as her teammates jumped on top of her. Jill Ellis patted Tony Gustavsson and smirked.

Two minutes later, the Americans got a free kick from a wide position—another set piece—and Japan hadn't learned their lesson. Again, Lloyd was left unmarked outside the box. This time, Lauren Holiday lined up to take the kick, but again, it was a low, driving strike instead of the usual air service. Lloyd, looking for a seam to run through unnoticed, ran for the back post this time. Julie Johnston got to Holiday's ball first but flicked it past her with a nifty back heel tap. It fell for Lloyd again, who smashed it. Goal, USA again!

Lloyd ran from the goal to the American bench on the other end of the field and brought all the substitutes in for a group hug.

The players shouted at one another to stay calm. One of the most popular clichés in soccer is that 2–0 is the most dangerous lead. It's easy to assume you have a match won already and take the foot off the pedal.

That's how leads are blown—by complacency. The Americans weren't going to let that happen in a World Cup final.

The clock hadn't even hit the five-minute mark, and the Americans were already up by two goals. Fans who were still taking their seats after getting through the bottlenecked lines for admission probably did a double take at the score. The Japanese team huddled together, trying to regroup.

President Barack Obama would later joke that the match was over as soon as he sat down to watch it at the White House: "I had gotten my popcorn, I was all settling in. I'm thinking I've got a couple hours of tension and excitement and—poof! It was over."

BC Place was rocking. Chants of "U-S-A! U-S-A!" rung around the stadium. Then the fans started chanting, "We want three! We want three!" Whether they wanted three goals or a third World Cup win, it wasn't clear, but they would get both.

It took a mere eight minutes more for the Americans to score again. On a poor clearance from Azusa Iwashimizu, the ball popped into the air and Lauren Holiday tracked it until it fell. She later said the ball looked huge at that moment, and she smashed it for a gorgeous volley. Goal, USA! The score was 3–0, and the clock had not yet hit 14 minutes.

It was right about at this moment that the match took on a surreal feeling. Everything was falling the Americans' way. A Japan team good enough to land in the final looked stunned and unsure of what to do. But the game hadn't reached its peak of absurdity. That would take about another 30 seconds.

Lloyd got the ball in the USA's half. She turned and flicked it past a Japanese defender and then ran around the player to receive the ball, almost as if Lloyd passed it to herself. When she got the ball back at her feet, she picked her head up and noticed goalkeeper Ayumi Kaihori was way out of goal.

In a moment of pure audacity, Lloyd took a full swing at it from the center line and kicked the ball nearly 50 yards. Kaihori desperately tried to scramble back in place but could barely get a hand on the ball. Goal, USA! It was the sort of goal that was so brazen it would happen once in a while in a random high school game—no one would ever try such a thing in a World Cup.

But Lloyd did. She had a hat trick . . . in 15 minutes . . . in a World Cup final. That sort of performance on the world's biggest stage was simply unheard of. It looked like the USA had been playing a video game on easy mode.

Hope Solo, who had precious few touches by that point, ran from her goal to hug Lloyd, something the goalkeeper rarely did. She looked at Lloyd and said: "Are you even human?!"

"I've dreamed of scoring a shot like that," Lloyd later said. "I did it once when I was younger on the national team in a training environment. Very rarely do you just wind up and hit it. When you're feeling good mentally and physically, those plays are just instincts and it just happens."

Now, Ali Krieger jokes that the most exhausting part of the final was celebrating Lloyd's goals: "We had to chase Carli after she scored all her goals. I was like, *Can she not run around the entire field?*"

There was still another 75 minutes left to play. It didn't matter. Those 75 minutes would end up as a footnote on Carli Lloyd's stunning performance—one of the most dominant displays in a championship game anywhere, ever. The Americans won the World Cup, 5–2, but it was the performance of a lifetime for Lloyd.

When the whistle blew, Lloyd dropped to her knees and cried. Heather O'Reilly ran from the bench straight to Lloyd and slid into her. Soon all the players found their way to one another for a frantic mishmash of hugs.

Afterward, in the post-match press conference, Japanese coach Norio Sasaki told reporters: "Ms. Lloyd always does this to us. In London she scored twice. Today she scored three times. So we're embarrassed, but she's excellent."

Lloyd, for her part, almost downplayed the performance. She believed she could've scored one more goal.

"I visualized playing in the World Cup final and visualized scoring four goals," Lloyd said. "It sounds pretty funny, but that's what it's all about. At the end of the day, you can be physically strong, you can have all the tools out there, but if your mental state isn't good enough, you can't bring yourself to bigger and better things."

* * *

This time, when the players stepped into the locker room, no one had to remove all the protective plastic wrap. Goggles were handed out to players so they didn't get champagne in their eyes.

They danced, shouted, and doused themselves in booze, just like the world champions they were. They took turns passing around the World Cup trophy and posed for photos.

Tobin Heath, with tears in her eyes, told reporters after stepping out of the mayhem for interviews: "It's wild in there."

The players didn't know it quite yet, but their win was historic—not just because they were the new world champions but because of the match's impact.

The USA-Japan final was watched on television by a whopping 25.4 million Americans, smashing the TV record for the most-viewed soccer game by an American audience. Even more stunning, 43.2 million Americans watched at least part of the final.

It beat every game of the NBA finals, happening around the same time, and beat the primetime average of the Sochi Olympics the year before. With 39 percent higher ratings, it destroyed a record set by the U.S. men's team when it faced Cristiano Ronaldo and Portugal during the 2014 World Cup group stage. The 1999 World Cup final, which had held the record for 15 years before that, had been watched by 17.8 million Americans.

On social media, the moment was just as big. According to Facebook, 9 million people posted 20 million interactions to the platform about the final during the game. Tweets about the tournament had been seen 9 billion times across all of Twitter, with the final match earning the most engagements. Carli Lloyd's half-field goal was the most-tweeted-about moment of the match.

The national team's victory touched millions of people—and that probably included plenty of little girls who had no clue who "the '99ers" were and never saw Brandi Chastain twirl her shirt in the air. For the first time, millions of young girls saw the women of the national team as heroes.

Just like that, a new generation of female soccer players was created. Statistical analysis has shown that events like a Women's World Cup encourage young girls to sign up for sports. U.S. Soccer's own analysis showed that after the 1999 Women's World Cup, registration numbers among girls boomed, especially in the cities that had hosted World Cup games. In all likelihood, the future stars of the national team were watching the 2015 World Cup final.

"I think every little girl who watched last night believes that they can do this and inspire a nation," coach Jill Ellis said the next day. "That's what they've done. Remarkable."

Before the team flew back to the United States with the trophy, they first had to take a phone call from President Barack Obama.

"Carli, what have you been eating?" he said. "I want to do what you're doing."

When the team landed in Los Angeles, it was off to a huge victory rally that filled downtown LA.

"They only had 24 hours to tell people about it. I thought, *Hopefully we'll get a couple thousand and some of my family will come*," Alex Morgan said. "But they were cramming in there like sardines. There were so many people."

New York City wanted to honor the players, too. Mayor Bill de Blasio announced that the city would hold a ticker-tape parade for the players, making them the first women's team ever to be given the historic celebration.

Within two days, there the players were at Battery Park on their respective floats, waiting for the parade to start. They couldn't see up Broadway and had no idea just how many people were waiting to catch a glimpse of them.

Then, the procession turned the corner. The sidewalks were packed 30-people deep in places—and it continued all the way up Broadway as far as the eye could see. There were thousands and thousands of people lining Broadway into the horizon.

"We turned onto the street and it was like, *Are you fucking kidding me? All these people are here for us?*" Ali Krieger says, laughing.

None of the players had seen anything quite like it. Office workers on Broadway were opening their windows and throwing paper shreds out. The air was filled with paper, floating over the parade route like some sort of festive fog.

When the parade reached its destination, City Hall, the players got off the 12 floats they had been riding. They waited in a room at City Hall, finally together again and able to talk about what they'd just seen, and the players became emotional. Some players were crying. Some were in shock.

"I never quite understand the following this team has until it's thrown in my face, and the ticker-tape parade epitomizes that," says Becky Sauerbrunn, who has nearly 150 caps for the USA. "I was like, *Is anyone going to be at this parade? What if no one shows up?* It blew me away."

CHAPTER 19

"It Is Our Job to Keep on Fighting"

In the days after the national team won the World Cup, the players were the most in-demand athletes in the entire country.

After a sleepless night in Vancouver following the final, they did a round of media for Fox Sports, the broadcaster of the World Cup, and then zipped off to Los Angeles for a victory rally that U.S. Soccer had set up for the next day. Two days later, they needed to be in New York City for an appearance on *Good Morning America* and the ticker-tape parade.

Within 24 hours of the parade, U.S. Soccer expected the players to report to their clubs in the U.S. Soccer–backed NWSL for games the very next day. For the players, who had been on the road and flying across the continent for more than two months nonstop, it was a harsh request. They had to be in Los Angeles again in four days for the ESPY Awards, and in less than a month, a 10-game victory tour across the country was scheduled to start.

"We weren't allowed to go home first. We were at the mercy of whatever media appearances they wanted us to go to," goalkeeper Ashlyn Harris says. "It was more exhausting after the tournament than during it. You didn't have a choice—it was mandatory."

The players weren't upset to have all these obligations. There was genuine excitement amongst the team that people across the country wanted to celebrate their success. But everything was taking a toll, and not everyone on the team was convinced that the players' interests were being put first.

Hope Solo couldn't help but notice that Don Garber—the commissioner of MLS, the men's pro league—was on one of the floats for the national team's ticker-tape parade. When it came time for the rally outside City Hall at the end of the parade route, many of the people who came up to the podium to speak were as expected: Mayor Bill de Blasio, coach Jill Ellis, and U.S. Soccer president Sunil Gulati. But the commissioner of the NWSL, Jeff Plush, who was there, never got up to speak. Instead, Garber spoke after de Blasio.

MLS was one of the corporate sponsors that helped New York City pay for the parade, but representatives from Nike and EA Sports, who sponsored the parade as well, didn't get up to speak.

"Things just didn't look right," Solo says. "Everywhere we looked it was Don Garber, it was MLS, it was U.S. Soccer's sponsors. It wasn't necessarily about us when they were using our success to promote MLS and U.S. Soccer but not the women. It felt like they were using us."

Another mandatory appearance the next day at NWSL games didn't make sense to players who were exhausted and needed a break. Usually leagues build gaps into the schedule for major tournaments— international breaks, they are called—but the NWSL played through the World Cup. Many members of the national team wouldn't be able to play in their NWSL games the next day anyway, with such a short turnaround from both playing in the World Cup and the cross-country travel, and players generally don't go to games they can't play in. So, that's what the players told U.S. Soccer.

"They wouldn't work with us at all," Solo says. "They demanded that every player had to be at her NWSL game that weekend."

Coming off the World Cup win with the most leverage they'd ever had, the players felt confident enough to push back.

"When we put our foot down, I think they got a little bit nervous," Solo says. "They said, *Okay, what will it take to get you guys at all the NWSL games this weekend?*"

In the end, the federation treated it as an appearance fee of sorts. The players would get $10,000 each to attend their NWSL games, and they would be flown first-class, a distinct upgrade from their usual travel. It was a relatively small victory, but it set the stage for the players to stand up for themselves more assertively. The women of the national team proved they were the best in the world, they captured the country's attention, and now they had leverage.

"It was really the first time where we were like, *Okay, we are worth something to the federation and we know it, so now we have to keep this going*," Solo says. "That's what really empowered us. All of a sudden, we got a $10,000 fee, first-class tickets to fly to our NWSL games, and it was right before we were going to negotiate our new contract."

But things didn't get better just because the federation paid the players a $10,000 fee. In less than a month, the players had to set out on the road again for a 10-game victory tour as World Cup champions and, as it turned out, the venues weren't exactly befitting of a World Cup–winning national team.

Eight of the 10 victory-tour games in 2015 were scheduled on artificial turf. Over the course of that year, U.S. Soccer scheduled the women to play 57 percent of their home games on artificial turf but scheduled zero of the men's games on artificial turf. In fact, the men played at five venues that had artificial-turf surfaces, and in all five cases, the federation paid to have temporary grass installed.

The last time the federation had scheduled a men's home friendly match on artificial turf had been in 1994. In that same time span since 1994, the women played dozens of U.S. Soccer–hosted matches on artificial turf. Now, even as World Cup winners, they were stuck on turf again.

"It just wasn't good enough," says Carli Lloyd, who has more than 250 caps. "Here we are, world champions, we come home and not only do we have to play all these games on artificial turf, our current CBA says we have to play 10 games to earn another bonus. We won the World Cup, great, but in order to earn a bonus, we had to play 10 games. We just thought the whole structure of it wasn't good enough and we needed to change a lot of things."

The crowds that greeted the national team on the victory tour were unprecedented for inconsequential friendly matches. On August 16, six weeks after the World Cup ended, more than 44,000 people packed Heinz Field in Pittsburgh to see the U.S. steamroll past Costa Rica, 8–0. When, in the following game, they sold out Finley Stadium in Chattanooga, Tennessee, with a crowd of 20,535—for a 7–2 win over Costa Rica—the federation tried to schedule upcoming games in larger venues. In Birmingham, Alabama, nearly 36,000 people showed up at Legion Field on September 20 as the U.S. beat Haiti, 8–0.

But while U.S. Soccer was making a windfall with higher ticket prices, the players didn't see anything from it other than the $1.20 per ticket they'd negotiated in 2013. While U.S. Soccer's merchandise for the national team flew off the shelves, the players didn't get anything from that. The team's popularity was surging, but they weren't in any position to capitalize on it.

"I thought it was bullshit," says defender Meghan Klingenberg, who played every minute of the 2015 World Cup as a left back. "All these people are making money from our likeness and our faces and our value, but we're not. We're only getting money from our winnings, and that doesn't seem right."

"We didn't have any rights," she adds. "We had basically assigned our likeness rights, for sponsorships and licensing, to U.S. Soccer to do with them whatever they wanted."

The final straw for the players was a game scheduled in Hawaii at Aloha Stadium during the victory tour. No one from U.S. Soccer had gone to inspect the facilities before scheduling the national team to play there. The practice field was grass, but it was patchy, bumpy, and lined with sewer plates that had plastic coverings. It was on that sub-par practice field that Megan Rapinoe tore her ACL, which meant she might have to miss the 2016 Olympics the next year.

Then, the next day, the players got to the stadium where they were supposed to play the game. Not only was it artificial turf, but the players were concerned by the seams on the field where parts of the turf were pulling up off the ground. Sharp rocks were embedded all over the field. If someone from U.S. Soccer had been there beforehand to inspect it, there's no way they could've believed it was an appropriate venue for a national team soccer match.

The players unanimously agreed to boycott the match and stand up to the federation together. The federation officially cancelled the match, and Sunil Gulati, the president of U.S. Soccer, publicly apologized, calling it "a black eye for this organization."

The players seemed more determined than they had been in a long time to fight for themselves.

"The team needs to be a little more vocal about whether this is good for our bodies and whether we should be playing on it if the men wouldn't be playing on it," Alex Morgan said after the Hawaii cancellation. "We've been told by U.S. Soccer that the field's condition and the size of the field are the first two talking points of when they decide on a field, so I'm not sure why eight of our 10 victory tour games are on turf whereas the men haven't played on turf this year."

* * *

Though winning the 2015 World Cup finally gave the players the confidence to speak up in a way they hadn't before, the groundwork had been laid the year before. The players were ready to start changing tactics in their contract negotiations, and that's when they fired John Langel, the man who had led the national team through their most important previous legal battles.

It happened in September 2014. By then, some of the players had already felt the deal negotiated under Langel's guidance a year earlier didn't do enough.

The deal he spearheaded in 2013, which was set to expire at the end of 2016, largely rolled over many of the terms of their previous contract, which was negotiated back in 2005. Rather than put together a new collective bargaining agreement, the 2013 contract came in the form of a memorandum of understanding, or an MOU. It was a hastily put-together document so a deal could be done in time for the NWSL's launch in March 2013. In some places, final terms weren't even set—for instance, it specified that marketing rights were "an issue that remains to be discussed." That became the source of repeated squabbles between the team and the federation.

But still, it included what Langel saw as key wins. It increased the number of players U.S. Soccer had to put under contract—

which guaranteed year-round salaries, injury protection, and pregnancy protection—to 24 players, up from 20. It raised salaries significantly, with different compensation increases built in regardless of whether there was or wasn't a league for the players.

The players could also earn larger bonuses and, for the first time, they could earn a bonus for finishing in fourth place of a World Cup or an Olympics at $10,000 per player. A provision set a minimum of 10 dates for the team's victory tour, which essentially served a bonus because the team would also earn $1.20 per ticket sold to every U.S.-based friendly game. That marked the first time the team had gotten a direct cut of ticket sales.

But the players weren't sure they'd gotten everything they could have, and some players wondered if the team was outgrowing the basic structure of the contract. After all, the contract was built on what the team first bargained for in 2000, and an exhausting 10-game victory tour, when these players were more in-demand than ever, didn't make sense anymore to some players.

The MOU also left too many gray areas, even beyond the parts that were unfinished. The tier system for players was confusing, and the national team was constantly questioning the federation about which players were on which salary tier. With a $36,000 difference between the top tier and the bottom tier, players wanted something more concrete to guarantee their compensation.

"The way we read clauses in that MOU was different than the way U.S. Soccer read the MOU," Becky Sauerbrunn says. "Looking back, we should've fought for something more comprehensive than the MOU, but as players we didn't demand that, and that's on us."

It wasn't about any one specific thing, though. Some players felt Langel had grown out of touch with the team's needs ever since Mia Hamm and Julie Foudy had retired. Others felt that John Langel and U.S. Soccer president Sunil Gulati had gotten far too chummy.

"He had been in it for so long, he had a close relationship with Sunil—a very good relationship with Sunil, in fact," Hope Solo says. "He'd go up to Sunil's suite every game and sit with him."

"Some say it was a working relationship," Solo adds. "Others say it was a little too close of a relationship to really stand up and fight for us."

That too-chummy impression hung over Langel's final meeting with the team before he was fired. In September 2014, Langel and Gulati met with the players in Rochester, New York, where the team had a friendly match against Mexico.

The meeting wasn't unusual—the national team's contract called for regular meetings between the players and U.S. Soccer to discuss how things were going in the NWSL. The players would send Langel their concerns about things like coaching, travel accommodations, field conditions, medical treatment, and other issues, and then he'd compile them to get club owners' responses. U.S. Soccer's job was to intervene and make sure improvements happened. But the meeting reinforced for players their impression of Langel and Gulati's relationship.

At a hotel in Rochester, Gulati sat in the front of the conference room and all the players sat facing him while Langel sat off to the side. It was Gulati who ran the meeting. He didn't have a copy of the player memos in front of him—he conducted the meeting without any notes—while Langel, notes in hand, would interject at times. It was a meeting for the players' benefit, but Gulati was the dominant figure in the room.

After the meeting, the players got ready to head to training, and Langel and Gulati broke off to have lunch together at the hotel. As far as some players were concerned, that was something Langel and Gulati had done too often—getting a meal or a cup of coffee together like old friends. Some players said goodbye to Langel on their way out of the hotel.

Rich Nichols, another attorney, was there in Rochester, too. He had already been in contact with the players as far back as late 2012 through Hope Solo, who was frustrated with the team's hesitance to take a stronger stance against U.S. Soccer. Solo didn't know Nichols when she called him for the first time. She believed the national team needed a stronger voice in negotiations, and after asking around, she eventually got Nichols's name.

His highest-profile experience in sports came from representing Olympic track star Marion Jones in doping allegations and serving as general counsel for the American Basketball League, a women's league that preceded the WNBA. Nichols's expertise isn't quite as a trial lawyer, but he speaks with the cadence and tempo of one, knowing which words to emphasize and where to pause for effect.

As the players of the national team were debating how to move forward in contract negotiations, Solo called Nichols on her own to see if he could help. Their first conversation centered largely around the idea that the women should demand the same pay as the men's national team. Nichols and Solo felt a philosophical connection right away. Both outspoken and unafraid to ruffle feathers, they had the same ideas about the tack the national team needed to take.

"She was a tiger," Nichols says of that first conversation. "It was clear she was going to do whatever was required to get some equality with regard to compensation."

It wasn't until September 2014—after that meeting with Langel and Gulati—that enough players were ready to hire Nichols. They had decided John Langel was no longer able to stand up to U.S. Soccer and Sunil Gulati in the way that they needed. The players held a vote in Rochester by show of hands on whether to hire Rich Nichols. It wasn't unanimous, but it was enough.

Christie Pearce, the captain of the team, was tasked with breaking the news to Langel. She told him the players needed to be sure their lawyer would not have allegiance to the federation. The firing didn't entirely surprise Langel. Before then, he had a growing sense the players didn't trust Gulati, and he didn't share that view, which the players knew. It still hurt, Langel admits, but he would've never wanted to continue without unanimous support from the national team.

"As far as I'm concerned, I would not want to represent the players on an 11-to-10 majority vote or 12-to-9 or whatever it was," Langel says. "That's not a recipe for success."

Rich Nichols became the attorney for the players and the new head of their players association. With that, the tone of the relationship between the national team and the federation was about to take a sharp turn.

* * *

Nichols's first major action in his new role was to tell U.S. Soccer that, as far as the players association was concerned, there was no collective bargaining agreement in place and the players could strike if they wanted. U.S. Soccer got the letter on Christmas Eve of 2015.

His argument went back to Langel's memorandum of understanding. An MOU isn't a CBA, his argument went, and therefore it could be canceled at any time. If that was true and the MOU was canceled, the no-strike provision of the previous CBA would not be in effect, and the players could threaten to boycott the 2016 Olympics.

The national team was trying to get back the leverage of a potential strike.

It was a bold strategy devised, in part, by Jeffrey Kessler and his colleagues at Winston & Strawn, who were hired as outside counsel for the national team. Kessler had been involved in a number of high-profile cases in the world of sports, such as overturning Tom Brady's infamous "Deflategate" suspension from the NFL and successfully appealing Ray Rice's indefinite suspension from the NFL for a disturbing domestic-violence incident. Kessler had also won the case that paved the way for free agency in the NFL in the 1990s.

Weeks later, as negotiations for a new national team contract began, the issue came to a head. In a February 3, 2016, meeting, federation lawyers asked Nichols to reassure them that the players wouldn't strike. Nichols refused—he said the players wouldn't forfeit their legal right to strike. That, as far as U.S. Soccer was concerned, was tantamount to a threat, and the federation immediately went to federal court asking a judge to rule the players couldn't strike.

The 2016 Olympics in Rio were six months away, and both sides were digging in their heels.

"We didn't expect them to jump to court," Kessler says. "But the federation obviously decided that they were going to come in like tough guys and with lots of resources and spend a lot of money, which they did, and require the players union to spend money to fight it. And it was all part of their strategy to head off any possibility that there would ever be a strike."

Meanwhile, there were still contract negotiations to do—contract negotiations that had to take place no matter what the federal judge decided.

At the start of substantive negotiations in February 2016, Nichols presented an 18-page financial proposal. It essentially demanded that the women's team be paid the same as the men's team.

"What we got back is what all professional players associations get when they ask for more money from management—you get what I call the Poverty Presentation," Nichols says. "In our first negotiation, the financial officer gets up and they walk us through their last few years of their financial history and, as always, they arrive at: *Well, we don't have any money.* That's what we got in the first negotiation session."

Negotiations continued on March 5, and they remained at a standstill: Nichols said the national team wanted to be paid what the men's team was making and the federation, again, said that wasn't possible.

"The tone of those negotiations was very contentious," says Becky Sauerbrunn, who served on the national team's CBA committee and participated in most of the negotiation sessions. "They didn't go anywhere. We would go into those meetings and say we want equal pay and they would say you're not really generating the revenue to deserve equal pay to the men. And it just went around and around like that."

But then on March 7, Rich Nichols saw something that caught him by surprise. It was an article by Jonathan Tannenwald of the *Philadelphia Inquirer* that broke down financial numbers contained in U.S. Soccer's General Annual Meeting report. The report itself was released quietly on U.S. Soccer's website without fanfare—Tannenwald was the only journalist for a major newspaper who picked up on it.

What the U.S. Soccer report showed—and what in turn the *Philadelphia Inquirer* explained—was that U.S. Soccer initially budgeted a $420,000 loss for 2016 but changed their numbers to expect a profit of almost $18 million, based largely on the gate receipts and merchandise sales of the women's national team during the 2015 Women's World Cup victory tour.

That's not all the report showed, though. The women's team was projected in 2017 to earn more than $5 million in revenue for the federation. The men's team, meanwhile, was projected to lose about $1 million. That was even as U.S. Soccer planned to spend about $1.5 million more on the men's team.

"I couldn't believe my eyes," Nichols says. "I said: *This is what we need. This is what we thought was the real story, and here it is.* They basically provided us the financial data we needed to prove our premise that the women are the economic engine of U.S. Soccer. We knew that but we didn't have the numbers to prove it. And the men are a losing proposition despite the fact that U.S. Soccer tries to sell the story that the men drive the revenue. The women drive the revenue, period."

U.S. Soccer was largely under no obligation to open its financial books to the players association, according to Kessler—the players association could have requested more specific information, but once they saw the financials U.S. Soccer had released publicly, they knew that wouldn't be necessary. The numbers the federation put out supported the premise the players association had all along. They had everything they needed.

When the next negotiation session came around on March 15, Nichols confidently pulled out a printed copy of the report and confronted U.S. Soccer's representatives with it. U.S. Soccer responded that the jump in profitability for the women's team was an aberration—not part of the larger pattern in the federation's finances.

"An aberration?" Nichols responded. "Aberrations don't occur multiple years in a row. Aberrations aren't projected. You guys have projected profitability. You projected the women to bring in more than the men."

What U.S. Soccer's executives told him, and have maintained in the federation's defense ever since, is that over the previous four-year cycle—which includes World Cups for both teams—the men brought in more revenue than the women. Both sides agree that is true.

The gap in revenue between the national teams *had* historically been large—but the long-term trend showed the gap was shrinking. Since the 2015 World Cup, the gap had flipped and the women had been bringing in more money.

No one knew it at the time, but in a little over a year, the men would fail even to qualify for the 2018 World Cup, dealing a massive blow to their ability to generate revenue. But no one needed to know that yet. For two straight years in 2016 and 2017, the women were going to be more profitable than the men, and yet—as far as Nichols and Kessler were concerned—U.S. Soccer was acting in negotiations as if the men would always be more profitable.

"We did not believe their claim that there was a financial justification for discriminating against the women this way," Kessler says.

The negotiations reached their trigger point. The national team had a Plan B—a bombshell strategy—and now they were going to use it.

* * *

The national team players were in camp in Orlando, Florida, preparing for a pair of friendlies against Colombia when Rich Nichols and Jeffrey Kessler scheduled a conference call with the players on the team's CBA committee. It was then that Hope Solo, Carli Lloyd, Alex Morgan, Becky Sauerbrunn, and Megan Rapinoe were presented with the idea of filing a wage-discrimination complaint with the Equal Employment Opportunity Commission, or EEOC, against U.S. Soccer.

If the players agreed to sign on, they would be asking a government agency to investigate whether U.S. Soccer was violating U.S. laws against workplace discrimination. In other words, the players were going to publicly accuse U.S. Soccer of discriminating against the women's national team. It was a move guaranteed to ratchet up the tension between the national team and the federation.

"I was nervous about that call the entire week because, in essence, what we were asking these great players to do was to sue their current employer for wage discrimination," Nichols says. "That takes huge courage from anybody."

"Think about that: To file a complaint with the Equal Employment Opportunity Commission, which is a public body, alleging that your employer is discriminating against you on wages, it's a serious thing for anybody to do. It's even more serious for the five top women professional soccer players to do in full public view."

The wage-discrimination complaint was a legal strategy—an idea that lawyers conjured up—but it fell in line with what the players had already been discussing for a while. Even if the players weren't familiar with the EEOC, they had already committed themselves to standing up against what they believed was unequal treatment between the women's national team and the men's team.

Nichols said only one player needed to sign on, but the call ended with all five of them agreeing to do it, as long as the rest of the national team wasn't against it.

"For the last several years, we had team meetings every single camp," says Alex Morgan. "A lot of the issues with equitable pay, equal treatment, and equal opportunity for the women's team in comparison to the men's team surfaced and were the sticking points. We weren't aware of the EEOC and the possibility of them coming to our defense before it was brought up by Rich Nichols and Jeffrey Kessler, but that was something that, as a team, we decided to move forward with."

Because the national team was in camp, the players on that call—except Megan Rapinoe, who was out injured after tearing her ACL in Hawaii five months earlier—were able to talk to the rest of the players about the plan. Although the five players filed the EEOC claim on behalf of the team and, as they saw it, to take a stand for all the women playing for U.S. Soccer, the complaint was filed on an individual basis, meaning no players outside of that group were directly involved. Still, the five players agreed they wouldn't move forward unless at least a majority of the team supported it.

The rest of the players had questions. Would the federation retaliate against the entire team? What would happen if the EEOC ruled in the players' favor? Was there a different route the players should take?

After a round of discussions, including a big all-player team meeting the night before the complaint was going to be made public, the five players had the backing from the rest of the team.

Within five days of the conference call, the players filed the complaint and booked a spot on the *Today* show to explain their reasoning for taking such a drastic step. All of the players were seasoned pros at media appearances by then, but this was different. It was a live interview where they would have only a few minutes to try to get their point across on what had become a complicated, polarizing issue.

"The preparation was so last-minute," Morgan says. "We wanted to be firm on the point of why we were filing the charge and get that across in a three-minute segment. We wanted to speak up in the right moments and there was five of us—five very strong women representing the team and trying to have this voice in unison—so there was a lot of preparation within a short period of time with our lawyers guiding us through that."

Most worrying, it was in the middle of a national team camp, and the players were going to criticize their boss, the U.S. Soccer Federation. Morgan remembers the questions that ran through her mind: "Are we going to have consequences for doing this within camp? Are they going to feel like we are distracted? What will come of this?"

The players admit they were scared of what the consequences could be, but they believed the fight was bigger than just themselves.

"For me, who hasn't really had a contentious relationship with anyone before, to basically make this proclamation, it was nerve-racking," Sauerbrunn says. "But we also knew we were doing it not just for the five of us but for the entire team, so that bolstered us."

From their hotel in Orlando, Florida, before team training on March 31, 2016, Hope Solo, Carli Lloyd, Becky Sauerbrunn, and Alex Morgan, joined by Jeffrey Kessler, spoke live with Matt Lauer over a video feed at the *Today* show studio in New York City.

"Carli, you don't just wake up one morning and say, *We're going to file a claim with the EEOC*, and point a finger at U.S. Soccer," Matt Lauer said to open the segment. "This has been simmering for a while. But why does it come to a head now?"

"The timing is right," Lloyd said. "We've proven our worth over the years, just coming off of a World Cup win, and the pay disparity between the men and women is just too large. We want to continue to fight. The generation of players before us fought, and now it is our job to keep on fighting."

Lauer then asked the rest of the group: "Ladies, you complained to the U.S. Soccer Federation in the past. What's been their response when you talk about these equal pay issues?"

"You know, Matt, I've been on this team for a decade and a half," said Hope Solo. "I've been through numerous CBA negotiations and, honestly, not much has changed. We continue to be told we should be grateful just to have the opportunity to play professional soccer and to be paid for doing it."

Officials from U.S. Soccer braced themselves for the appearance. The *Today* show had reached out to head of communications Neil Buethe the night before to get a statement. Lauer read the statement on air: "While we have not seen this complaint and can't comment on the specifics of it, we are disappointed about this action. We have been a world leader in women's soccer and are proud of the commitment we have made to building the women's game in the United States over the past 30 years."

With the short heads-up, the federation arranged a conference call with a small, select group of trusted reporters to take place after the *Today* show aired. They sent information to those reporters showing how the men's team brought in more revenue and more value to the federation. The men's team had higher gate receipts and higher TV ratings, which made the men more attractive to sponsors, the federation said.

Sunil Gulati—the U.S. Soccer president who had avoided some of the very public fights of his predecessors with the women's national team—told reporters he was surprised by the filing.

"I'm cordial with Sunil, and this wasn't to spite him," Lloyd says now. "We just knew we had to step up as a leadership group to make things better for the future. The only way that was going to happen was if we spoke our minds."

Meanwhile, the reaction to the *Today* show appearance was already spreading quickly on social media—and it was largely in the favor of the women. After all, a record audience had watched them win the World Cup not even a year earlier. Many fans surely assumed the women were being treated like champions.

"The press picked up on it in about half a second," says Eva Cole, an attorney at Winston & Strawn who worked on the EEOC filing with Kessler. "We received close to 100 press inquiries from not just press in the United States but all over the world—inquiries from Europe, South America, anywhere that has any kind of interest in soccer. It was across the globe."

"What I think a lot of people picked up on was this notion that they could identify players on the women's team and they couldn't do it for the men because the men's team just simply wasn't as successful," she adds. "You had players who were popular in the public eye and that's a lot of what drove the interest. People knew who these women were, they knew they were the best in the world, and they were captivated."

The lawyers at Winston & Strawn who worked on the filing saw their email inboxes flooded with messages from young girls who wanted to contact the players. Some of them were writing papers for school projects. Some just wanted to let the players know they supported them. Others were saying thanks.

"It was a moving response," says Jeffrey Kessler.

Sauerbrunn says she is still getting requests from young fans working on school projects about equal pay and women's soccer.

"We wanted it to be public," Morgan says. "We wanted everyone in the country to realize why we were doing this. It wasn't just for us five players, but for all the national team players and for the future of the team as well."

Fans who had only just seen the team win the 2015 World Cup probably weren't aware of what the players had been through in the past—boycotting games to earn comparable pay to the men, threatening to retire in the face of a lawsuit, asking the U.S. Olympic Committee to intervene, and so on. These sorts of battles were built into the DNA of the team. Their drive to win and their drive to stand up for themselves seemed to go hand in hand.

For Lloyd, the appearance on the *Today* show and the public decision to file the EEOC claim gave the players a chance to help people understand that this sort of substandard treatment was the reality of the women's national team. She laments that some people mistook the players' stance as fighting against the men's team itself, but she says it shined a light on the issues confronting the women's team.

"A lot of people didn't realize the history of this team and what we've had to fight for," Lloyd says. "When I first joined the team in 2005, they were fighting for salaries, healthcare, pregnancy leave—basic stuff."

Like many American women, the players had their own struggles with equal pay, fair treatment, maternity leave, and other issues that are as endemic in the United States as they are disheartening. As it turned out, even World Cup champions faced the same challenges as other women.

* * *

The complaint itself came down to hard numbers. The players' argument was, essentially, that the federation was paying the women cents on every dollar their male counterparts earned. What the women wanted was equal pay: a dollar for every dollar the men got.

But "equal pay" in this situation was more complicated than that. The men and women weren't just paid different amounts—they were paid via entirely different compensation structures that they each had negotiated for in separate collective bargaining agreements. Critics argued that "equal pay" was not possible because the women and men were paid in different ways. Not only that, the players *asked* for the different structure.

In the hastily arranged conference call with reporters the day of the team's *Today* show appearance, U.S. Soccer's outside counsel Russell Sauer made a similar point.

"It quite frankly seems odd from a legal perspective that the players are complaining about a compensation system that they insisted upon," he said.

The women were paid salaries they negotiated in their last CBA—the most veteran players earned a $72,000 salary, second-tier players earned $51,000, and the lowest-tier players earned $36,000. That was guaranteed payment regardless of how many games they played. The men, meanwhile, were not paid salaries at all. Instead, they were paid on a per-roster basis, and each roster appearance was worth thousands of dollars. A male player had to be called in and make a roster to earn anything, so if he was injured or fell out of favor with his coach, he received nothing from the federation.

The per-roster payment structure is common for national teams around the world—particularly for men's national teams—so why did the women push for a salary structure? Because given how the women's game lagged behind the men's game globally and how women's leagues were still playing catch-up, the women's national team didn't have much of a choice. Male players make their livings from their clubs, not from their national teams, but when John Langel negotiated the earliest contracts for the U.S. women, the women had no professional league to play in and no way to earn a living as soccer players. They couldn't fully commit themselves to the national team if the federation didn't offer year-round financial stability.

The lack of viable women's leagues that could pay salaries wasn't due to lack of trying. The slower development of leagues for women around the world has been reflective, to some extent, of a landscape where decision-makers haven't wanted women taking over the sport. Women were up until relatively recently banned from playing soccer in two of the world's most famous soccer countries: England, until 1971, and Brazil, until 1979. Globally, women's soccer and the institutions around it were still young and growing compared to the male version of the sport.

The U.S. men's team, meanwhile, didn't have to worry about having a league to play in for at least the last several decades. Whether it was stateside in MLS or a bevy of top-tier leagues around the world, the men had hundreds of clubs that could pay them a steady paycheck. In other words: The men's national team simply didn't need to rely on the federation for a guaranteed salary.

But even with the different salary structures, both teams were eligible for performance bonuses. It was those bonuses that created the biggest discrepancy in compensation and became the heart of the players' wage-discrimination complaint. If a female player won a game, she earned a $1,350 win bonus. If a male player won a game, depending on the opponent, he could earn a bonus ranging from $6,250 to $17,625.

It was the huge discrepancy in performance bonuses that allowed the women to earn a fraction of every dollar a male player made. Even though the men and women were paid differently, the bottom line was that the federation had been paying more compensation overall to the men's player pool.

In eight years, from 2008 to 2015, the federation's five top-paid male players made more money than the five top-paid female players. Going down the list of the federation's highest-paid players, the advantage flipped and the female players earned slightly more than the men through the rest of the top 20. But after that point, the men earned far more than the women straight down the line. For instance, the 25th highest-paid man earned almost double the 25th highest-paid woman. The 50th highest-paid man earned nearly 10 times the 50th highest-paid woman.

The question posed to the EEOC was whether the discrepancy in compensation was justifiable. The players say that because the discrepancy came from performance bonuses—whether or not a team wins—a revenue-based justification wasn't valid.

On the conference call the day the EEOC complaint was filed, Grant Wahl of *Sports Illustrated* asked U.S. Soccer president Sunil Gulati directly: "Do you think the U.S. women deserve to be paid equally to the U.S. men by U.S. Soccer and, if not, why not?"

Gulati replied: "I don't know if I want to use the word *deserve* in any of this. I guess I'd reverse the question, Grant. Do you think revenue should matter at all in determination of compensation in a market economy?"

Part of the difference in compensation was based on revenue, he said. Another part of it was how successful each team had been and how much in incentives each team needed to perform well. The implication was, of course, that the No. 1–ranked women needed fewer incentives to win than the perennially mid-tier men's team.

Then, Matthew Futterman of the *Wall Street Journal* followed up on the conference call. There's no other federation the women can play for—they can't shop around for a better employer in international soccer—so how, he asked, is a "market economy" argument fair?

Gulati, an economics professor at Columbia University, replied: "Happy to have you sit in on a class up here, Matt. You're right, in terms of their national team performance, there's only one employer. That's why you have a collective bargaining agreement that's fairly negotiated between the two parties."

U.S. Soccer would stick to its talking point that the players negotiated the compensation structure they received, and thus, the federation didn't understand why the players were now complaining about wage discrimination. But the legal team backing the players' EEOC complaint disagreed—they argued the individual players who filed the claim could never collectively bargain away their rights not to be discriminated against.

One of U.S. Soccer's key arguments—if not in a legal sense, then for public relations—was that it had invested far more in its women's program than any other country in the world. That was the argument Hank Steinbrecher made back in 1996 when the national team threatened to boycott the Olympics over bonus pay, and it remained an argument 20 years later. Neither side disputes that it's true: U.S. Soccer *does* invest more in its women's program than any other nation in the world. The federation had also set up a league for the women to play in.

But for the players, who see themselves as offering guidance and leadership to other women's teams around the world, that didn't matter. Just because U.S. Soccer hadn't treated them worse didn't mean the players should stop pushing for equal treatment.

For the EEOC, investigating the complicated financial comparisons between teams and determining whether there was legal basis for discrepancies would be a long, arduous task. Noneconomic factors, like the disparity in grass versus turf for the men and women, could be considered too, and it would take years to determine if U.S. Soccer had, in fact, discriminated against the players.

The court of public opinion wouldn't take that long, though. The women were winning straight out of the gate.

The *Today* show appearance spread like wildfire, and the story was featured by major outlets around the world in no time. Fresh off having just watched the women win a World Cup in dominating fashion, pundits and opinion columnists lined up to take their side in the public fight. The U.S. Senate, which rarely agreed on much, unanimously voted to pass a nonbinding resolution asking U.S. Soccer to pay the women equally to the men.

But part of what made the "equal pay" argument so compelling were some of the smaller disparities that seemed impossible to justify.

If U.S. Soccer asked a player to appear at an event for a sponsor and that player was male, he got paid $3,750. If the player was female, she got $3,000. For every ticket sold to a women's game, $1.20 went into the team's coffers. For the men, it was $1.50 of every ticket.

The women got a domestic per diem of $50, while the men got $62.50. When traveling internationally, the women got $60, while the men got $75. In a *New York Times* op-ed, Carli Lloyd quipped: "Maybe they figure that women are smaller and thus eat less."

The federation seemed particularly embarrassed about the difference in per diem and appearance fees. Though they said it was due to the men and women negotiating their CBAs at different times, they vowed that the next women's CBA would include language that guaranteed the women would get the same payment in those situations as the men.

Sources at the federation now say if John Langel had still been the team's attorney, he would've just called up Sunil Gulati and asked that the women get whatever was in the new men's contract. It would've been an easy sell, they say: the discrepancy in per diems, for instance, was worth only about $40,000 per year, a drop in the bucket. The issue would've never been part of a public fight. But John Langel wasn't the team's attorney anymore, and the discrepancies in favor of the men were powerful ammo in the equal pay campaign.

* * *

The players were still under contract with U.S. Soccer while all of this was going on and they still had to go back to the negotiation table to try to get a new deal done.

"It made the negotiations way more public—probably more public than U.S. Soccer wanted them to be," Becky Sauerbrunn says. "In that respect, the public leaned toward us, and it put more pressure on U.S. Soccer."

But the tone of negotiations didn't change after the EEOC claim. The wide gulf between the two sides that was there before still remained and they weren't any closer to getting a deal done. On top of that, the leverage the players were hoping for—the threat of boycotting the Olympics—soon disappeared.

On June 3, 2016, a judge ruled in favor of U.S. Soccer over the question of whether the memorandum of understanding bound the players to their previous collective bargaining agreement and its no-strike clause. Testimony and old emails from John Langel convinced the judge that the MOU was intended all along to keep the CBA in effect until December 31, 2016, and the players had approved it. The ruling meant the players could not strike heading into the Olympics.

If the national team was going to compel U.S. Soccer to give them a new contract with equal pay, a threat to boycott wasn't going to do it. The best leverage they could find would be in the form of a gold medal in Rio.

CHAPTER 20
"We Played a Bunch of Cowards"

Since the national team had just won the 2015 World Cup, picking a roster for the 2016 Olympics in Rio de Janeiro should be easy, right? Not quite.

Before Jill Ellis selected her final roster, she chatted with U.S. Soccer president Sunil Gulati about her plans. There was one of two ways she could approach the Olympics, she told him. Either she could treat it as an extension of the World Cup cycle and bring in largely the same team that won the 2015 World Cup. Or, she could start preparing for the 2019 World Cup immediately, even as she tried to win in Rio.

Ellis, who had earned a multiyear contract extension after her World Cup win, wanted to take a long-term approach. She wanted to set up the team not just for the upcoming Olympics but for the next World Cup, too.

"You're not going to cost us a medal, are you?" Gulati asked.

"I don't plan on it," Ellis told him.

In some ways, the roster was going to change because there was no other choice. For certain players who had made the squad for the World Cup a year earlier, it was never expected that they would return for the Olympics.

Shannon Boxx, Abby Wambach, Lori Chalupny, and Lauren Holiday all retired after the World Cup. That created some roster spots, but not too many. The rosters for the Olympics had five fewer players than those for the World Cup. There was no room for luxury players—everyone would need to be able to contribute.

Mallory Pugh, then just 18 years old, was in great form, but she didn't have any experience in a big tournament. Nevertheless, she figured to be an important part of the team for years to come and made the roster. Crystal Dunn was lighting it up in the NWSL and earned a spot for her first major tournament, too.

For Ellis, the biggest roster decision came down to whether she should take Megan Rapinoe or Heather O'Reilly. Both were wingers. Both were veterans. Both had delivered memorable, game-changing, last-gasp crosses on the world stage.

But Rapinoe hadn't played a game since December, eight months before, when she tore her ACL in Hawaii. She was only just starting to return to full-contact training, and she wasn't fully fit.

On a roster as small as the one for an Olympics—just 18 players, two of them goalkeepers—every single field player would need to be able to contribute. The question wasn't whether Rapinoe was good enough—it was whether she could really make her return in the middle of a major tournament.

Taking Rapinoe was risky, but something told Ellis that Rapinoe was too special of a player to leave at home.

Rapinoe, a native of Northern California who settled in the Pacific Northwest, was the type of player who could change a game. She sparked the first bit of momentum for the Americans at the 2015 World Cup, scoring the team's first goal in Canada. She could create magic out of nothing, and when she was having a good game, defenders were helpless to stop her. She was also an effervescent personality who kept the mood light, even amid the rigor of a major tournament.

"With Rapinoe, it obviously was not her form, because she hasn't been playing," Ellis told reporters after she had selected her roster. "But she's got set pieces, crossing—the pieces where, I think, late in a game or against a certain team we have to break down, she can help us with."

After more than a decade of Heather O'Reilly serving as a key cog in the national team's system, it was hard to imagine the team without her. Though she wasn't the type of creative flair player who dazzles, like Rapinoe, she covered a ton of ground, she ran harder than anyone on the field, and she had a way of producing special moments through brute force.

Rapinoe made the final roster and O'Reilly was named an alternate, a player who could be added to the roster in case of a tournament-ending injury, but who would really just be there to train with the Olympic team in Brazil.

"In the 230 games that I have played for the USWNT so far," O'Reilly wrote on social media after the roster was announced, "I have done it with my whole heart, with every ounce of me, regardless of the role, to help us win. Whether I was a starter, or a substitute, or even the times that I did not see the field. . . . And next month, I will travel to Rio with the team as an alternate. Once again, whatever I need to do to help the U.S. win, I will do with my whole heart."

* * *

Before the tournament even started, Hope Solo had already unwittingly managed to turn Brazilian fans against the Americans.

Worries about the Zika virus had led some athletes to pull out of the Olympics, and others expressed concerns. Soccer teams would play most of their games outside of Rio de Janeiro, including in far-flung Manaus, where Zika cases via mosquitos had been reported.

Before the national team left for the tournament, Solo posted pictures on social media of the mosquito repellant and mosquito nets she planned to bring to Brazil with her, with the hashtag #ZikaProof. The posts offended soccer fans in Brazil, who were already upset with how American media had portrayed their country.

Much of the Brazilians' bitterness toward Americans wasn't Solo's fault, but she became the target of it. From her first goal kick in the USA's opening match versus New Zealand in the group stage, fans shouted "*Oooooh*," holding the sound as Solo prepared to strike the dead ball. Then, at the moment Solo's foot hit the ball, they shouted "*Ziiikaaa!*" Anytime she touched the ball, the stadium filled with boos.

But if the Brazilians hoped to get into Solo's head or the heads of her teammates, it didn't appear to be working. The national team started the 2016 Olympics in the dominant fashion everyone expected. The Americans comfortably rolled past New Zealand, and afterward, there wasn't much of a story for the media to cover. The Americans were winning again—same old, same old. So, the focus turned to the Zika chants and Solo. She was diplomatic and unfazed.

"It's the Brazilians—they love soccer, they love football, it's part of the culture, so I expect it, but they're having fun," Solo told reporters. "I mean, at least it's loud in the stadium—I'd rather have that than hear a needle drop."

The Americans faced France next, and again Solo was the storyline—but this time it was because she had a spectacular game in goal. She denied a header from towering French defender Wendie Renard with a full-stretch, fingertip save. Later, she made a point-blank save on Marie-Laure Delie, who had a breakaway. Solo denied two other good Delie shots.

With a goal scored by Carli Lloyd, the Americans beat France, 1–0, but Hope Solo was the hero, despite the loud boos from the crowd.

"Hope is ice," Lloyd said afterward. "Nothing can rattle her. She had a fantastic game tonight—huge saves and came up really big."

Solo was arguably the national team's most consistent and reliable player. But then, the match against Colombia happened.

Heading into the final match of the group stage, there was little reason to think anything other than a win was ahead for the Americans. In their previous meetings, Colombia had never even scored a goal and the U.S. always won by multiple goals.

But after 25 minutes, it became clear that everything the U.S. counted on—the precedents set with Solo and against Colombia—had turned on its head. Megan Rapinoe fouled Liana Salazar, conceding a free kick, and Catalina Usme stood behind the ball just outside the box. A wall of six American players shielded Solo on the near-post side. Usme struck the ball around the wall at the center of the goal. Solo only had to take one step to be in perfect position—it was an easy catch—so, she crouched, ready for the ball. But the shot dropped right before it reached her hands and bounced off the grass, through her legs, and into the net.

It was a shocking misjudgment of the ball's flight from the world's best goalkeeper. Such a hard-to-watch goalkeeper error is called a "howler" in soccer lingo—and it was definitely a howler.

Becky Sauerbrunn, the team's leading centerback and cocaptain, turned to Solo and told her not to worry.

"We're good," she told Solo. "We'll get it back."

They did eventually get it back. Carli Lloyd fired a long-range shot that was blocked, but Crystal Dunn tapped it in for the equalizer. Later, Mallory Pugh became the youngest-ever goal-scorer for the national team in an Olympics at 18 years old with a lovely dribbled run and strike.

The clock ticked past the 90th minute and the Americans held a 2–1 lead, but there was enough stoppage time left for a surprise from Colombia—or rather, a surprise from Hope Solo. On another free kick outside the box, again Catalina Usme stepped up behind the ball. Christen Press and Crystal Dunn formed a two-woman wall while the rest of the Americans tried to man-mark in the box. Usme wasn't looking for her teammates, though—she had an eye for goal. She struck the ball and Solo rose into the air to punch it away with her left fist. But Solo missed. The ball fell into the back of the net. The match ended, 2–2.

The Americans still topped Group G, even with the draw to Colombia, which meant they should face a weak team in the quarterfinal. On paper, it was still mission accomplished, but it was a demoralizing result. The players, including Solo, were determined to look ahead.

"I've been around the game long enough to know that it's part of the position," Solo said of her mistakes. "I don't wish it on anybody. Being a goalkeeper is extremely difficult. I've been around long enough to know that these things do happen—they've happened to me before."

"I have also learned to have a short-term memory," she added. "So I'm just going to put this behind me and move on."

* * *

Pia Sundhage and the Swedish team didn't have much reason to feel confident going into the quarterfinal.

The only reason they were facing the Americans, who had won their group, was because the Swedes had played so poorly in the group stage and barely advanced. But for Sundhage, there was nothing to lose by facing her former team. She went into the match with a sense of calm.

"We're going to play the best team in the world," Sundhage told reporters the day before the game. "All the pressure is on the Americans."

She added: "We're going to the quarterfinal, and everyone knows when you get to a quarterfinal, anything can happen."

After Sundhage's press conference, it was Jill Ellis's turn to face the media. A Brazilian reporter asked the first question: What did the Americans need to worry about going against Sweden?

"They will park the bus," Ellis said. "They will sit as low as they possibly can and then look to transition, and they're going to try to kill the game off that way and not give up space. I imagine they'll play a 4–5–1 and be very compact."

When the game arrived, it was exactly as Jill Ellis had forecasted.

At Estádio Nacional Mané Garrincha in Brasília, a tense chess match of tactics was playing out. The Americans were persistent in launching the ball forward, but the Swedes were happy to absorb pressure and bide their time.

The stalemate continued until the 61st minute, when Sweden finally found an opening to attack. Allie Long lofted a ball up the field, trying to find Alex Morgan's run, but it fell short and was headed away by Nilla Fischer toward Kosovare Asllani.

Then, the game sped up a few notches: Asllani tapped a short lateral pass to Lisa Dahlkvist, who knocked a perfectly weighted onetime pass up the field toward a sprinting Stina Blackstenius, splitting centerbacks Julie Johnston and Becky Sauerbrunn. Blackstenius beat the defenders and fired a low shot to the far corner, well out of Hope Solo's reach.

Pia Sundhage smiled ear to ear and high-fived her coaching assistants. It was just as she had drawn up.

Once the Swedes got the lead, they weren't going to give an inch. They put all their players behind the ball to defend, and any attacks forward were half-hearted at best. Up to that point, the Americans had been playing aggressive attacking soccer, and they weren't about to change now.

A few minutes after Sweden's goal, coach Jill Ellis made an attacking substitution. Defender Kelley O'Hara came off and winger Megan Rapinoe came on. This moment was the reason Ellis brought Rapinoe to the Olympics. The Americans needed some service to create goal-dangerous chances. Rapinoe, the player who had lofted a ball onto Abby Wambach's head in 2011—one of the most spectacular goals in the team's history—was being asked to do something heroic again.

She made an impact quickly. In the 77th minute, with a high-booted challenge, Rapinoe plucked a poorly cleared ball out of the air, kicking Kosovare Asllani in the process. Asllani went down in a heap and the crowd booed, wanting the ref to blow the whistle, but the game played on with Rapinoe winning the ball.

With a couple of quick passes to the other side of the field, Tobin Heath then lofted a ball into the box that took a deflection and landed in front of Alex Morgan's left foot. Morgan drilled a shot into the corner. Goal, 1–1. The Americans had found their equalizer.

But the Brazilian crowd seemed to think it was a cheap goal, booing through the celebrations and well after play restarted. Meanwhile, Asllani went to the sideline to be briefly looked at by medical trainers before she returned to the field.

In the first half, when a Swedish player was down, the Americans, in an act of common but unnecessary soccer etiquette, kicked the ball out of play so she could get medical attention. It's an unwritten rule—a polite act—but it's not required. The Americans didn't do it again once they were down a goal.

"It's a nice thing to do, but you're losing a game," said Kate Markgraf, who was calling the match live for NBC's broadcast. "Would you rather go home because you're playing nice, or do you follow the rules of the game and let the referee decide when play will cease?"

The fans didn't care. The Americans had a tendency to win over crowds wherever they went because of their tenacity and flair, but not here in Brazil. The negative energy hung over the team like a fog. It had been there since the first match when fans had started chanting "Zika!"

every time Solo kicked the ball. And now it was turning the momentum against them.

The Americans desperately tried to find their game-winner, but with the score locked at 1–1, the match moved into extra time. The players started to look sluggish, and that especially applied to Megan Rapinoe, who came on as a substitute in the 72nd minute. Ellis subbed her out in favor of forward Christen Press.

The decision to use up two substitutions on Rapinoe over the course of the game—sacrificing a pair of fresh legs in the process—could come back to haunt Ellis if the Americans didn't win this. The knock-on effect of putting Tobin Heath, one of the USA's most creative attacking players, on the defensive line to allow Press to replace Rapinoe was also going to be criticized if the U.S. lost.

Carli Lloyd should've scored in the 115th minute, but the referee incorrectly ruled it offside. A minute later, the same thing happened to Lotta Schelin on the other side of the field: Sweden was wrongly called offside on a goal.

The match seemed destined to continue into penalty kicks, and so it did.

* * *

Momentum in sports is a funny concept.

So often, players and coaches talk about gaining momentum or losing it. Even fans in the stands and journalists in the press box can see who has the momentum on the field. But it's not as if a snowball is rolling down a hill, pulled by the force of gravity, accumulating new layers of snow. Momentum, at least in sports, is just a state of mind.

The inertia—the negative energy holding the Americans back—had been there in Brasília all day. From the boos and the Zika chants, to the team's barrage of 26 shots that didn't result in a goal, to the tired legs and makeshift lineup on the field. Things just weren't going right.

So when Alex Morgan stepped up to the spot, took the first kick in the shootout, and had her shot blocked, it felt like momentum had something to do with it.

The Swedes and the Americans then exchanged goals—Lotta Schelin, Lindsey Horan, Kosovare Asllani, and Carli Lloyd all buried their attempts. When Linda Sembrant took her shot, Hope Solo guessed the right way and punched the ball over the net. Was there still time to shift the momentum back?

Morgan Brian and Caroline Seger each scored. Then Christen Press stepped up. She looked nervous and took a deep sigh before she finally approached the ball. Her foot got too far under it—her shot sailed over the goal.

When Lisa Dahlkvist stepped up to the spot, everyone knew: If she scored this, Sweden would win and the U.S. was going home. Hope Solo did what she could—she stalled, just like she had at the 2015 World Cup one year earlier. She had a trainer bring her a new pair of gloves. Perhaps she wanted to keep Sweden's momentum at bay. But Dahlkvist, standing at the spot with the ball in her hands, laughed, as if to say: *Take as much time as you want—I'm fine.*

Finally, Dahlkvist took her spot and Solo took hers. Dahlkvist shot to the right while Solo guessed to the left. Goal. Just like that, the unthinkable had happened: The Americans were knocked out of the Olympics in the quarterfinal, their earliest exit in a major tournament ever.

The Americans looked stunned. While the Swedes cheered and danced in a huddle, the Americans mostly just stood in silence in the spots they had been standing during the shootout, tears welling up in their eyes.

What happened in the loss was something that would seem to haunt coach Jill Ellis. It was something that she would spend the next couple of years trying to solve with endless tinkering and tactical experiments. Sweden played defensively—they "bunkered"—and even though Ellis forecasted it in the pregame press conference, she still couldn't stop it.

For the American players, it was a devastating loss. They outplayed Sweden in every category except one: the score.

Never had the U.S. team been knocked out of a major tournament so early. Never had the team failed to make the semifinal of a major tournament. A 25-year streak of top-three finishes in major tournaments had reached its end.

It was an embarrassment, it was a shock, and it was painful. But pretty soon, that's not what anyone would be talking about.

* * *

After the players emerged from the locker room, they walked through the mixed zone, like they always do, so reporters could ask them questions.

This mixed zone in Brasília was quiet and low-key. Most reporters covering the Games were in Rio, the host city, and the only reporters eager to speak to the U.S. players were a small handful from major American outlets, plus one Swedish journalist. After all, it was still early in the tournament, and no one had expected the USA to be knocked out so soon.

Alex Morgan walked through with tears in her eyes. She looked as though she had been crying hard and held it together just enough to talk to reporters.

"I'm really just heartbroken right now for the girls and the federation," Morgan said, her voice breaking. "It's just unfortunate. I feel like we were prepared, but so were Sweden. Today could go either way. Sweden came to play and I feel like they did well and stepped up."

The team press officer, Aaron Heifetz, escorted her away after a few minutes.

Hope Solo then stopped, and the reporters swarmed to get her reaction. Grant Wahl from *Sports Illustrated* asked the only question you ever need to ask a player after a game—a question that just lets the player get whatever they want off their chest. His question: "Your thoughts on the game?"

Hope Solo had a lot to get off her chest.

"I thought we played a courageous game. I thought we had many opportunities on goal," she said. "I think we showed a lot of heart. We came back from a goal down. I'm very proud of this team.

"But I also think we played a bunch of cowards. The best team did not win today. I strongly, firmly believe that. I think you saw Americans' heart. You saw us give everything that we had today and unfortunately the better team didn't win."

Why, Wahl asked, was the Swedish team a bunch of cowards? Solo obliged to elaborate.

"Sweden dropped off. They didn't want to open play. They didn't want to pass the ball around," Solo said. "They didn't want to play great soccer, entertaining soccer."

"They didn't try and press. They didn't want to open the game. And they tried to counter with long balls. We had that style of play when Pia was our coach. I don't think they're going to make it very far in the tournament. I think it was very cowardly."

She continued: "Pia is somewhat of a tactician. They could only really score on the opportunities for a long ball and set pieces. So I guess you can say it's smart, but I don't think it's respectful to the game."

Rather than wait to publish a full article, reporters rushed to get the quote out on social media. Kevin Baxter of the *Los Angeles Times* was the first—he left the mixed zone while Solo was still being interviewed so he could get a reaction from Pia Sundhage.

While Solo was still in the mixed zone, Baxter tweeted a snippet: *#USWNT's Hope Solo "we lost to a bunch of cowards. The better team did not win" #Rio2016.* His tweet gained traction instantly. ESPN showed a screenshot of it on television.

Not long after, Wahl tweeted a screenshot of her full quote to his hundreds of thousands of Twitter followers. Anne M. Peterson of the Associated Press included the "cowards" quote in her postgame write-up, which was sent over the wire to hundreds of newspapers and web-sites around the world.

The comment spread like wildfire and Solo was roundly criticized for being a sore loser and defying the competitive spirit of the Olympics.

Solo says now: "The media said I was the selfish one, that I was the poor sport. But I cared. I went home heartbroken and some of the players went to Rio to party. It's all how you want to tell the story."

While the internet buzzed with reactions to Solo's comments, Sundhage was sitting in a press conference. There, Baxter relayed Solo's comments to the Sweden coach for the first time.

"According to Hope Solo, I think you should define what is a good team," she said. "Well, usually—especially with the Americans—a good team is when they're winning."

She added: "It's okay to be a coward if you win."

Sundhage was asked about it again as more reporters trickled into her press conference, not aware the question had been asked already, and Sundhage said in Swedish: "I don't give a crap. I'm going to Rio. She's going home."

Now, years removed from that 2016 press conference, Pia Sundhage says she regrets what she said. What got buried in all the controversy was what Sweden accomplished: No one had ever bested the Americans so early in a major tournament. Never had the Americans failed to come in at least third place.

"That just came out of my mouth," Sundhage says now. "I apologized the next day. The fact is, I don't think that people understand what we did. The U.S. had been winning a medal every single time since '91. Sweden was the first team to kick them out. I could tell all the American players were devastated."

It was perhaps a twist of irony: The coach who had brought Hope Solo back into the national team when Solo had been exiled was now the coach responsible for the loss that was about to end Solo's career.

While Solo's remarks were ricocheting around every corner of the media landscape, Solo got on the team bus, went back to the hotel, and then went to the meal room, where she saw Sunil Gulati, the president of U.S. Soccer. They sat down to chat.

"He said one of his friends in real estate in Seattle saw that my home was up for sale," Solo remembers. "He saw a photo of it and said, . *You have a really beautiful home,* and he made a joke about how, *We must be paying you well*, and we kind of laughed. He said, *I know it hurts*—he empathized with the loss. We talked like everything was normal and said, *I'll see you tomorrow*. It wasn't anything."

Gulati confirms that encounter happened, but he says he hadn't yet known about her controversial remarks.

Later, Solo sought out Lotta Schelin, the captain of the Swedish team, who was staying in the same hotel. Solo and Schelin had played together for the same club in Gothenburg, Sweden, in 2004, where they became friends. Schelin later told Swedish press about the encounter—that Solo had apologized and there was no problem.

"It was in the heat of the moment," Schelin said of Solo's comments.

The news of Schelin and Solo's amicable meeting didn't make the rounds in the American press, and Solo still laments that some people still don't know she had made amends directly with the Swedish team.

"When American media still wanted to take my head off, I addressed the people who I wanted to address," she says.

The next morning, with the U.S. national team's Olympics officially over, it was time for the players to disperse. While a few of them stuck around to visit Rio and experience the rest of the Olympics, Solo was ready to get out of Brazil and return to Seattle, Washington. The U.S. players who opted to leave Brazil had tickets on the same flight to the U.S., and then everyone had connections to their final destinations.

Solo arrived at the gate early, still upset and teary-eyed about the loss to Sweden, and was the first passenger on the plane. Not far behind was Jill Ellis, who boarded after her.

Before the other players boarded, the national team's goalkeeper and coach had time to chat. They talked about the future.

"It was just Jill and I and on the plane for 15 minutes before anyone else came on," Solo says. "We talked about where the game was headed in the future, things we need to look for in the next World Cup to get around a team that bunkers. She talked to me about how much I'm going to be needed in the next World Cup."

"It was a really positive conversation, but knowing we had to address different strategies on how to beat a team that's bunkering and what we're going to do with our defenders and why she needed me in the back because we were probably going to push more defenders up," Solo says. "It was a turning of the page. We lost an Olympics and now we need to look forward at how were going to learn from this."

Solo says she brought up her "cowards" comment—she asked Ellis if she saw it. Ellis said she had but didn't seem worried about it, as far as Solo could tell.

"She said, *Can't you just apologize on Twitter or something?*" Solo says. "She didn't care at all."

So on August 13, 2016, Solo flew home, still devastated about the loss to Sweden but thinking the fallout from her postgame interview was over.

That same day, Grant Wahl published an interview with Sunil Gulati where Wahl asked about Solo's comments. Gulati was critical, telling Wahl: "While we are all very disappointed with the results of the match, Hope's post-game comments were highly inappropriate and not in line with the expectations of U.S. Soccer or the ideals of the Olympic movement."

Gulati says he also sent Solo a text message that day—the day after the game—expressing his disappointment in what she had said.

Over the next few days, Solo's teammates distanced themselves from her sentiment. Megan Rapinoe said when the team loses, "we need to handle that graciously." Asked pointedly about Solo's comments, Alex Morgan said: "I saw her comments, but I feel like those are opinions I don't share."

Soon enough, Solo got an email from Jill Ellis asking her to come to a meeting with U.S. Soccer CEO Dan Flynn in Seattle on August 24, 2016. When Solo didn't respond quickly, Ellis texted her.

"When she texted me, that was really weird and I knew something was up," Solo says. "I wanted to say, *No, I'm not going to be there*, but I knew something was going on and I had to deal with it. It was important, so I made sure I was in town. When Dan Flynn comes to town, it's for a hiring or a firing. I knew someone's being fired."

On that Wednesday afternoon, Solo went to meet the people who were effectively her boss and her boss's boss in the conference room of a Seattle-area hotel.

When Solo greeted Flynn, she joked that they couldn't stop meeting under these circumstances—a nod to her previous run-ins with the federation. They both laughed. But this meeting felt tense and awkward in a way that no other meeting of hers with U.S. Soccer had.

While Flynn got the meeting set up to begin, which included getting U.S. Soccer's lawyers on speaker phone, Solo sat silently next to Jill Ellis.

"I think she was so uncomfortable with the silence that she finally looked at me and was like, *So, you're going to play in the NWSL game this weekend?*" Solo recalls.

Solo's team, the Seattle Reign, was hosting the Portland Thorns. It was a big rivalry game and her first club game on the schedule since an NWSL break for the Olympics ended.

"I just laughed," Solo says. "It was like, *Jill, you fucking tell me. Here I am in this meeting, I have no idea what it is about or if you're going to fire me, and you're asking me if I'm playing?* I laughed because it was a really dumb question. She just looked away."

It was there that Flynn told her that she had effectively been fired, on top of a suspension. He handed her a letter notifying her that her contract was terminated and that she was entitled to three months of severance pay, per her contract.

"That was it. I didn't say much or ask any questions," Solo says. "I knew that the decision was made and I wasn't going to talk my way out of it, nor would I stoop to the level of begging for their mercy or anything like that. I took the paper, I thanked Dan, I thanked Jill, and I walked out."

Outside of the meeting room, Solo's husband and her publicist were waiting for her.

"Six months suspension, no pay, terminated contract effective immediately," she said through tears. "Terminated contract—not just a suspension!" she added as she forcefully tapped on the desk in front of her for emphasis.

"How can it be both?" her husband asked, confused why it was both a suspension and a termination.

Solo threw her arms up: "It's both!"

U.S. Soccer swiftly issued a press release titled: "HOPE SOLO SUSPENDED FOR SIX MONTHS FROM U.S. WOMEN'S NATIONAL TEAM." It made no mention of Solo's contract with U.S. Soccer being terminated—the press statement only said she had been suspended for six months and that she'd be eligible to return to the national team in February 2017. In his statement, Sunil Gulati said Solo's comments "do not meet the standard of conduct we require," which he had previously spoken to Solo about privately.

Solo believes U.S. Soccer portrayed the situation as a suspension, not a termination, because otherwise it would've looked like an overreaction.

"They didn't want people to know I was terminated for something so dubious and gray," Solo says. "U.S. Soccer knew they would look bad if they terminated me and didn't just suspend me, so they leaked that I was only suspended."

A federation spokesman says her termination was clarified for reporters, but U.S. Soccer announced only her suspension because a termination alone couldn't prevent her from being called back in.

Solo, however, alleges Dan Flynn told her in the meeting that if she didn't share that she had been terminated, she may be allowed back on the team. Instead, Solo shared a photo of the termination letter she received with the media so everyone knew it wasn't only a suspension.

"They told me if I don't tell anyone it's a termination and it's just a suspension, I might be able to come back," she says. "I was like, *Do you know who I am? I've always been honest.*"

Before she even knew it, Hope Solo had played her last game of soccer—not just with the national team, but ever. The deadline for her suspension came and went without coach Jill Ellis calling her back in. U.S. Soccer said they would not cancel the NWSL portion of Solo's contract, but she took a leave of absence from the Seattle Reign. She never returned.

Solo left the national team holding not just the program record for most shutouts but the world record in shutouts, at 102. She was arguably the greatest female goalkeeper the world had ever seen. But, just like that, the Hope Solo era of the national team was over.

CHAPTER 21

"The Power of Collective Bargaining"

With Hope Solo no longer on the team, contract negotiations were about to change again.

Rich Nichols issued a swift reaction to her ouster, telling reporters that it was "excessive, unprecedented, disproportionate, and a violation of Ms. Solo's First Amendment rights."

"She was fired for making comments that a man never would have been fired for," he said.

The timing of Solo's firing certainly raised a few eyebrows. After all, Hope Solo had always been an outspoken member of the team and never shied away from controversial statements. Amid all her previous controversies, the federation supported her. How was a comment calling Sweden "cowards" the final straw?

Solo is convinced it is because of her role in fighting for equal pay, even though the federation has adamantly denied that.

"When I filed the EEOC claim, I knew these things could happen," Solo says. "U.S. Soccer praised me for so many years and they celebrated my strong personality, and as soon as I started to go after the money, I saw things flip and change with U.S. Soccer."

After all, she was the one who had brought in Rich Nichols. She voted in favor of striking. She demanded the appearance bonuses after the World Cup. She was one of the players who filed the wage-discrimination claim. She was often the loudest voice pushing back against U.S. Soccer.

Even her teammate Megan Rapinoe had a similar thought. Rapinoe was being filmed as part of a documentary during and after the Olympics, and she told the camera: "As a member of the team and of the CBA group and of the PA [Players Association], I'm pretty unhappy with a sort of arbitrary six-month suspension for calling someone a coward. I think that there's probably some legal strategy going on with it all."

Whether there was a legal strategy or not, once Hope Solo was out of the way, Rich Nichols soon followed.

"There was no doubt in my mind then and there's no doubt in my mind now that Hope getting fired was the federation's way of taking the strength away from the team," Nichols says.

"When you're in a CBA negotiation, management is always trying to find a way to dilute the power and authority of the executive director of the union," he adds. "It happens all the time. It's a question of when it's going to start happening. So, how do you do that? You find a couple of employees who are vulnerable and you pressure them. You get rid of the internal leader of the union, and that was Hope."

By now, it was late 2016, and negotiations for a new collective bargaining agreement were at the same standstill they'd been in since 2015. The federation and the national team weren't just failing to see eye to eye in negotiations—it was as if they were each on different planets.

While the wage-discrimination complaint sat with the EEOC, the players of the national team had one of two choices: they could either just stop playing until the equal-pay dispute was solved, which could take years, or they could somehow end the standstill and get a deal done that offered some progress, even if it didn't include equal pay.

They chose the option that allowed them to keep playing soccer.

With three days left before the national team's collective bargaining agreement was set to expire on December 31, 2016, the players voted to fire Rich Nichols as their legal counsel and head of their players union.

"The way negotiations had transpired to that point, it was too far gone," says Becky Sauerbrunn. "There was no way to turn the tone of it around to get to a place where it could be more collaborative rather than a win-lose situation."

While players don't speak negatively about their former general counsel, Nichols had clearly been a thorn in U.S. Soccer's side because of his obstinate, pugnacious negotiation style.

One U.S. Soccer official, speaking only on the condition of anonymity, feels the players had been ill advised by Nichols and their legal team. The official regrets the federation didn't directly communicate with the players earlier in the process before it devolved into legal fights, adding that negotiations had "ugly moments."

Another anonymous source, a U.S. Soccer board member who sat in some negotiation sessions, adds: "They were some of weirdest negotiations I'd ever been in in my life, and I've been in a lot. Only when a player was in the room did they halfway behave themselves. It wasn't a hard-nosed negotiation—it was like they didn't understand what we were talking about."

Regardless of whatever had gone wrong in negotiations, the players set out to make things right.

* * *

The players decided they wanted to be more involved in everything—negotiating the new contract with the federation, running the players association, understanding the business side of being athletes, everything. Part of that meant determining they had left too much control to the likes of John Langel and Rich Nichols. The players of the national team were plenty capable of taking on these issues themselves.

They restructured the players association to reflect that. They already had an existing CBA committee led by Becky Sauerbrunn, Christen Press, Alex Morgan, and Megan Rapinoe and one for finance led by Meghan Klingenberg, Heather O'Reilly, Whitney Engen, and Morgan Brian, but they got more players involved with new subcommittees on various topics they cared about, including alumni engagement, the NWSL, member relations, commercial business, and the social impact of soccer.

"Our big goal is to have as many of the players cued in, and involved, and invested, as possible," Megan Rapinoe said after the changes were announced. "That's something that can be really special about this."

The players also brought in a management consultant, Becca Roux, to be their new players association director. Roux had previously volunteered to help the players find ways to improve their commercial revenue after the 2015 World Cup. Instead, once she saw how their players association was being operated, she suggested the players association itself needed to be restructured to lay the groundwork for the team to capitalize on commercial opportunities.

Once the players decided to start restructuring, after looking at other candidates for the job, they asked Roux to lead the association. Roux, who holds degrees in both law and business administration from Northwestern University, came aboard in February 2017.

With the end date for their CBA having passed at the end of December, the players were now operating on an expired contract. That meant the no-strike clause had officially expired and the players were ready to wield that power. They weren't shy about publicly hinting at the possibility.

"To force a change sometimes you need to stand up," Alex Morgan said when asked about striking. "You know what you're worth, rather than what your employer is paying you. We're not scared. To move the women's game ahead we need to do what's necessary. I feel other national teams are looking at us for that guidance."

The problem with striking, however, was that its impact on the NWSL wasn't clear. Playing in the U.S. Soccer–backed NWSL was part of the players' duties as employees of the federation, even if it was a different job than playing for the national team. Could they boycott the national team and still play in the NWSL? Legal experts gave them differing opinions.

"We weren't sure how it was going to affect the NWSL," Becky Sauerbrunn says. "If the league folded because of this, we could be responsible for putting so many of our fellow teammates out of a job. We had to weigh that. We weren't just fighting for the players in the national team pool, we were also potentially affecting NWSL players."

The best-case scenario for everyone was that a new deal would be worked out with U.S. Soccer. So, on February 4, 2017, more than one month after their existing CBA expired, the players resumed negotiations. Becky Sauerbrunn, Christen Press, and their new players association director, Becca Roux, presented a new proposal to U.S. Soccer outlining their broad goals.

The overarching theme of the proposal was respect—or, more specifically, the same level of respect the men's team has gotten over the years. The players wanted a collaborative relationship with U.S. Soccer, one where the federation and the national team were partners and communicated about decisions regularly.

In the interest of getting a deal done, the players shifted their focus from equal pay to equitable pay. Initially, based on the strong projected revenue growth of the team, they proposed a revenue-sharing model that U.S. Soccer rejected. Even if the tone of negotiations had improved, progress was still difficult.

"We were in the room, across the table from each other for weeks straight, every day for hours, fighting over every little thing and seeing real-time responses to our proposals," Sauerbrunn says. "It was quite draining. Not least of all because we're professional soccer players and we were training, too. So, they were long days."

Within the second week of resumed negotiations, the federation still refused to offer compensation near what the players wanted. Then, on February 10, 2017, with negotiations stuck, the national team let U.S. Soccer know they had made a decision: All the players' licensing and sponsorship rights that U.S. Soccer controlled in previous contracts were now off the table. The national team players were taking all of them back for themselves to monetize how they saw fit.

"When we did that, U.S. Soccer seemed stunned," Roux says. "They called off the rest of bargaining that night. They made us come back the next morning and then delayed the session."

At first, U.S. Soccer told the players that the value of those rights was already part of the salaries the federation paid them. But the players didn't buy it—they believed their salaries were for playing soccer and the federation just took the additional commercial rights for granted.

Under the previous CBA, any licensing agreements involving the players—things like featuring the players in the popular video game *FIFA 16* or on collectible Panini stickers—were mostly split down the middle between the players and U.S. Soccer. Whoever initiated the deal got a 10 percent bonus of the revenue as a finder's fee, but otherwise proceeds were split in half.

What ended up actually happening, however, was most of these deals went through the federation, because that was who companies contacted. The federation could negotiate whatever terms they wanted, and the players felt the federation wasn't valuing them highly enough.

The players had never had full control of these sorts of commercial rights before or the ability to try to capture the full value of them on their own. But with the federation unwilling to budge on compensation, it became a key bargaining chip. While the team's lead negotiators, defender Becky Sauerbrunn and striker Christen Press, pushed for those rights, defender Meghan Klingenberg worked behind the scenes to lay the groundwork so the players association would be ready to capitalize.

"It's a very hard thing to be across the table and be fighting for something the other side doesn't think you should get," Sauerbrunn says. "We had to get creative and progressive and think of new ways to generate revenue. We fought for sponsorships and licensing—we had to fight to take things back that we hadn't had before so we could find different revenue routes than straight-up salary."

In the end, the national team granted some group-image rights that both the federation and the NWSL could use for promotion—group photos of players for marketing materials, for instance. But the national team took back exclusive control of licensing rights, which covers any merchandise sold featuring national team players. For the rights to commercial uses, such as advertisements for a U.S. Soccer sponsor, the federation agreed to pay the team $350,000 annually.

With compensation a sticking point in negotiations, the players were willing to reevaluate the contracted salary structure that had been in place for years. For many years, those guaranteed salaries were the financial security players needed to even be part of the national team, but the new contract negotiations marked an evolution away from that.

The federation sought to lower the number of contracts, and the players wanted to keep the minimum at the level Langel had negotiated, 24 contracts. Instead, the two sides reached a compromise that changed the compensation structure dramatically. While the potential for more money overall ended up on the table, it was going to be spread more evenly amongst the players, and less of it would be guaranteed.

The number of national team contracts was cut significantly to 20 contracts in 2017, and the number drops by one every year to hit 16 contracts by 2021. The core of the team will shrink over time, but the rest of the player pool will benefit from significantly higher bonuses that can be earned by any player who makes a roster, veteran or not.

The friendly win bonus increased from $1,350 per player in the previous contract to bonuses of at least $5,250 and as high as $8,500, depending on the quality of the opponent. Players never used to receive bonuses just for making a friendly roster, but now noncontracted players will get $3,500 per game until 2021, when it goes up to $3,750—it's closer to what the men's team earns ($5,000 per player), though still not equal. Contracted players won't get game-appearance fees because they will instead earn a $100,000 base salary.

The players fought to keep their NWSL allocation contracts intact, however. The CBA ensures that 22 national team players will be allocated at all times throughout the life of the contract. That clause signals a commitment from both U.S. Soccer and the national team to have allocated players in the NWSL through 2021, regardless of whether U.S. Soccer is the league operator or not. It also signals a shift where club play becomes more important for the careers of national team players. NWSL salaries were raised for the 2017 season to between $62,500 and $67,500, depending on each player's tier, with a $2,500 yearly increase.

Samantha Mewis, one of the younger players to participate in some of the negotiation sessions, says the reduction of contracts gives more opportunities to more players, which ultimately expands the player pool and helps the sport as a whole.

"Someday, the league will ideally provide high annual salaries, leaving U.S. Soccer free to call in the players who are in form and pay them per game," Mewis says. "With more contracts, there is certainly more security for the players on those contracts, but there is less opportunity for other players, as U.S. Soccer is incentivized to call in players who they are already paying."

The issues went well beyond compensation, though. The players remembered the 2015 victory tour, which was mostly on artificial turf, and boycotting the Hawaii game because U.S. Soccer hadn't inspected the field beforehand. The players didn't want to rule out turf entirely—some key soccer markets have good artificial-turf venues—but they secured language in the new contract that any games on artificial turf be inspected by the federation and deemed to be "in safe condition" and "conducive to soccer on game day." The players can request "photographs of the turf and a report on its condition" and offer input on venue selection, too.

The 10-game victory tour—the one the 1999 team fought so hard to create—was something the national team had outgrown. With the NWSL looking stable and viable for years to come, the players wanted to prioritize club play and asked for the victory tour to be cut drastically. The two sides agreed on a post-tournament victory tour of just four games that would be held only within FIFA windows to avoid disrupting the NWSL.

"The movement between line items was so small, it would take days," Sauerbrunn says. "There was never a day where we got everything we wanted. Every proposal was so carefully countered and movement was very incremental. It was a daily chess match."

With the biggest hurdles out of the way, a deal was getting closer as April 2017 approached—three months after their previous CBA had expired. Both sides were eager to get a deal done, and U.S. Soccer seemed to be particularly anxious. By the time the players had to report to camp in Texas for a pair of friendlies versus Russia, the federation insisted the team continue negotiations there.

"Camp is the players' time to do their work," Roux says. "It felt disrespectful to hold negotiations between training sessions such that players were sitting in chairs for hours—for some players, until midnight—rather than doing proper recovery."

If negotiation sessions had to be held during camp, then all of the players eligible to vote on the contract—not just the CBA committee—decided they should show up. Mallory Pugh, who was in college at the time, and Rose Lavelle, who had just joined the team, were not eligible to be in the session, but the rest of the team showed up in matching Nike T-shirts that read "Equality" and sat around a large conference-room table. Players who weren't at that camp called into the session over the phone. Alex Morgan, who was playing for Olympique Lyonnais, called in from France, even though it was late at night there. Julie Ertz, formerly Johnston, called in from her honeymoon.

The last negotiation session to finalize the terms was on April 3, 2017. At the last minute, U.S. Soccer asked for a clause allowing for an "identification camp" to be held every January that would not be tied to any games and would only feature so-called floaters—players who were new and not under contract. That camp could be held during a new six-week annual rest period for veterans built into the CBA for every winter. The players, who throughout the negotiations had generally supported expanding the player pool, agreed.

With that, the deal was finally done. The new agreement was ratified on April 4, 2017, two days before their two-game series versus Russia was set to begin.

It wasn't the deal the players truly wanted—it didn't include equal pay—but it was something that allowed the players to continue to do their jobs and play soccer while the EEOC investigation continued. They couldn't have known that, more than two years after the EEOC claim was filed, it would remain unresolved as the calendar turned to 2019. But they knew it would take long enough that they needed a new contract. Now they had one.

* * *

With the negotiations over and a new contract in place, a new batch of work was set to begin.

Perhaps most pressing, the national team players now had to figure out what to do with those commercial rights they took back from U.S. Soccer. It was the first time the national team had full control of those rights—and that meant they had to essentially build up a new business from scratch. It's not as simple or as immediate as collecting a salary from U.S. Soccer, but the national team believes it sets them up in the long term.

"With licensing merchandise, the players controlling those rights going forward is a huge deal," Becca Roux says. "It gives them an ability to monetize something that otherwise wasn't being monetized. Just because there wasn't any authorized product doesn't mean it wasn't happening—it was being done in an unauthorized way and players weren't capturing the royalties."

Nine months after the new CBA was finalized, the national team launched a new licensing and branding agency with players from the WNBA and the NFL called REP Worldwide. The agency was the first step in maximizing those new commercial rights. Meghan Klingenberg, the player who'd pushed hardest for control of the licensing rights, was elected in 2018 by her teammates to sit on the board as the national team's athlete representative. In that role, she has helped the team build its new business operations.

The players association signed three of its first deals in April 2018, for player-specific scarves with the brand Ruffneck, socks with Strideline, and giant decals of the players' faces with Build-A-Head.

For the first time, not only can fans buy U.S. Soccer scarves with all the royalties going to U.S. Soccer, but fans can also buy an Alex Morgan–branded scarf and have 100 percent of the royalties go directly to the players. If the Alex Morgan scarf has a U.S. Soccer logo, the players and the federation each get cuts.

By September 2018, the team added deals to sell T-shirts through the company Represent, digital collectibles called Player Tokens, and perhaps most important, official jerseys customized with players' names, via Fanatics. In the past, U.S. Soccer and other retailers sold unauthorized player-specific jerseys and reaped the profits, but now fans can buy an authorized jersey with their favorite player's name and a portion of that sale will go back to the players.

The players don't know exactly how much these group-licensing rights could be worth—it's a gamble, to be sure—but they think the value will exceed whatever they got out of their previous CBAs. After all, for instance, when the USA women's team appeared in *FIFA 16*, it ranked as the 23rd most-played team in the game out of 600 teams—not just in the U.S., but around the world.

"It's a good outcome to get away from the federation's belief that there is no value in the women's game," Roux says. "Now we can test the market and prove them wrong."

Even as more contracts are signed and more revenue streams are put into place, the players are keenly aware it will take time to see the benefit of this new business they are building. But, like much of the new CBA, the focus has been on building for the future.

"The real potential will probably be long after I'm done playing, but I think the potential is massive," says Megan Rapinoe, who has been on the national team since 2006. "Right now, we're still in an experimentation period of figuring out what it is, what it means, how do we do it, and how do we capitalize, both individually and as a group. We have a million questions every day."

The new CBA created a lot more work for other people, too—specifically NWSL owners, who were tasked with changes immediately and in the years to come. That's because all the problems in the NWSL that national team players had to take on—bad playing surfaces, locker rooms without basic amenities, sub-par staffing—were addressed in the national team's new CBA. With U.S. Soccer running the NWSL, the national team players saw an opportunity to use their CBA to improve the league.

"We understood that we can't fight for the NWSL players, because we're not the NWSL Players Association—we're the U.S. National Team Players Association," says Becky Sauerbrunn. "But we knew that we wanted to help women's soccer as a whole as much as we could. So we said we need to have these minimum standards for the NWSL. We did that knowing it wouldn't just benefit the national team players, it would benefit all the players."

The new CBA called for immediate changes in 2017, including that all NWSL locker rooms should, at a minimum, be clean. But those requirements were set to expand over time. By 2020, every NWSL team will be required to have a designated on-site locker room with showers, an on-site training room with equipment, and a medical treatment room. From 2019 onward, every NWSL team will need to play its home games on either natural grass or on artificial turf that meets specific, high standards, unless an ongoing stadium lease prevents it.

Roster sizes in the NWSL will increase, too, which will allow teams to rest players more and better mitigate injuries. By 2020, the minimum roster size in the NWSL will jump to 22 players from the 18 players it was in the years prior. That will also give more national team hopefuls a chance to prove themselves in the NWSL.

The CBA also set out to ensure that if the national team experiences unprecedented success off the field, like it had in 2015 and 2016, the team will reap the benefits.

If the average TV viewership for U.S. Soccer–hosted games increases by 10 percent over the previous calendar year, it will trigger bonuses for the players of $15,000. If the team sells out U.S. Soccer–hosted games, the players will earn bonuses of either $15,000 or an additional 7.5 percent per average ticket price for all sales beyond a threshold of 17,000 tickets, whichever is more.

The players may have forfeited some of their security, but they increased the potential rewards. It was a dramatic shift from the early years: The team wasn't so worried about avoiding the downside—they wanted to be able to capture the upside. The hope was that they'd found a way to capitalize on their success in a way no previous generation of the national team had.

After all, Kate Markgraf can recall her son asking her why she still has to work when she is one of the most-capped players in the world and has won World Cups and Olympics medals. She had to explain to him it's because she's a woman: "I'd probably have enough saved by now if I were a male athlete," she told him.

Brandi Chastain remains one of the most famous female soccer players ever, but when she thinks back to the $500 check she received for winning the 1991 Women's World Cup, she remembers how grateful she felt then and how differently she feels now about it.

"The farther I get away from that moment, the more I realize, *Man, I still have to work really hard to earn a living and I hustle every day*," she says. "I do think sometimes, if I had been born a male and I had the success I had, financially I'd be a much bigger tax bracket."

The team's new CBA doesn't figure to change all the harsh realities that female soccer players face, but the current players hope it offers a few steps in the right direction.

* * *

For the national team, stats alone can tell a story. Kristine Lilly, the iron woman of the team, has a record 354 caps, which is about 100 more than just about anyone else. Abby Wambach, the goal-scoring leader, has the most international goals of any soccer player on the planet, male or female. Mallory Pugh, the teenage prodigy, became the youngest American to score a goal at an Olympics in 2016. And so on.

Off the field, the national team's collective bargaining agreements have told a story in a similar way. In 2000, it was about being treated like professionals at the most basic level. In 2005, it was about financial security and making a living. By 2012, things like pregnancy protection, sharing revenues on ticket sales, and building a league came into play. In 2017, it was about taking control and ownership of the future.

The national team's current collective bargaining agreement is the latest chapter in a story that has been told over more than three decades. Now, it's a story that has inspired other women's sports teams to carve out similar paths. In that sense, the players of the national team have emerged as a different kind of role model—not just to girls who play soccer but to female sports teams around the world who demand equal treatment.

When the U.S. women's national hockey team boycotted their biggest event of 2017—the world championships hosted for the first time in the United States—it was a page taken out of the soccer team's book. But more than that, it was a decision made with the close guidance and input from those who fought the same fights in soccer.

One day in 2015, out of the blue, John Langel got a call at his desk in his Ballard Spahr office. The USA women's hockey team had gotten his name from Heather O'Reilly, who happened to work out at the same gym as Meghan Duggan, a forward for the hockey team. The hockey players had asked O'Reilly about how the soccer team had made the advancements it did throughout the years, so O'Reilly recommended they call Langel. He spoke with Duggan and the Lamoureux twins, Monique and Jocelyne, who described treatment as bad as what the soccer team experienced when Langel first came on board in 1998.

"Every issue and every protection we engineered for the soccer women over 16 years was an issue that had to be addressed in hockey," Langel says.

By September 2015, Langel and his law partner, Dee Spagnuolo, had started working with the hockey team on a pro bono basis and put together a wish list with the players of things they should fight for. It was the same thing he had done with the soccer players in 1998, a process that started when Kristine Lilly had to run out and get her teammates food in between training sessions.

The hockey players' wages were paltry—USA Hockey paid compensation as low as $6,000 per player for every four-year cycle. It was paid out $1,000 per month for six months before the Olympics, and the players got paid $0 for the rest of the three and a half years, even as USA Hockey expected them to train and compete in games the entire time. They also had no protections for injury or pregnancy. Their working conditions and treatment were well below what the men's team received.

But hiring a lawyer alone wasn't enough. Julie Foudy remembers the last time the hockey team had tried to hire a lawyer and stand up to USA Hockey. She remembers it because it was around the same time she, Mia Hamm, and the rest of the soccer team were fighting a similar battle with U.S. Soccer.

"When we were doing our fighting, we tried to get the hockey team to do the same, but they couldn't pull it off because they couldn't stay unified," Foudy says. "This current group of hockey players came to understand that history."

Throughout 2016 and into 2017, USA Hockey was uncooperative and negotiations went nowhere. With nothing to lose and everything to gain, the hockey players notified the federation they planned to boycott the world championships in 2017. It was their biggest event of the year, and one year before the Olympics, it was a major statement that they were willing to take a stand.

It mirrored the story already told by the soccer team in 1999 when the players threatened to retire if U.S. Soccer took them to court over the indoor victory tour.

"That moment when Mia turns to Julie and says, *I won two World Cups, an Olympics—I'm prepared to give it all up. How about you?* That's the same conversation the hockey players had amongst themselves," Langel says. "They knew they were going to bypass a world championship, and if they do that, they might not have been invited to play in the Olympics. It was the same commitment."

It was a decision the hockey team made only after constant conversations with players from the soccer team, past and present. Duggan, the Lamoureux twins, and Hilary Knight all sought advice from Foudy and Hamm, who walked them through what the soccer team did in the late 1990s and early 2000s to unify younger players and use the leverage they had.

But not all the conversations were about legal strategy. Sometimes it was just about getting the perspective of someone who had been through this before.

"Was it scary?" Foudy remembers the hockey players asked her. She told them: "Hell yeah, it was scary."

Some hockey players were afraid of the negative consequences, and they weren't sure about the boycott.

"You just have to bring them back into the fold and tell them: If we stay together on this, we're fine," Foudy would tell the hockey players. "We knew they couldn't fire the whole team as long as we stayed together."

The hockey team convinced potential alternates not to accept invites to play during the boycott and, two days before the 2017 world championships were set to begin, USA Hockey and the team reached a deal. The terms were not released, but the players got living wages, and the federation agreed to better promotion for the women's team. Only one year later, the hockey team would win a gold medal in the 2018 Olympics in South Korea.

The hockey team wasn't the only one that gained inspiration from the soccer team. Canada's soccer team sought advice on getting maternity coverage into contracts. WNBA players asked the soccer players how to ask for better standards across the league for travel accommodations and trainers.

But what may perhaps be most important is that the soccer team's lessons—the story of its hardest struggles in the fight for equality—will continue on no matter what happens with the soccer team. What the team started decades ago has slowly spread and touched other teams around the world. For the youngest players on the soccer team, it may be what ensures they never forget the history of the team, even if they weren't around to see it happen.

For the new soccer players who have never had to strike for anything and stepped onto a national team that already offered a living wage, they are still able to see the effects of what the generations before started.

Samantha Mewis—one of the soccer team's up-and-coming players who could make her World Cup debut in 2019—happened to train with a group of the hockey players during the offseason before the hockey team went on strike. The conversations sometimes turned to equality, and she later got to see the hockey team turn that conversation into action.

"We often discussed our roles in the landscape of professional sports—how could we continue to fight for our own rights and further create opportunities for the next generation?" Mewis says. "Their resolve to go on strike before their world championship until they received fair compensation was extremely admirable and taught me so much about the power of collective bargaining."

For John Langel, fighting for the hockey team allowed him to reprise a familiar role. The soccer team may have eventually outgrown his guidance, but with the hockey team, he again got to build something from scratch.

"Being fired by soccer hurt," Langel says. "I didn't like it. I look back on it and say I'm glad I was fired because several players needed new representation, but I didn't like it when it happened. Going on to being as successful as we were in hockey—going on strike and getting what the players wanted in the face of criticism that we hadn't been tough enough with U.S. Soccer—that made me feel good."

CHAPTER 22

"We Had to Turn the Lens on Ourselves"

With the failure of the 2016 Olympics still fresh, coach Jill Ellis sat down and wrote an email to the players of the national team.

This email wasn't a usual update or a motivational pep talk. It was distinctly the turning of a page for the national team. The team would play two friendlies after the Olympics, but once those were done, it was time to hit the reset button.

"Some of you will not factor in our plans for 2019 and I will share that with you in a timely manner," she wrote, in part. "For some of you, it will mean you will not be on a specific roster so I can rotate and evaluate other players. But what everyone must understand is that performance becomes the precedent of selection. Whether you have 1 cap or 300 caps, gold medals or no medals, you will be measured by what you do on the training field and what you do on the playing field in this, and your professional environments."

It signaled for some players that their guaranteed starting spots of the past were now up for grabs. For others, it signaled their career with the national team was over.

Whitney Engen, who had served as a depth piece on both the 2015 World Cup and 2016 Olympic rosters, was among the players cut from the team. After the two post-Olympics friendlies in September 2016, the 28-year-old centerback got a phone call from Ellis informing her of the decision.

"I was extremely surprised at the timing and to say I am devastated is an understatement," Engen said in a letter to fans.

Heather O'Reilly, who had been on the national team since she was 17 years old, was no longer getting minutes for the national team and clearly didn't fit into Ellis's long-term plans. She played her last game for the national team on September 15, 2016, in an emotional farewell from the international game. Mia Hamm, her former teammate, came out before the game and presented her with a framed jersey.

The new normal on the national team would now be seeing less experienced, unfamiliar names on every roster while Ellis called up players from college, the NWSL, and youth national teams. A core of veterans would no longer be starting every single game. And, notably, now that Ellis had won a World Cup, she would have a longer leash than someone like Tom Sermanni did, even after failure at the Olympics.

This new approach that Ellis insisted upon was a break from tradition and it certainly wasn't what American fans or players were used to, and once the new collective bargaining agreement was ratified, she would end up with even more flexibility.

"The rest of the world deals with how you play for your club, and that's how you get a call-up," Ellis said. "It's about shifting the mind-set."

Mia Hamm retired in 2004 with 276 caps to her name, and Carli Lloyd, who debuted for the national team in 2005, has around 270 caps. But the new era of the national team means no player should ever come close to matching those numbers, at least as far as Ellis is concerned.

Mallory Pugh may have gotten a head start because she broke into the national team and became a starter at just 17 years old, but Ellis thinks someone should replace her before she starts hitting jaw-dropping career stats.

"If she reaches 200 caps, I don't think we're doing our job," Ellis told reporters. "When I used to recruit in college, my sole job was to out-recruit what I had. And if I did that, I knew we would grow and be successful."

So, with the players on notice, Ellis set out on a mission to leave no stone unturned. After the dust had settled from the 2016 Olympics, she began calling in a carousel of new players and tinkering with her tactics endlessly.

But what if she tinkered and tested but never found a team as good as the one at the 2015 World Cup?

* * *

When the 2019 World Cup arrives, the Americans will have a new goal-keeper in goal for the first time since 2007, when Greg Ryan benched Hope Solo and accidentally blew the team up.

Solo has not returned to the team, even though her six-month suspension came and went. In late 2017, the federation eventually settled a grievance with the national team players union over her suspension. The terms aren't public, but sources with knowledge say it included a monetary settlement.

Instead, the national team will turn to a goalkeeper who has never featured in a major tournament.

"Hope played every minute of every game, and now we have a starting goalkeeper with 12 caps," Ellis admitted in 2017.

At the 2019 World Cup, that new goalkeeper will most likely be Alyssa Naeher, who had just six caps at the time Solo was kicked off the team and has quickly earned start after start to gain reps. Ashlyn Harris, a longtime backup for the national team, is another option. Any other goalkeepers in the pool won't have more than a small handful of international caps.

"As a goalkeeper, there are a lot of scenarios and situations that you can't fully train for," said Naeher after she became the new No. 1 goal-keeper. "The only way to gain those experiences is in games."

For her part, 37-year-old Solo thinks she still has plenty to give to the game. She got long-needed shoulder surgery after the 2016 Olympics, and even though she hasn't played club soccer, she says she's been ready to return. But, although the assault case against her was finally dismissed for good in May 2018, she's hardly endeared herself to the federation since her termination, becoming a vocal critic of the organization.

In the unlikely event the federation and Ellis would invite her back, Solo says she'd turn it down.

"I know they need some defensive leadership and some good goal-keeping," Solo says. "I would never work for a federation, at this point, that doesn't pay their women equally. I won't work for someone like Jill who is part of the problem—I think she's a weak leader and essentially another puppet for U.S. Soccer."

"Have stranger things happened? Yeah," she adds of a possible return. "There's a possibility if Jill wasn't there and U.S. Soccer came to terms with paying the women equally. There's a possibility, but it's pretty slim. I'm not holding my breath."

* * *

The national team's performance in Seattle on July 27, 2017, had not been a good one—not by any stretch.

Two years removed from a World Cup victory in Canada, the national team was now losing to opponents it had never lost to before. On this day, it was Australia who beat the Americans, 1–0, for the first time in 28 games.

The starting lineup, like most that year, looked experimental, with some players in new roles and usual starters watching from the bench. Taylor Smith, a fullback who had shown well in the NWSL, made her debut for the national team, becoming the 17th player under coach Jill Ellis to get a first cap. New defenders Abby Dahlkemper and Casey Short joined her on the back line. A defensive breakdown allowed Australia's Tameka Butt to score.

Alex Morgan and Crystal Dunn, both second-half substitutes, each had golden opportunities to score that they couldn't finish. Lloyd came on as a second-half substitute, as well, but couldn't find a way to change the game.

Morgan, walking through the stadium from the field after the match, in a rare outward display of frustration, whipped a Sharpie at the wall before disappearing into the locker room. Presumably, she had the marker in her hand because she had to sign memorabilia for VIP ticket holders, who line up in the tunnel for autographs after games. It was the only thing she had in her hand that she could throw.

Her display of emotion was in plain view of the mixed zone, where journalists stood, waiting for the players to walk through. It was a glimpse of consternation from a team that was often polished and upbeat—a team that was not only media savvy but used to winning.

Jonathan Tannenwald of the *Philadelphia Inquirer*, wh among the press corps to see it, tweeted about it. It was well a night on the East Coast, but it took only minutes for his tweet to s amongst the national team fans, who shared Morgan's frustration.

Morgan wasn't being criticized by fans for being angry—far fron. it. Fans, who were equally frustrated with the national team's recent struggles, felt comforted the players shared their same feelings.

"I love this, to hear about the frustration and emotion from these players who are upset with themselves and the situation," said one fan. "Glad to see an emotional response—maybe it'll lead to a more fiery USA squad," wrote another. "She has every right to be angry. This team is SO MUCH BETTER than their coach is allowing them to be," another said.

When Morgan walked through the mixed zone later to speak with reporters, she lamented the "lull" the Americans got into as the first half wore on. It was plainly obvious to the journalists in Seattle that day that the Americans didn't really start to threaten Australia until the second half, but the goals never came.

"We're not going to forget what happened tonight," Morgan said. "We need to learn from this, for sure."

At this point, some of the players had become worried enough about the team's performances to say something to the federation. A small group of veteran players in Seattle went to Sunil Gulati, the president of U.S. Soccer, to express their concern about the direction of the team under Jill Ellis, according to sources close to the team.

That loss in Seattle was only the USA's third in 2017, but the losses that year were especially demoralizing.

In March, the national team had lost 3–0 to France. It was the USA's worst, most lopsided loss in a decade—the last time the team lost by such a wide margin was that infamous 2007 World Cup semifinal versus Brazil. The loss to France also came after a 1–0 loss to England a few days earlier, marking the team's first time losing back-to-back games since 2014, when Tom Sermanni was fired as coach shortly thereafter.

Adding to the embarrassment of the losses to France and England, they came during the SheBelieves Cup, a tournament that U.S. Soccer had created as an upgraded replacement for the Algarve Cup. The Americans came in last place in their own tournament.

When the group of veteran players went to Gulati in Seattle, they were mainly concerned about the team's recent string of dropped results. Some of these veterans who were complaining to Gulati had seen their playing time scaled back significantly and could only helplessly watch the team struggle.

There was a new and obvious economic reason to be upset by the losses: the players' compensation was more directly tied to winning than it had ever been before because of their new CBA. But this was also a team that viewed nothing less than winning as acceptable. Winning was a defining part of the national team's identity.

As Alex Morgan told the media right before the loss in Seattle: "We do have the best team in the world, and not even on our best day, we should still beat the best teams."

Results aside, however, players expressed to Gulati concerns about a lack of communication from Ellis off the field. Some players felt that they learned more about Ellis's plans from reading her comments in the media than from speaking directly with their coach. Instead of the team feeling confident and cohesive, it felt unstable and in flux.

The team's losses in 2017 were easily attributable to Ellis's coaching decisions, including experimental tactics and constant lineup changes. Throughout the March 2017 SheBelieves Cup, Ellis had put the team into a new, unfamiliar formation that used three defenders instead of four. On top of that, she rotated in new players and asked others to play in new positions.

So when the French team easily penetrated the American back line to score, it wasn't surprising. The Americans looked disorganized and out of sync. No one seemed quite sure of their positioning. It was unclear who was supposed to track certain runners into the box. And the Americans, who wanted to play the ball out of the back, struggled to connect lines.

Eventually, Gulati told the players he wouldn't consider a coaching change until after the 2019 World Cup. A source with knowledge of the situation says the federation asked other players on the team about the veterans' complaints, and the players who hadn't met with Gulati were fine with Ellis staying in charge.

For the players in the primes of their careers who had been playing well for the national team all along, off-cycle tinkering was just something they'd have to weather.

"It is difficult because you want to continue maintaining a really high level both individually and collectively as a team," Tobin Heath said after the SheBelieves Cup when asked about coping with such experiments. "That's where you can grow and stretch the most—under that intense pressure. At times during this process, it doesn't necessarily feel as much like that because there are so many changes. But as much as it can be frustrating, it's important to remain focused and positive about the fact that we're trying to go somewhere. "

There can be value in losing, after all. The national team had started losing more often before the 2015 World Cup. They went to Brazil in December 2014 and lost to Brazil, 3–2. Their next trip on the schedule was to France in February 2015, where the Americans again lost to the host, 2–0. Ellis credits those losses with hardening the team before the World Cup.

"I wanted them to struggle," Ellis later said. "It was going to be a challenge. It was hot, adverse, hard, and we lost the game. From there, I took them to France and we struggled, we lost."

"In those hardships, we learned more about ourselves," Ellis added. "I'm going to say that without those struggles and losses, I don't think we win the World Cup. We really had to turn the lens on ourselves, and we needed to be exposed and find answers."

The question may be whether the national team will learn enough from their latest string of struggles before the 2019 World Cup.

The thing about the national team is that there have always been setbacks. There have been losses and embarrassments and steps backward. There have been coaches who have come and gone again.

There have been lulls when the media and fans stopped caring about the team.

But the national team always eventually comes back stronger, better, fiercer. The culture of the team—its DNA, its fighting mentality—has outlasted every player, every coach, every World Cup, every Olympics, every collective bargaining agreement, every fight.

Whether they can win another Women's World Cup in 2019 or an Olympic gold medal in 2020 almost doesn't matter. They'll be back eventually, because they always are.

That's just the national team.

Acknowledgments

As a journalist who has followed and covered the U.S. women's national team for many years, I always aspired to one day write a book about them—a story of defying the odds, of changing the sports landscape, of inspiring women. I'm grateful that my editor at Abrams Press, Jamison Stoltz, presented me that opportunity. He believed in me, and this book would not be possible without him, or without his assistant, Alicia Tan, and the entire team at Abrams.

I'd like to thank all the national team players who spoke to me on the record for this book and generously shared not just their time, but their memories and insights: Julie Foudy, Brandi Chastain, Briana Scurry, Kate Markgraf, Ann Orrison (Germain), Shannon Higgins (Cirovski), Tracey Bates (Leone), Shannon MacMillan, Tiffeny Milbrett, Danielle Slaton, Angela Hucles, Heather O'Reilly, Cat Whitehill, Heather Mitts, Hope Solo, Shannon Boxx, Becky Sauerbrunn, Carli Lloyd, Ali Krieger, Ashlyn Harris, Meghan Klingenberg, Alex Morgan, Megan Rapinoe, and Samantha Mewis.

My gratitude also extends to the players I've interviewed previously over the years. The players of the national team have always been gracious with the media and eager to promote the game they love. Years of interviews I've conducted—that I thankfully archived along the way—helped fill in this book.

I would also like to thank the coaches, administrators, team attorneys, and others I interviewed as well: Anson Dorrance, Lauren Gregg, Pia Sundhage, Tom Sermanni, Sunil Gulati, Robert Contiguglia, Alan Rothenberg, John Langel, Becca Roux, Rich Nichols, Jeffrey Kessler, Eva

Cole, Marty Mankamyer, Joe Elsmore, Mick Hoban, JP Dellacamera, Donna de Varona, Marla Messing, John Hendricks, Jim Kennedy, Amos Hostetter Jr., Ben Gomez, Joe Cummings, Arnim Whisler, Jeff Plush, Jim Gabarra, Mike Lyons, Merritt Paulson, Brian Budzinski, and Chris Canetti. Special thanks, as well, go to Anthony DiCicco, son of the late Tony DiCicco, and Dan Levy, Mia Hamm's agent.

In addition, I want to acknowledge those I interviewed off the record or anonymously for this book. I am incredibly grateful for the amount of time and candor people offered to help me tell the national team's story as truthfully as possible.

I'm indebted to the editors I've had the pleasure of working with over my career—they have all made me a better writer—and I owe a special thanks to Tom Lutz, who gave the opportunity to cover the 2015 Women's World Cup for the *Guardian*, which remains one of my most memorable experiences as a reporter.

I'd like to thank my fellow colleagues who have covered the U.S. women's national team as journalists over the years. Some offered me support and advice throughout the process of writing my manuscript, and many contributed via their excellent reporting on the team over the years. Among them were Anne M. Peterson, Grant Wahl, Jonathan Tannenwald, Beau Dure, Jamie Goldberg, Matt Pentz, Kevin Baxter, Andrew Das, Ann Killion, and many others.

Without the top-notch communications team at U.S. Soccer, particularly Aaron Heifetz and Neil Buethe, the coverage of the team would never be what it is today. I am grateful for their professionalism over the years and how they've enabled me to tell the players' stories along the way.

My greatest thanks of all go to my mom, Toni, my sister, Colleen, and my brother, Bill. They offered encouragement and motivation throughout the manuscript-writing process, especially when I needed it the most. I'm lucky to have such a supportive family in my life.

Sources

Although this book includes many new interviews conducted either specifically for the book or during the writing of the book, contemporaneous news sources were also crucial to capturing the story. I have covered the U.S. women's national team for a number of years, including throughout their run to winning the 2015 Women's World Cup in Canada, and I drew upon unused archive material of my own interviews, but the work of many journalists from 1985 through 2018 helped this book come together.

Every chapter includes new reporting and interviews I conducted exclusively for this book—a list of everyone I interviewed is in the Acknowledgments section—but here are many (not all) of the articles and sources that were part of my additional research.

Chapter 1

"Anniversary of First WNT Game." U.S. Soccer, August 26, 2005.

Bosley, Catherine. "Women's Football Has Come a Long Way in Germany." Reuters, October 15, 2007.

"FIFA Bans Mexico for Two Years—No Olympics, No World Cup in '90." *San Diego Tribune*, July 1, 1988.

Griendlin, Bob. "U.S. Soccer: The 17 Women Who Blazed an Amazing Trail." *Soccer America*, November 1, 2000.

"Hard-earned Success." *FIFA Weekly*, February 17, 2011.

"Increase in Participation and Competitions." FIFA: Women's Football Symposium, 2011.

Jones, Grahame L. "Women's Little Trip to Italy Was Start of Something Big." *Los Angeles Times*, July 10, 1999.

Margolis, Jason. "The Struggle for Female Soccer Equality in Brazil," Public Radio International, May 27, 2013.

Olmstead, Maegan. "Acknowledging the Importance of Title IX in the U.S. World Cup Win." Women's Sports Foundation, July 7, 2015.

Simpson, Jake. "How Title IX Sneakily Revolutionized Women's Sports." *Atlantic*, June 21, 2012.

Wallerson, Ryan. "Why Women's Soccer Was Banned in Brazil—Until 1979." *Ozy*, October 25, 2016.

"Why Was Women's Football Banned in 1921?" *BBC News*, December 12, 2014.

"Young Athlete Switches to Her Main Sport." Associated Press, July 30, 1985.

Chapter 2

"Akers-Stahl Kicks U.S. to World Title." Seattle Times, December 1, 1991.

"Boycott-Lockout Issue Threat to U.S. Women's Soccer." *Atlanta Journal-Constitution*, December 7, 1995.

Davidson, Gary. "U.S. Women's Team Takes Shot at First Goal; Play for World Crown Starts in China." *Baltimore Sun*, November 16, 1991.

French, Scott. "U.S. Gold Hopes on Hold?" *Long Beach Press-Telegram*, December 12, 1995.

HBO Sports. *Dare to Dream: The Story of the U.S. Women's Soccer Team.* 2005.

Jones, Grahame L. "Dispute Involving Top U.S. Players Hinges on Rejection of Contract Offers." *Los Angeles Times*, December 6, 1995.

Knight, Athelia. "Nine Players in Dispute with U.S. Soccer." *Washington Post*, December 8, 1995.

Longman, Jere. *The Girls of Summer: The U.S. Women's Soccer Team and How It Changed the World.* New York: HarperCollins, 2009.

Nance, Roscoe. "Contract Flap Keeps Nine from Camp." *USA Today*, December 7, 1995.

———. "Determined to Be No. 1, U.S. Women Quietly Build Soccer Power." *USA Today*, July 25, 1991.

Chapter 3

"FIFA Women's World Cups Support $493.6m in Economic Activity for Canada." Canada Soccer, November 5, 2015.

"How FIFA Shares Out Its Revenues." FIFA, May 22, 2002.

Longman, Jere. "1999 Women's World Cup: Beautiful Game Takes Flight." *New York Times*, May 20, 1999.

———. *The Girls of Summer: The U.S. Women's Soccer Team and How It Changed the World.* New York: HarperCollins, 2009.

"Sepp Blatter Loses His Appeal Against Six-Year Ban from Football." Associated Press, December 5, 2016.

U.S. Soccer Communications Department. "Women's National Team Media Guide." U.S. Soccer, 2018.

Chapter 4

HBO Sports. *Dare to Dream: The Story of the U.S. Women's Soccer Team.* 2005.

Longman, Jere. "U.S. National Team Has Redefined 'Soccer Mom.'" *New York Times*, May 9, 1999.

———. *The Girls of Summer: The U.S. Women's Soccer Team and How It Changed the World.* New York: HarperCollins, 2009.

Wahl, Grant. "How the U.S. Women Won the 1999 World Cup." Sports Illustrated, July 2, 2015.

Chapter 5

"And Strong TV Ratings, Too." *New York Times*, July 12, 1999.

Bennett, Roger. "Episode 10." June 11, 2018, in *American Fiasco*, produced by WNYC.

Erbe, Bonnie. "The Babe Factor in Soccer Team's Success." Scripps Howard News Service, July 12, 1999.

Gilligan, Amy. "Stripping Down to Sports Bra No Big Deal." Dubuque *Telegraph Herald*, July 18, 1999.

Haight, Abby. "U.S. Team Is Ready, Restless." *Oregonian*, June 18, 1999.

Harris, Elliott. "Uncover Story: Soccer Has Sex Appeal." *Chicago Sun-Times*, July 13, 1999.

Kimball, George. "U.S. Women's Team Looking Good: Sex Appeal Part of the Story." *Boston Herald*, July 9, 1999.

Kingsley, Barbara. "Men More Than Women Tune in to World Cup." *Orange County Register*, July 9, 1999.

Knott, Tom. "Get Real: Sex Appeal Does Count." *Washington Times*, July 6, 1999.

Longman, Jere. *The Girls of Summer: The U.S. Women's Soccer Team and How It Changed the World*. New York: HarperCollins, 2009.

———. "The Sports Bra Seen Round the World." *New York Times*, July 5, 2003.

"Now, It's the World at Their Feet." *San Diego Union-Tribune*, July 12, 1999.

Penner, Mike. "Success of the '99 Womens' World Cup Is . . . Looking Good." *Los Angeles Times*, July 8, 1999.

Powell, Shaun. "Momentum Won't Last for Women." *Newsday*, July 13, 1999.

Shipley, Amy. "Medals, Celebrity and Windfall for U.S. Women." *Washington Post*, July 12, 1999.

Vandecar, Annette. "U.S. Women Win World Cup and Promptly Tarnish It." *Northwest Indiana Post-Tribune*, July 13, 1999.

Chapter 6

Caparaz, Dean. "Women's Boycott: Behind the Pay Dispute." *Soccer America*, January 10, 2000.

Dure, Beau. "When Women Walked Out on Soccer." *Ozy*, May 9, 2016.

Fatsis, Stefan. "Nike Kicks in $120 Million to Sponsor Soccer in the U.S." *Wall Street Journal*, October 22, 1997.

Longman, Jere. *The Girls of Summer: The U.S. Women's Soccer Team and How It Changed the World.* New York: HarperCollins, 2009.

Shipley, Amy. "A Golden Moment Touched by Sorrow." *Washington Post,* June 8, 1997.

"Soccer Star Raising Goals in Women's Sports." CNN, 2001.

Ward, Bill. "Cup Champs' Tour May Face Legal Scrutiny." *Tampa Tribune,* July 27, 1999.

Chapter 7

Chapin, Dwight. "Fasten Your Seat Belts, It's Going to Be a Bumpy Ride." *San Francisco Chronicle,* June 18, 1999.

"Conference Call Quote Sheet from Announcement of April Heinrichs as U.S. Women's National Team Head Coach." U.S. Soccer, January 18, 2000.

HBO Sports. *Dare to Dream: The Story of the U.S. Women's Soccer Team.* 2005.

Longman, Jere. "Scurry Returns to World Cup in Peak Form. *New York Times,* September 21, 2003.

"Michelle Akers Bows Out of Olympics Due to Injury." U.S. Soccer, August 24, 2000.

Montville, Leigh. "Soccer Screwballs." *Sports Illustrated,* January 10, 2000.

Shipley, Amy. "After U.S. Storm, an April Shower of Change." *Washington Post,* March 12, 2000.

Ziegler, Mark. "Women's Soccer Coach Rose Despite Dysfunctional Upbringing." *San Diego Union-Tribune,* September 25, 2003.

———. "Women's World Cup Coach Could Lose Job." *San Diego Union-Tribune,* September 24, 1999.

Chapter 8

Almond, Elliot. "Pro Women's League to Begin in 1998?" *Seattle Times,* February 14, 1997.

Bondy, Filip. "Sporting Women Find Cup's Empty." New York *Daily News*, September 16, 2003.

Bradley, Jeff. "MLS Considering Weight-Loss Program." ESPN, September 14, 2001.

Eligon, John. "For M.L.S., the Sport's Future Is in the Eye of the Beholder." *New York Times*, November 11, 2005.

Kuhns, Will. "WUSA: Mutual Admiration." *Soccer America*, April 24, 2001.

Langdon, Jerry. "Women's League Gets $12M Pledge." *USA Today*, September 12, 1997.

———. "Women's Pro Soccer by '98." *USA Today*, February 13, 1997.

Murphy, Jarrett. "Women's Soccer League Kicks Bucket." Associated Press, September 16, 2003.

Reid, Scott M. "The U.S. Women's National Team Came Through on and off the Pitch, Attracting $64 Million to Get the WUSA Rolling." *Orange County Register*, April 14, 2001.

Shipley, Amy. "Women's League Falls Short of Goal." *Washington Post*, April 17, 1998.

Trecker, Jamie. "WMLS? No Way, Say U.S. Women." ESPN, September 14, 2001.

Trecker, Jerry. "No Net Profit with 2 Leagues of Their Own." *Hartford Courant*, April 13, 2000.

"U.S. Women's Soccer League Is Taking Its Best Shot, and It Just Might Score." *St. Louis Post-Dispatch*, April 14, 2001.

"WUSA Debuts with Pageantry and Symbolism." *Erie Times-News*, April 14, 2001.

"WUSA—Founding Players Take Pay Cuts." Soccer America, March 25, 2003.

Chapter 9

Jones, Grahame L. "Missing in Action," *Los Angeles Times*, August 20, 2004.

Lebreton, Gil. "Sequel May Be a Big Flop." *Fort Worth Star-Telegram*, September 21, 2003.

Robledo, Fred J. "U.S. Must Focus on Survivor Series." *Pasadena Star-News*, September 17, 2003.

Scripps Howard. "Winning the Cup Is More Vital Than Ever to U.S. Team." *Jackson Citizen Patriot*, September 17, 2003.

Voepe, Mechelle. "U.S. Women Putting Aside WUSA's Demise." *Kansas City Star*, September 17, 2003.

Wahl, Grant. "A New, Take-charge Mia Hamm Led the U.S. into the Cup Quarterfinals." *Sports Illustrated*, October 6, 2003.

———. "Kicked Out." *Sports Illustrated*, October 13, 2003.

———. "Going Out with a Bang." Sports Illustrated, August 30, 2004.

———. "Weathering the Storm." Sports Illustrated, September 29, 2003.

"Where's Tiffeny?" Associated Press, June 20, 2004.

Wilner, Barry. "Chastain, Hamm, Scurry Among 20 on U.S. World Cup Team." Associated Press, August 26, 2003.

Wyatt, Kristen. "Women's Soccer League Suspends Operations." Associated Press, September 16, 2003.

Chapter 10

Borzilleri, Meri-Jo. "Coach Has Team Looking Ahead." *Colorado Springs Gazette*, June 5, 2005.

Solo, Hope, and Ann Killion. *Solo: A Memoir of Hope*. New York: HarperCollins, 2013.

Ziegler, Mark. "U.S. Women's National Team Coach Steps Down Amid Pressure from Some Unhappy Players." *San Diego Union-Tribune*, February 16, 2005.

Chapter 11

Goff, Steven. "Solo Apologizes, but Won't Play for U.S. vs. Norway." *Washington Post*, September 30, 2007.

Lloyd, Carli, and Wayne Coffey. *When Nobody Was Watching: My Hard-Fought Journey to the Top of the Soccer World*. Boston: Houghton Mifflin Harcourt, 2016.

Paul, Erin. "Ryan's Goalkeeper Switch Backfires in a Big Way." *CBC,* September 27, 2007.

Ruibal, Sal. "USA Changes Goalkeeper in Surprise Move." *USA Today,* September 27, 2007.

"Ryan Breaks Silence Over Solo." *Washington Times,* January 12, 2008.

Solo, Hope, and Ann Killion. *Solo: A Memoir of Hope.* New York: Harper-Collins, 2013.

Wade, Stephen. "U.S. Switches Goalie for Cup Semifinals." Associated Press, September 26, 2007.

———. "Marta's Two Goals Help Defeat U.S. 4–0." Associated Press, September 27, 2007.

Wahl, Grant. "Hard Return." *Sports Illustrated,* June 30, 2008.

Wambach, Abby. *Forward: A Memoir.* New York: Dey Street Books, 2016.

Whitehead, Johnnie. "New Coach Lets Players Follow Instincts." USA Today, June 27, 2005.

Ziegler, Mark. "U.S. Soccer's Decision May Be Signal to Players." *San Diego Union-Tribune,* April 9, 2005.

Chapter 12

U.S. Soccer Communications Department. "Women's National Team Media Guide." U.S. Soccer, 2018.

Wahl, Grant. "Hucles a Pleasant Surprise for U.S." *Sports Illustrated,* August 18, 2008.

Wambach, Abby. *Forward: A Memoir.* New York: Dey Street Books, 2016.

Chapter 13

"Alex Morgan Fires Late US Goal to Beat Italy 10 in World Cup Playoff." Associated Press, November 21, 2010.

Assael, Shaun, and Peter Keating. "MagicTrick." *ESPN The Magazine,* September 13, 2012.

Bell, Jack. "For American Women, It's Win or Stay Home." *New York Times,* November 19, 2010.

"Company Behind MagicJack to Banish Calling Costs." Associated Press, August 13, 2010.

Dunbar, Graham. "Marta to Join LA Sol in New Women's Soccer League." Associated Press, January 12, 2009.

"Feeling Pinch, N.F.L. Will Cut About 150 Jobs." *New York Times*, December 9, 2008.

FitzGerald, Tom. "New League Opens with High Hopes." *San Francisco Chronicle*, March 27, 2009.

Goodman, Mark. "WPS: The New Game in Town." *Bolton* (MA) *Common*, July 29, 2009.

Jones, Grahame L. "New Women's Soccer League Takes World View." *Los Angeles Times*, March 29, 2009.

Kennedy, Paul. "Pro Sports' Worst-Run Franchise." *Soccer America*, May 12, 2011.

Ziegler, Mark. "Blame Federation for U.S. Performance in Women's World Cup." San Diego Union-Tribune, October 3, 2007.

Chapter 14

"Alex Morgan Fires Late US Goal to Beat Italy 10 in World Cup Playoff." Associated Press, November 21, 2010.

Boehm, Charles. "WPS Owners Decide to Cancel 2012 Season." National Soccer Wire, January 30, 2012.

Hirshey, David. "Hope and Glory for the U.S." ESPN, July 11, 2011.

Jones, Grahame L. "U.S. Names Roster for 2011 Women's World Cup." *Los Angeles Times*, May 9, 2011.

"USWNT Head Coach Sundhage Picks 21 Players for 2011 World Cup in Germany." *Goal*, May 9, 2011.

Wahl, Grant. "One Heady Moment." *Sports Illustrated*, 2014.

Ziegler, Mark. "Buehler and Her Wild Day in Germany." *San Diego Union-Tribune*, July 11, 2011.

Chapter 15

Baxter, Kevin. "U.S. Women's Soccer Team Annoys Some Foes with Goal Celebrations." *Los Angeles Times*, August 5, 2012.

Borden, Sam. "U.S. Women Unveil Victory Dance After Win Over North Korea." *New York Times,* July 31, 2012.

Bucholtz, Andrew. "Does Something Need to Be Done About the Epidemic of Olympic Qualifying Blowouts?" Yahoo News, January 21, 2012.

———. "Sydney Leroux Scores Five Goals in Memorable Homecoming, but Still Hears 'Judas' Taunts." Yahoo News, January 22, 2012.

"Canadian-Born U.S. Soccer Player Says She Was Racially Abused in Vancouver." *Canadian Press,* June 3, 2013.

Fitz-Gerald, Sean. "Christine Sinclair Still Seething Over Referee in Olympic Soccer Semifinal Loss to U.S." *Vancouver Sun,* August 10, 2012.

Kelly, Cathal. "The Greatest Game of Women's Soccer Ever Played." *Globe and Mail,* June 12, 2015.

Lloyd, Carli, and Wayne Coffey. *When Nobody Was Watching: My Hard-Fought Journey to the Top of the Soccer World.* Boston: Houghton Mifflin Harcourt, 2016.

Memmott, Jim. "Singing Her Way Toward Exit, Sundhage Steps Down as U.S. Coach." *New York Times,* September 1, 2012.

Stevenson, Chris. "Yanks Whining About Tancredi 'Stomp.'" *Toronto Sun,* August 8, 2012.

"U.S., Canada Women's Soccer Teams Set to Play with Bragging Rights on the Line." Associated Press, January 28, 2012.

"U.S. Trounce Canada Women's Soccer Team in Olympic Qualifying Tourney." *CityNews* (Toronto), January 30, 2012.

Wetzel, Dan. "Abby Wambach's Brains Provided Crucial Assist to U.S. Comeback Against Canada." Yahoo News, August 7, 2012.

Chapter 16

Arnold, Geoffrey C. "Fan Energy Awes Thorns." *Oregonian,* April 23, 2013.

Borden, Sam. "A U.S. Soccer Star's Declaration of Independence." *New York Times,* April 10, 2013.

Springer, Shira. "Why Do Fans Ignore Women's Pro Sports?" *Boston Globe*, September 24, 2014.

United States Soccer Federation, Inc. "2013 Audited Financial Statements." 2014.

Chapter 17

DiVeronica, Jeff. "Q&A: Abby Wambach Unplugged." *Rochester* (NY) *Democrat & Chronicle*, March 30, 2014.

"Hope Solo's Husband Busted for DUI." *TMZ*, January 20, 2015.

Morgan, Alex. *Breakaway: Beyond the Goal*. New York: Simon & Schuster, 2015.

"Tom Sermanni Named Coach of U.S. Women's National Team." U.S. Soccer, October 30, 2012.

Wahl, Grant. "U.S. Soccer President Sunil Gulati: On FIFA, World Cup, Copa America, and More." *Sports Illustrated*, July 3, 2014.

"Wambach: Players Didn't Have a Role in Sermanni's Firing." Associated Press, April 8, 2014.

Chapter 18

Armour, Nancy. "Lackluster Efforts at World Cup Bound to Catch Up to Americans." *USA Today*, June 22, 2015.

Bondy, Stefan. "Thierry Henry Doesn't Tolerate Turf Fields." New York *Daily News*, July 14, 2011.

Bousquette, MC. "What's Going On with USWNT? A Post-Colombia Primer." *Empire of Soccer*, June 25, 2015.

Child, Ben. "FIFA's *United Passions* Confirmed as Lowest-Grossing Film in US History." *Guardian*, June 18, 2015.

Doyle, John. "Doyle: The Insult of Artificial Turf at the Women's World Cup." *Globe and Mail*, June 1, 2015.

"FIFA Women's World Cup: USA Faces Flak for Dated Tactics." Reuters, June 24, 2015.

Filadelfo, Elaine. "The #FIFAWWC Twitter Data Recap." *Twitter* (blog), Twitter, July 6, 2015.

Foss, Mike. "The U.S. Women's World Cup Team Is a Shell of Its Former Self." *USA Today*, June 23, 2015.

Gayle, Branden. "2015 Women's World Cup Final on Facebook." *Facebook Media* (blog), Facebook, July 6, 2015.

Gold, Daniel M. "Review: In *United Passions*, a Fictionalized FIFA, Underwritten by the Soccer Group." *New York Times*, June 4, 2015.

"Group of Elite Players Led by U.S. Soccer Star Abby Wambach File Lawsuit." Associated Press, October 1, 2014.

Isidore, Chris. "Women World Cup Champs Win Waaaaay Less Money Than Men." CNN, July 7, 2015.

Litman, Laken. "Alex Morgan on Why Artificial Turf Is Tough for Players." *USA Today*, October 15, 2014.

Payne, Marissa. "Women's World Cup Players Withdraw 'Turf War' Lawsuit." *Washington Post*, January 21, 2015.

"Prize Money Doubled for World Cup Winners." BBC, December 20, 2014.

Rechtshaffen, Michael. "FIFA-Bankrolled 'United Passions' Kicks Far Wide of Its Goal." *Los Angeles Times*, June 4, 2015.

Roxborough, Scott, and Rhonda Richford. "FIFA Movie Director Breaks Silence on Bomb." Hollywood Reporter, June 17, 2015.

"Staggering 25.4 Million Viewers Witness USA Win." Fox Sports, July 6, 2015.

Terranova, Justin. "Clueless US Coach Threatens to Torpedo World Cup." *New York Post*, June 25, 2015.

Walters, John. "The US Women's World Cup Team Has a Goal Problem; and That May Not Matter." *Newsweek*, June 25, 2015.

"World Cup Turf Complaint Won't Get Human Rights Hearing." Associated Press, November 7, 2014.

Chapter 19

Ax, Joseph. "From NFL to Women's Soccer, Lawyer Is Thorn in Side of Sports Leagues." Reuters, March 31, 2016.

Borden, Sam. "Head of U.S. Soccer Apologizes for Cancellation." *New York Times*, December 8, 2015.

Cauterucci, Christina. "Senate Passed a Unanimous Resolution Supporting Equal Pay for U.S. Women's Soccer." *Slate*, May 27, 2016.

Das, Andrew. "Pay Disparity in U.S. Soccer? It's Complicated." *New York Times*, April 21, 2016.

"Equal Footing." *The Player's Tribune*, December 6, 2015.

Lloyd, Carli. "Why I'm Fighting for Equal Pay." *New York Times*, April 10, 2016.

Tannenwald, Jonathan. "Details of U.S. Soccer's Budget for National Teams." *Philadelphia Inquirer*, March 7, 2016.

Vecsey, Laura. "USWNT Match in Hawaii Cancelled Over Field Conditions." Fox Sports, December 6, 2015.

Chapter 20

Auerbach, Nicole. "Alex Morgan Discusses Hope Solo's Comments, Ex-Coach Pia Sundhage." *USA Today*, August 17, 2016.

"Hope Solo Blames US Media for Spreading Fear About Zika Virus and Rio Olympics." Associated Press, August 1, 2016.

"Megan Rapinoe Critical of Hope Solo Calling Sweden 'Cowards.'" Associated Press, August 18, 2016.

Palazzo, Chiara. "Rio Olympics: Which Athletes Have Withdrawn Over Zika Fears?" *Telegraph*, August 4, 2016.

"Schelin Avslöjar Hope Solos Ord Efter Motet." *Expressen* (Sweden), August 13, 2016.

"U.S. Soccer President Calls Hope Solo's Sweden Comments 'Highly Inappropriate.'" *Sports Illustrated*, August 13, 2016.

Chapter 21

Das, Andrew. "In Fight for Equality, U.S. Women's Soccer Team Leads the Way." *New York Times*, March 4, 2018.

―――. "U.S. Soccer Suspends Hope Solo and Terminates Her Contract." *New York Times*, August 24, 2016.

―――. "U.S. Women's Team Restructures Union in Effort to Revive C.B.A. Talks." *New York Times*, February 3, 2017.

Howard, Johnette. "The Shrewd Steps That Led U.S. Women to Landmark Deal." ESPN, March 31, 2017.

McRae, Donald. "Alex Morgan: 'If FIFA Starts Respecting the Women's Game More, Others Will Follow.'" *Guardian*, January 16, 2017.

Perez, A. J. "Five Things to Know in U.S. Women's Hockey Team Showdown with USA Hockey." *USA Today Sports*, March 27, 2017.

Chapter 22

Hayes, Graham. "Coach Jill Ellis Is Ready to Reboot the U.S. Women's Soccer Roster." ESPN, October 3, 2016.

Index